Kingdom Hearts Vol. 1
Adapted by
Shiro Amano

Associate Editor - Alexis Kirsch
Copy Editor - Peter Ahlstrom and Seraphina Wong
Retouch and Lettering - Adriana Rivera
Production Artist - Jose Macasocol, Jr. and Chris Anderson
Cover Layout - Gary Shum

Editor - Bryce P. Coleman
Digital Imaging Manager - Chris Buford
Production Managers - Jennifer Miller and Mutsumi Miyazaki
Managing Editor - Jill Freshney
VP of Production - Ron Klamert
Publisher and E.I.C. - Mike Kiley
President and C.O.O. - John Parker
Publisher and C.E.O. - Stuart Levy

A **TOKYOPOP** Manga

TOKYOPOP Inc.
5900 Wilshire Blvd. Suite 2000
Los Angeles, CA 90036

E-mail: info@TOKYOPOP.com
Come visit us online at www.TOKYOPOP.com

ISBN: 1-59816-217-9

First TOKYOPOP printing: October 2005
10 9 8
Printed in the USA

Kingdom Hearts

Disney SQUARESOFT

Volume 1

Adapted by
Shiro Amano

TOKYOPOP®

HAMBURG // LONDON // LOS ANGELES // TOKYO

KINGDOM HEARTS: VOLUME 1
TABLE OF CONTENTS

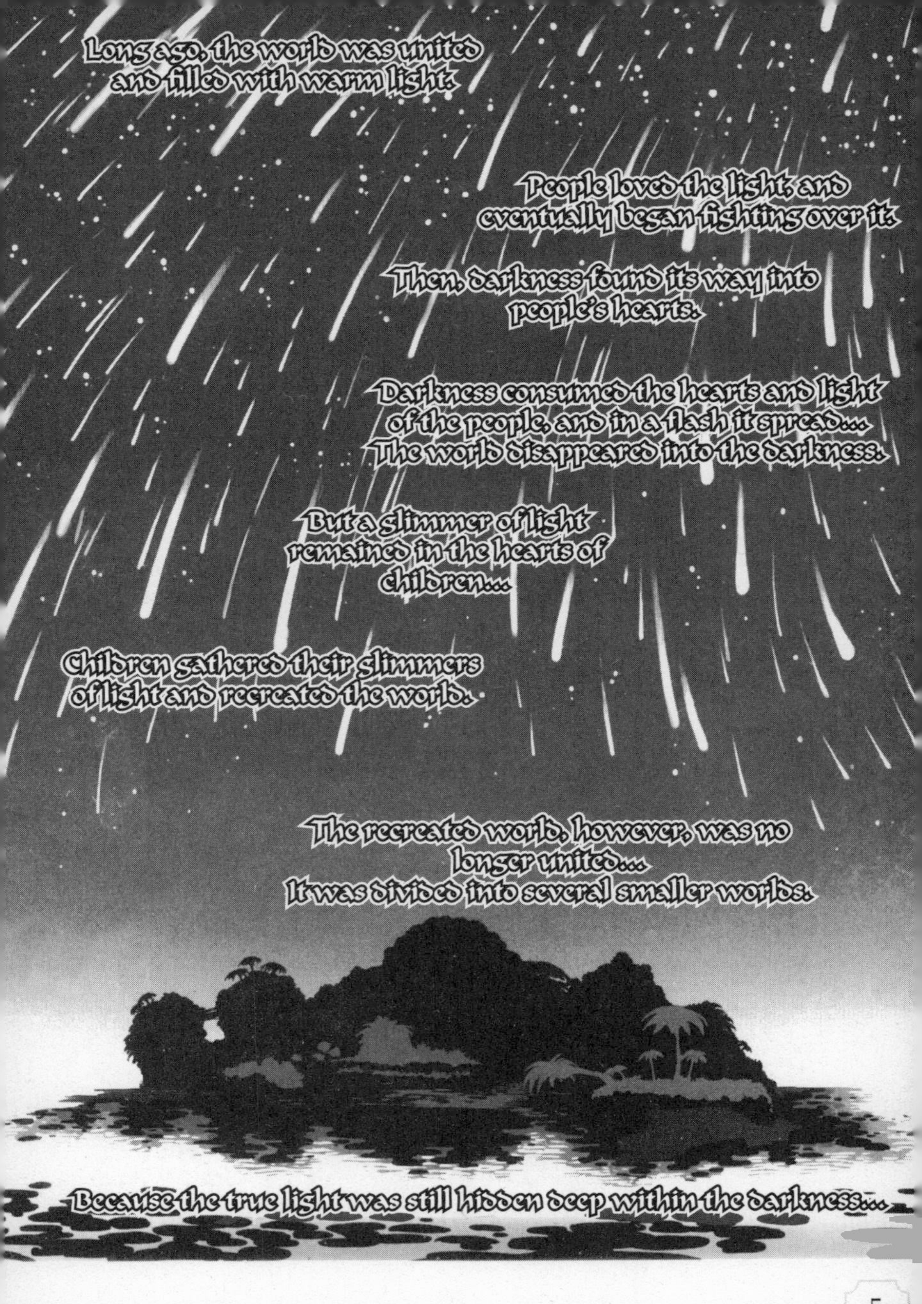
Long ago, the world was united and filled with warm light.
People loved the light, and eventually began fighting over it.
Then, darkness found its way into people's hearts.
Darkness consumed the hearts and light of the people, and in a flash it spread... The world disappeared into the darkness.
But a glimmer of light remained in the hearts of children...
Children gathered their glimmers of light and recreated the world.
The recreated world, however, was no longer united... It was divided into several smaller worlds.
Because the true light was still hidden deep within the darkness...

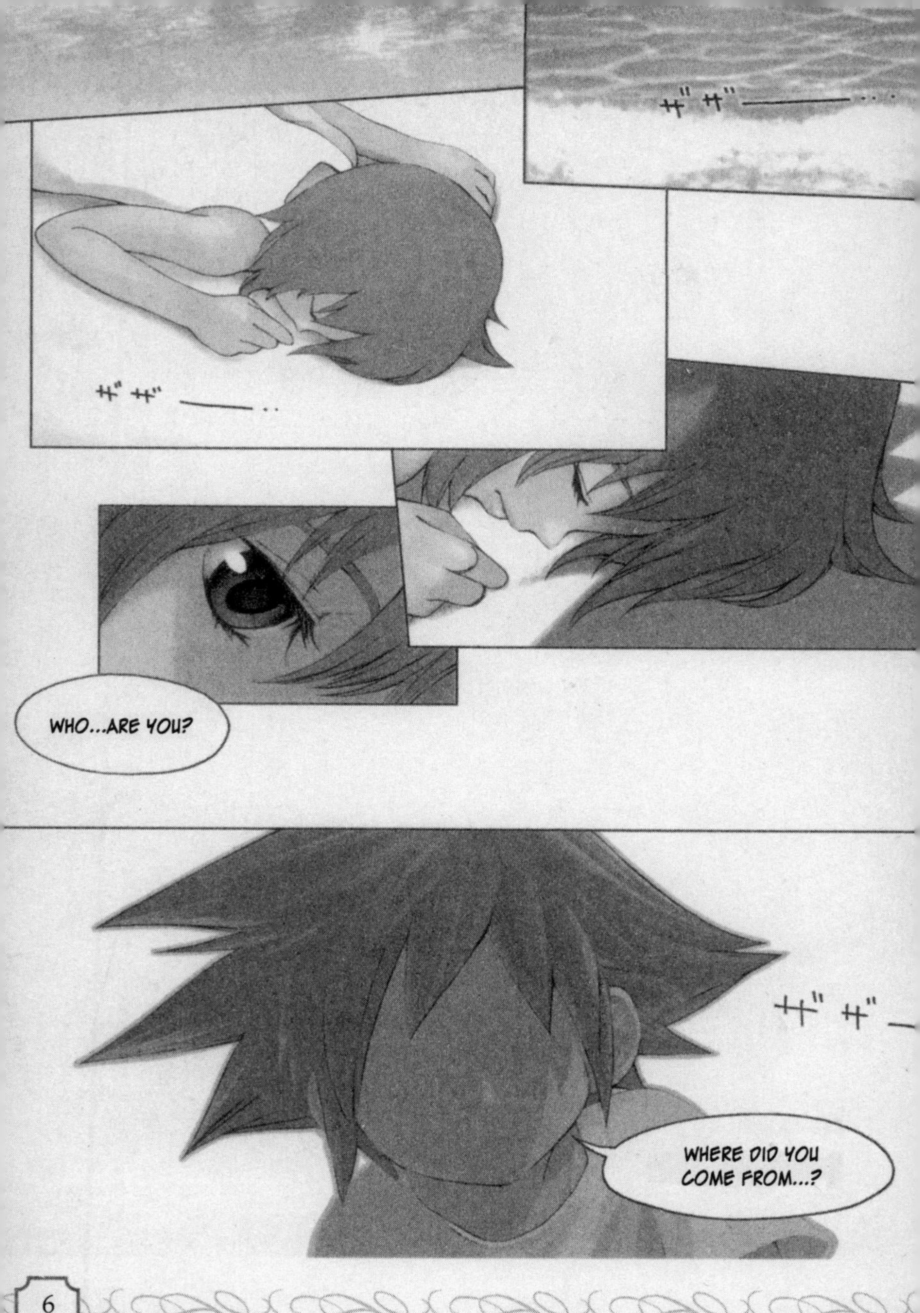
ザザ——..
ザザ———…
WHO...ARE YOU?
ザザ—
WHERE DID YOU COME FROM...?

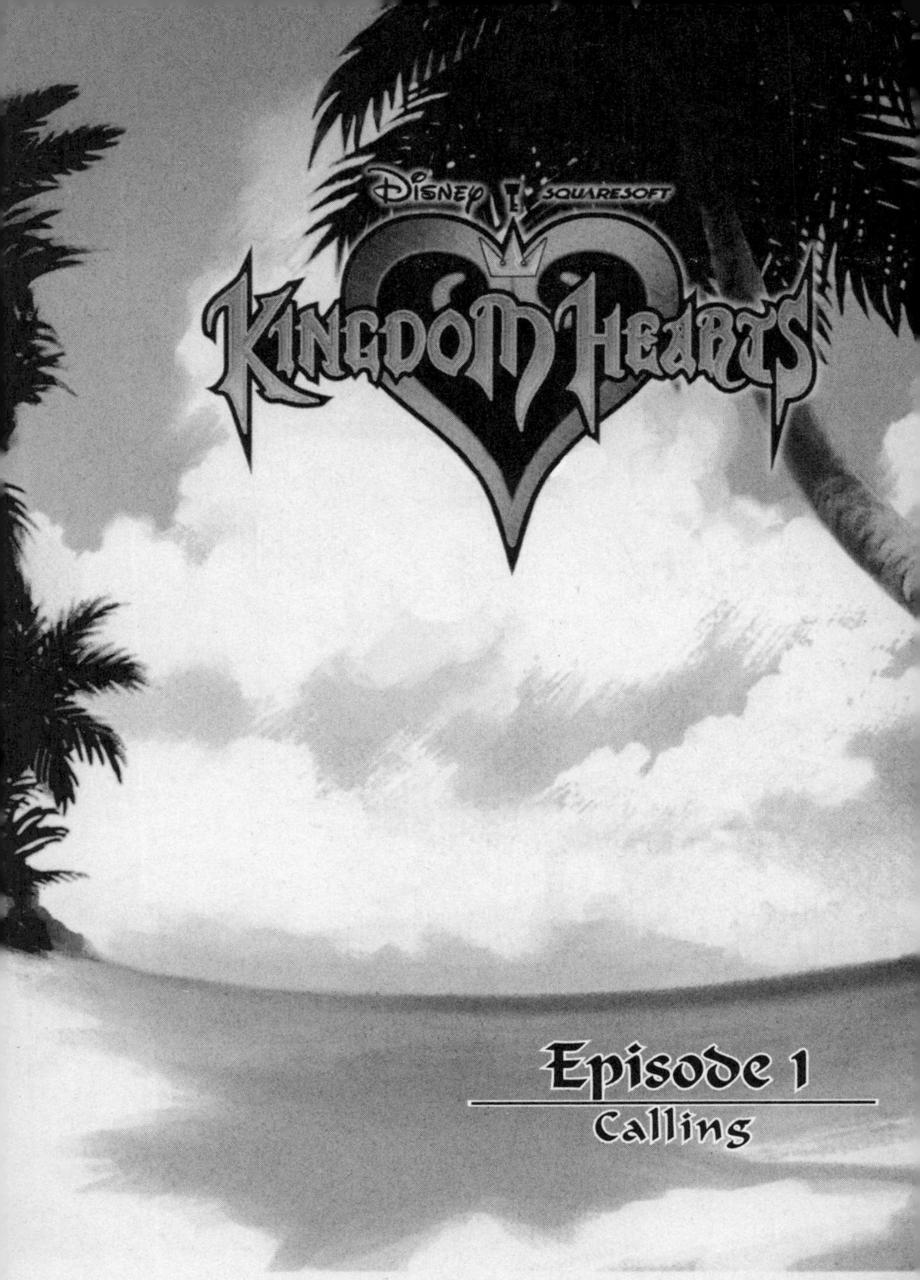
Disney
Squaresoft
Kingdom Hearts
Episode 1
Calling

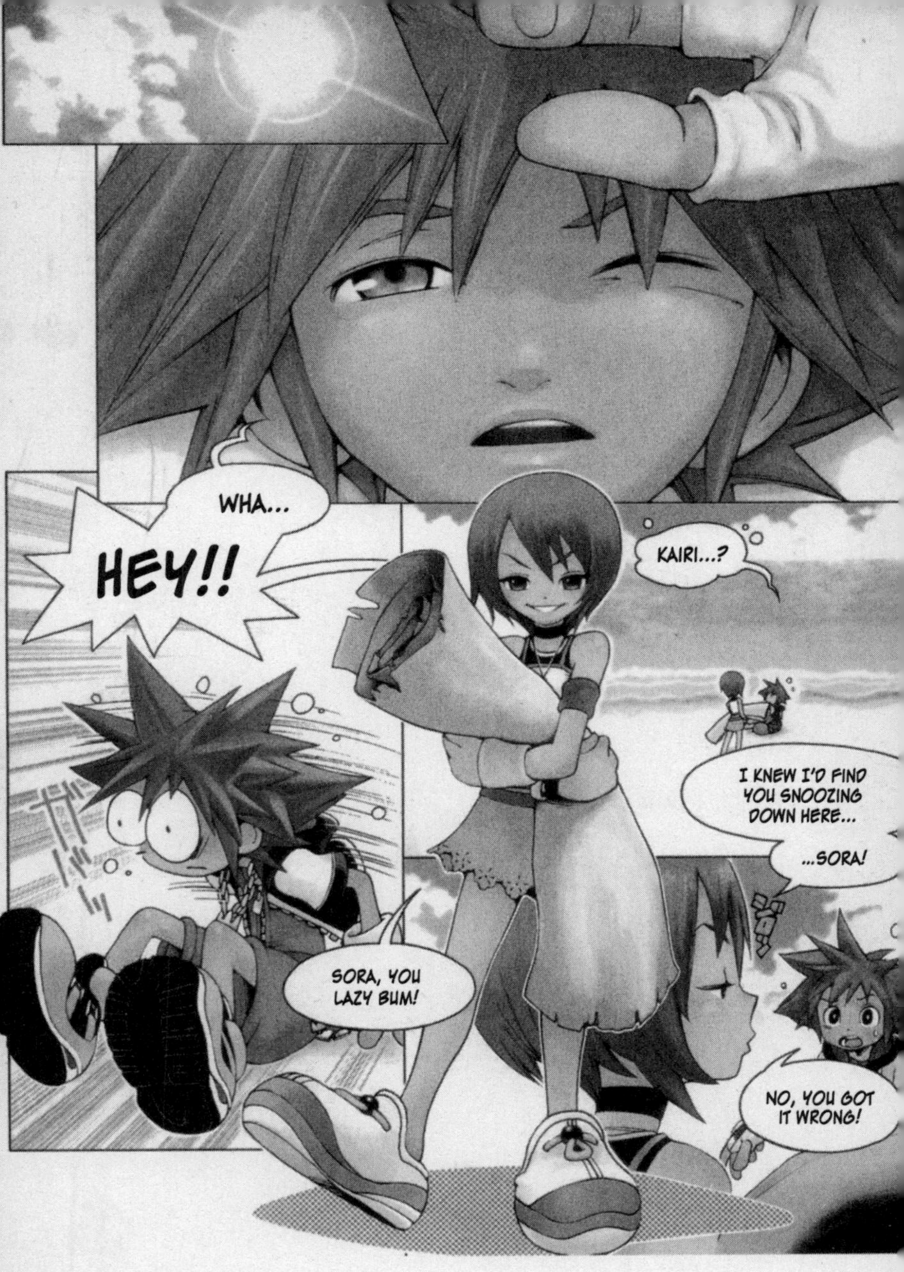

WHA...
HEY!!
KAIRI...?
SORA, YOU LAZY BUM!
I KNEW I'D FIND YOU SNOOZING DOWN HERE...
...SORA!
NO, YOU GOT IT WRONG!

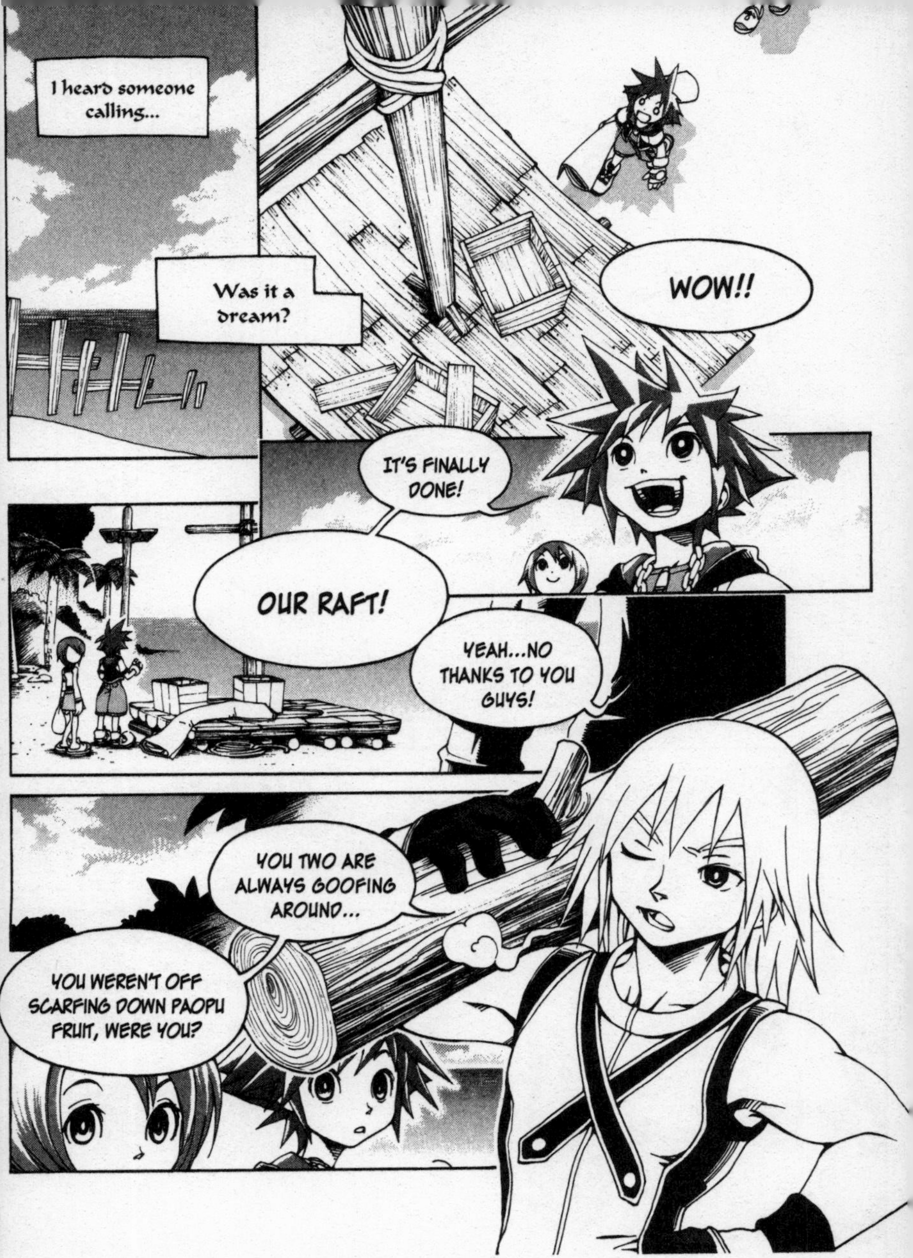
I heard someone calling...
Was it a dream?
WOW!!
IT'S FINALLY DONE!
OUR RAFT!
YEAH...NO THANKS TO YOU GUYS!
YOU TWO ARE ALWAYS GOOFING AROUND...
YOU WEREN'T OFF SCARFING DOWN PAOPU FRUIT, WERE YOU?

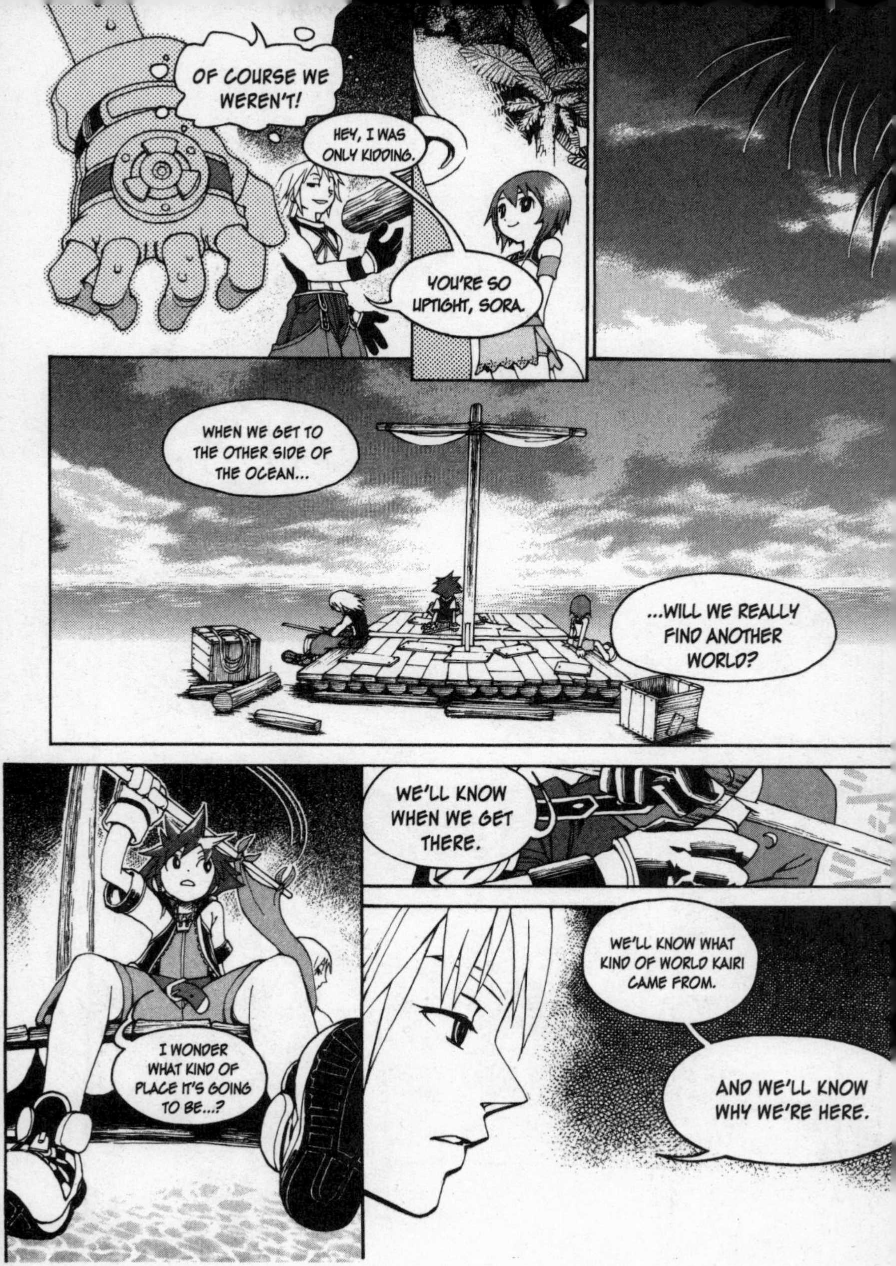

OF COURSE WE WEREN'T!
HEY, I WAS ONLY KIDDING.
YOU'RE SO UPTIGHT, SORA.
WHEN WE GET TO THE OTHER SIDE OF THE OCEAN...
...WILL WE REALLY FIND ANOTHER WORLD?
I WONDER WHAT KIND OF PLACE IT'S GOING TO BE...?
WE'LL KNOW WHEN WE GET THERE.
WE'LL KNOW WHAT KIND OF WORLD KAIRI CAME FROM.
AND WE'LL KNOW WHY WE'RE HERE.

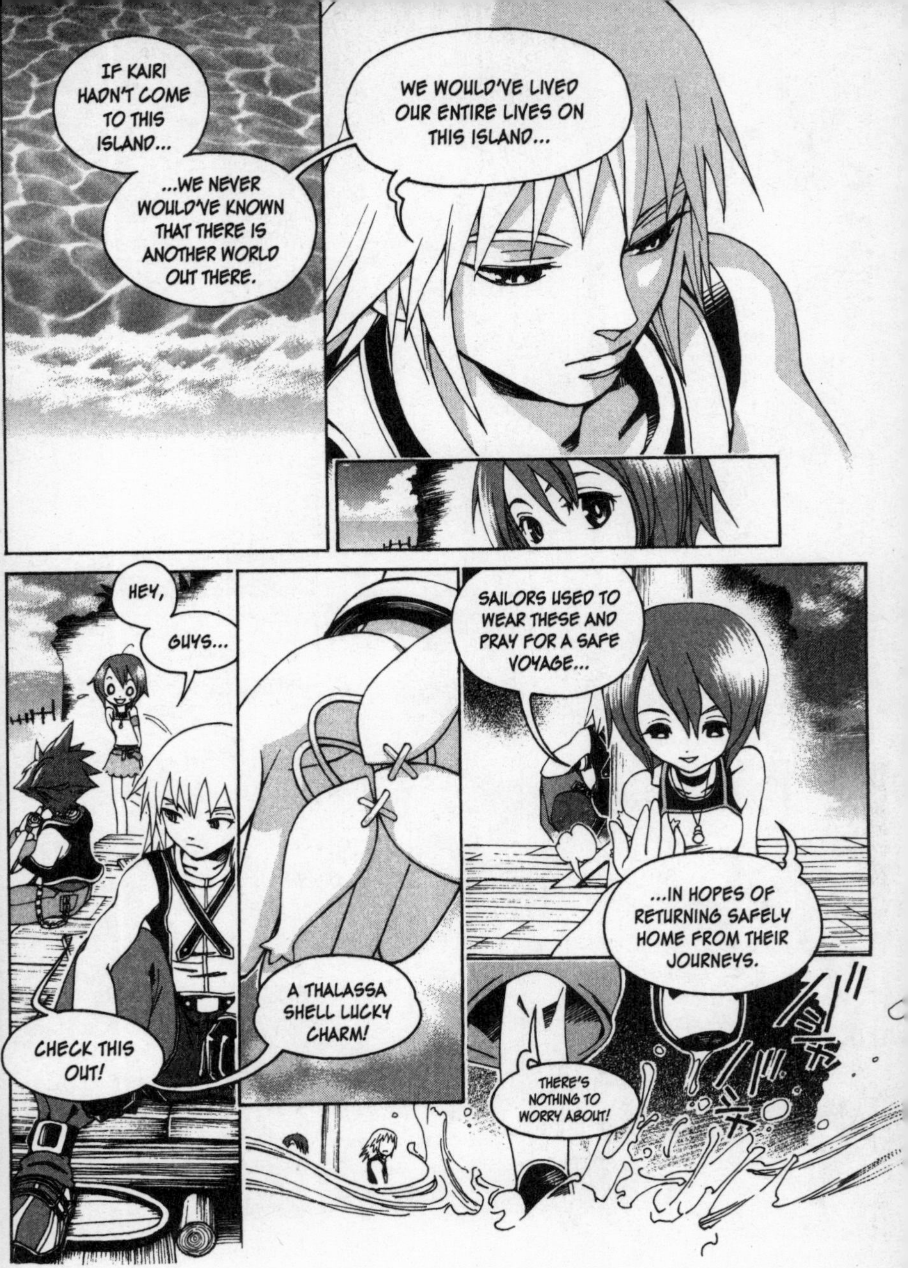
IF KAIRI HADN'T COME TO THIS ISLAND...
...WE NEVER WOULD'VE KNOWN THAT THERE IS ANOTHER WORLD OUT THERE.
WE WOULD'VE LIVED OUR ENTIRE LIVES ON THIS ISLAND...
HEY,
GUYS...
CHECK THIS OUT!
A THALASSA SHELL LUCKY CHARM!
SAILORS USED TO WEAR THESE AND PRAY FOR A SAFE VOYAGE...
...IN HOPES OF RETURNING SAFELY HOME FROM THEIR JOURNEYS.
THERE'S NOTHING TO WORRY ABOUT!

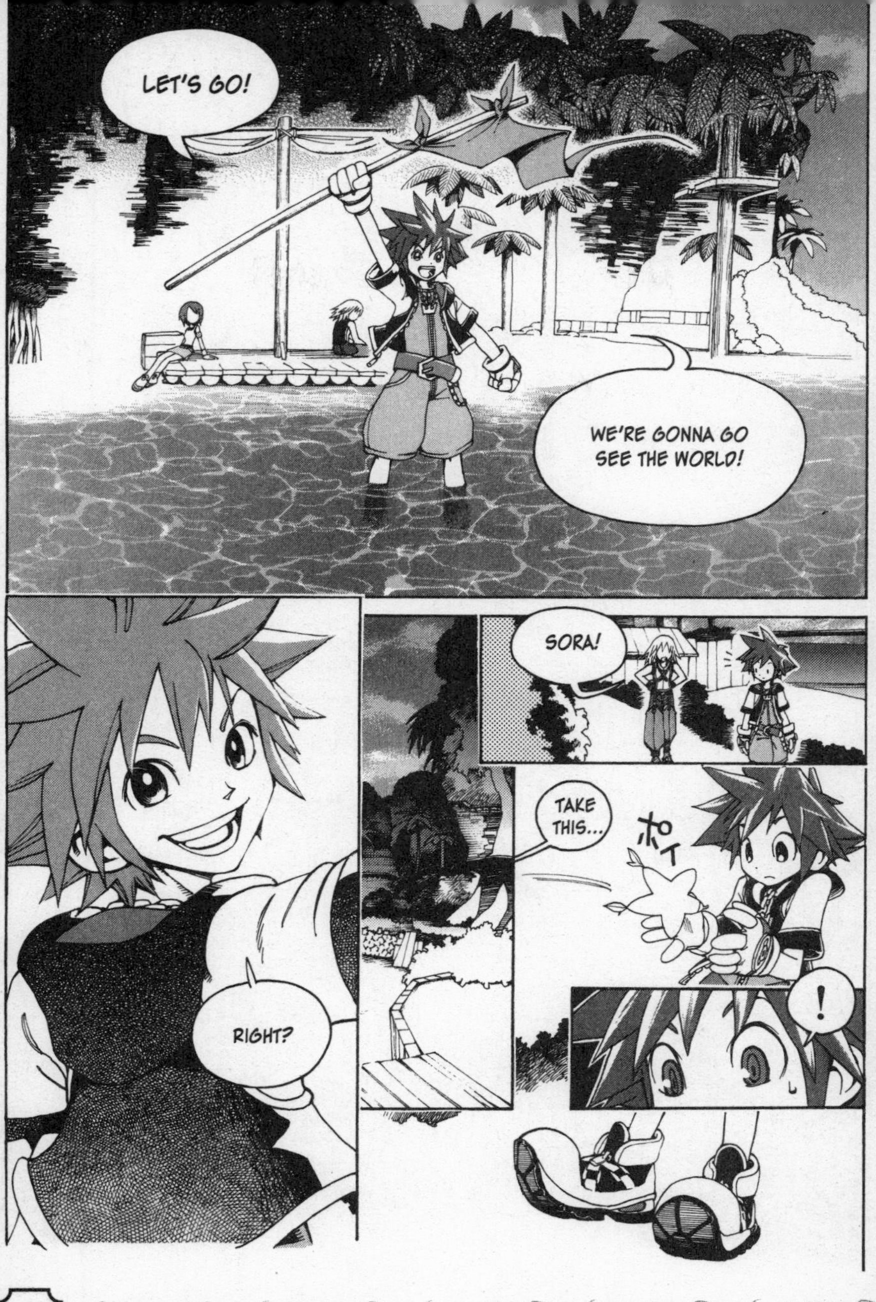
LET'S GO!
WE'RE GONNA GO SEE THE WORLD!
RIGHT?
SORA!
TAKE THIS...
ポイ
!

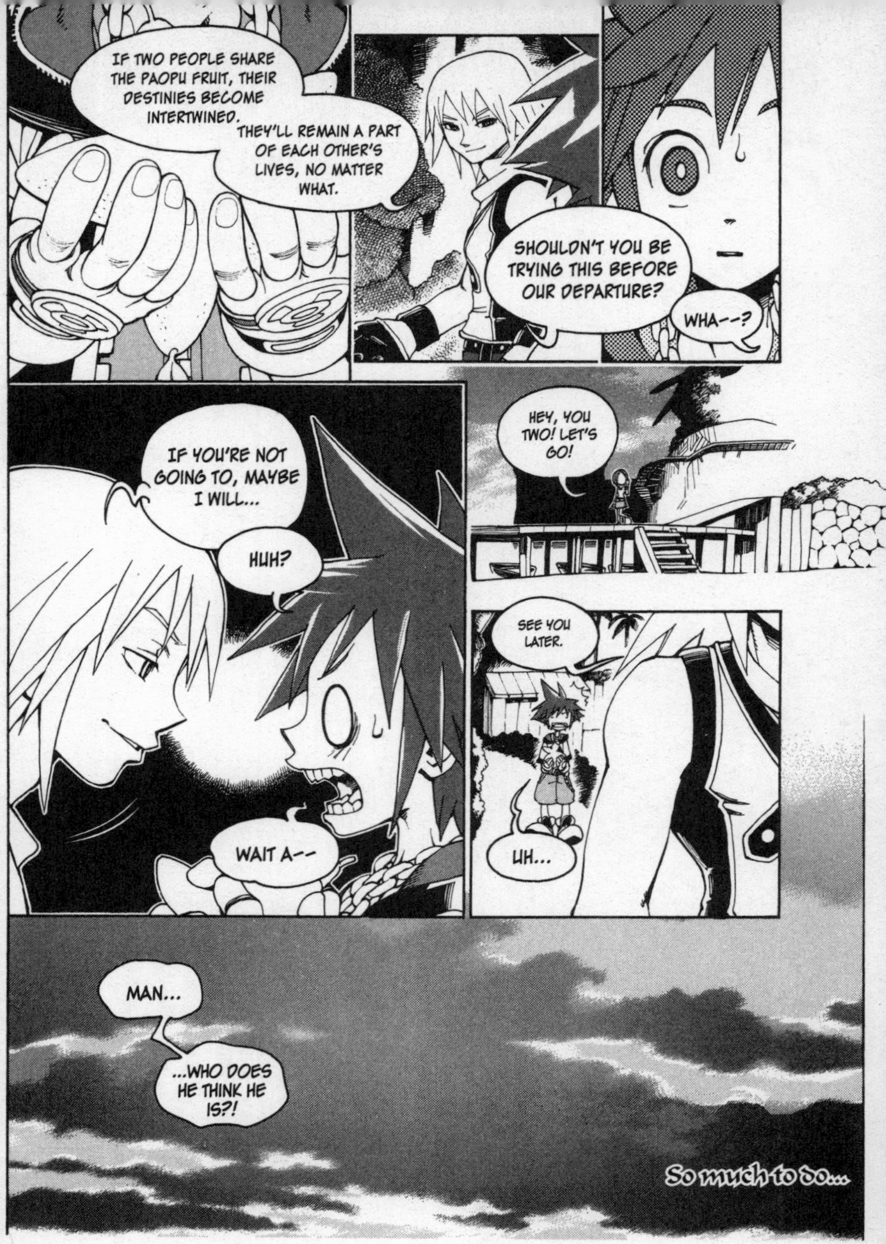
IF TWO PEOPLE SHARE THE PAOPU FRUIT, THEIR DESTINIES BECOME INTERTWINED.
THEY'LL REMAIN A PART OF EACH OTHER'S LIVES, NO MATTER WHAT.
SHOULDN'T YOU BE TRYING THIS BEFORE OUR DEPARTURE?
WHA--?
IF YOU'RE NOT GOING TO, MAYBE I WILL...
HUH?
WAIT A--
HEY, YOU TWO! LET'S GO!
SEE YOU LATER.
UH...
MAN...
...WHO DOES HE THINK HE IS?!
So much to do...

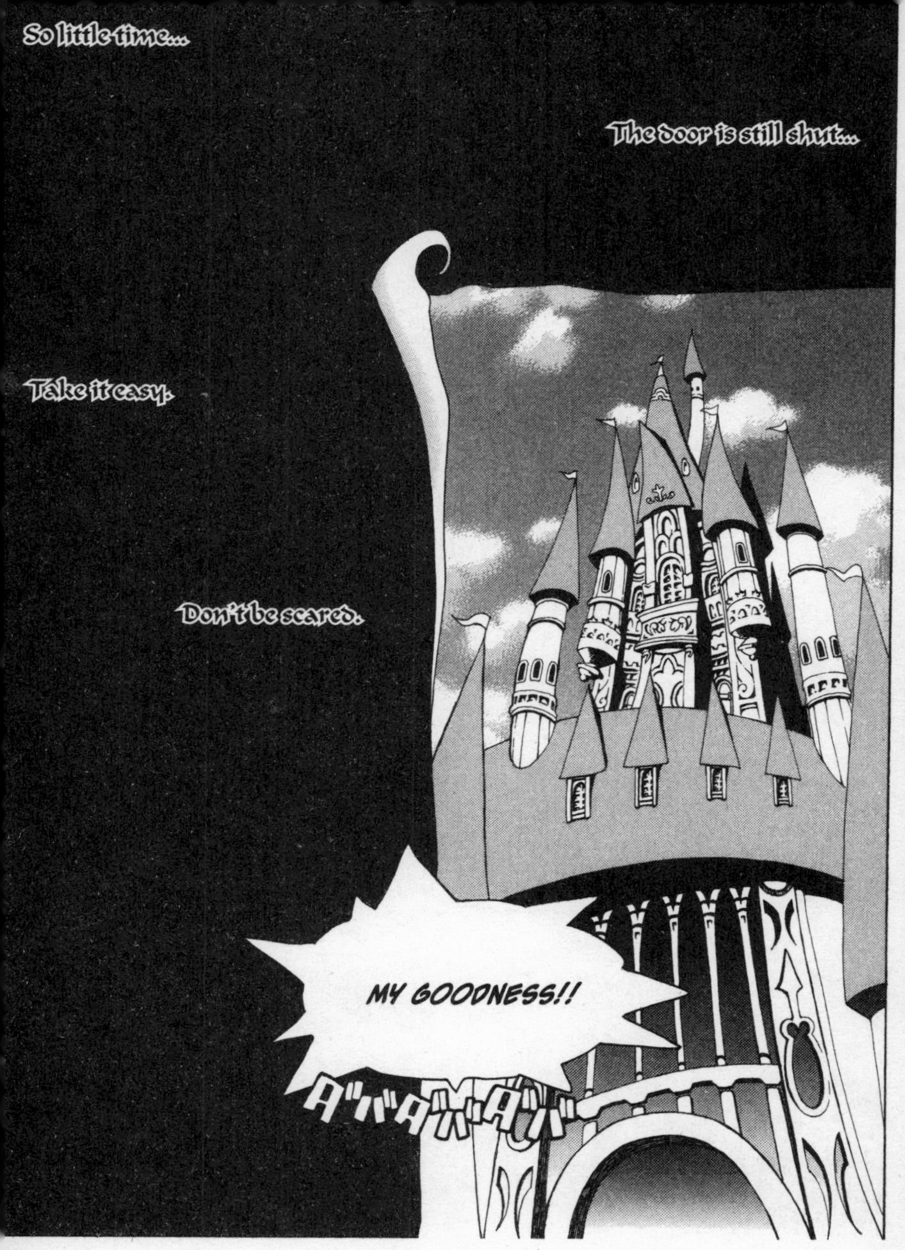
So little time...
The door is still shut...
Take it easy.
Don't be scared.
MY GOODNESS!!

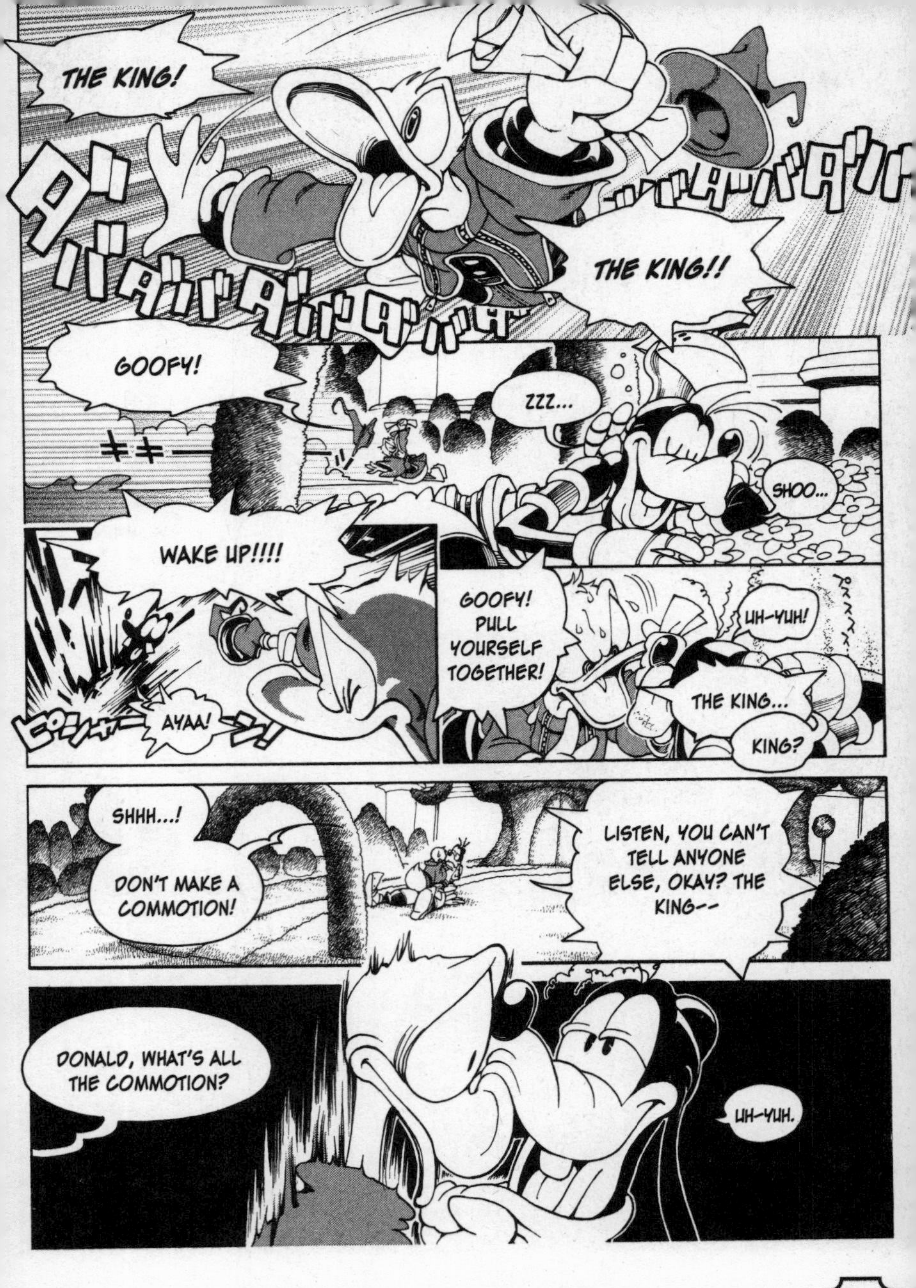
THE KING!
THE KING!!
GOOFY!
ZZZ...
SHOO...
WAKE UP!!!!
AYAA!
GOOFY! PULL YOURSELF TOGETHER!
UH-YUH!
THE KING...
KING?
SHHH...!
DON'T MAKE A COMMOTION!
LISTEN, YOU CAN'T TELL ANYONE ELSE, OKAY? THE KING--
DONALD, WHAT'S ALL THE COMMOTION?
UH-YUH.

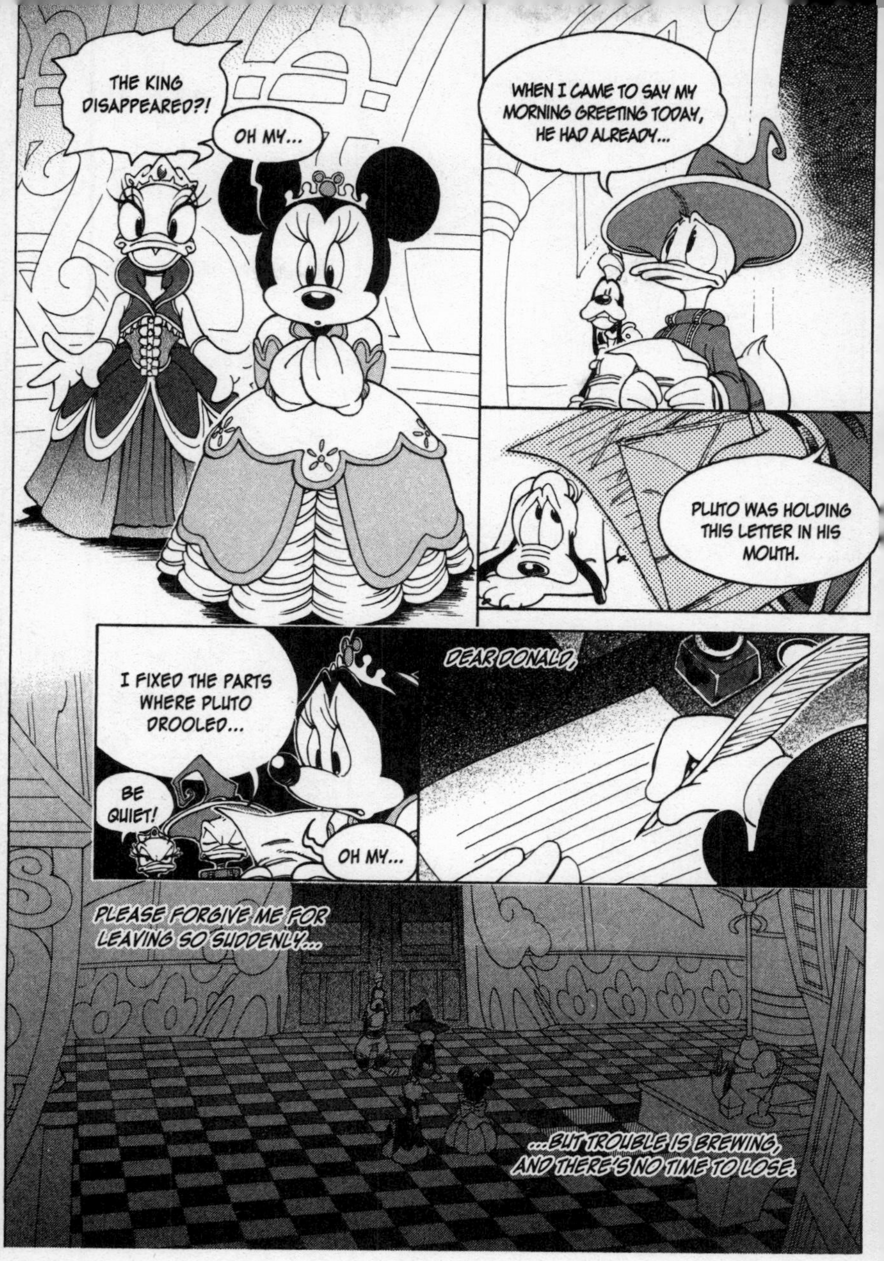
THE KING DISAPPEARED?!
OH MY...
WHEN I CAME TO SAY MY MORNING GREETING TODAY, HE HAD ALREADY...
PLUTO WAS HOLDING THIS LETTER IN HIS MOUTH.
I FIXED THE PARTS WHERE PLUTO DROOLED...
BE QUIET!
OH MY...
DEAR DONALD,
PLEASE FORGIVE ME FOR LEAVING SO SUDDENLY...
...BUT TROUBLE IS BREWING, AND THERE'S NO TIME TO LOSE.

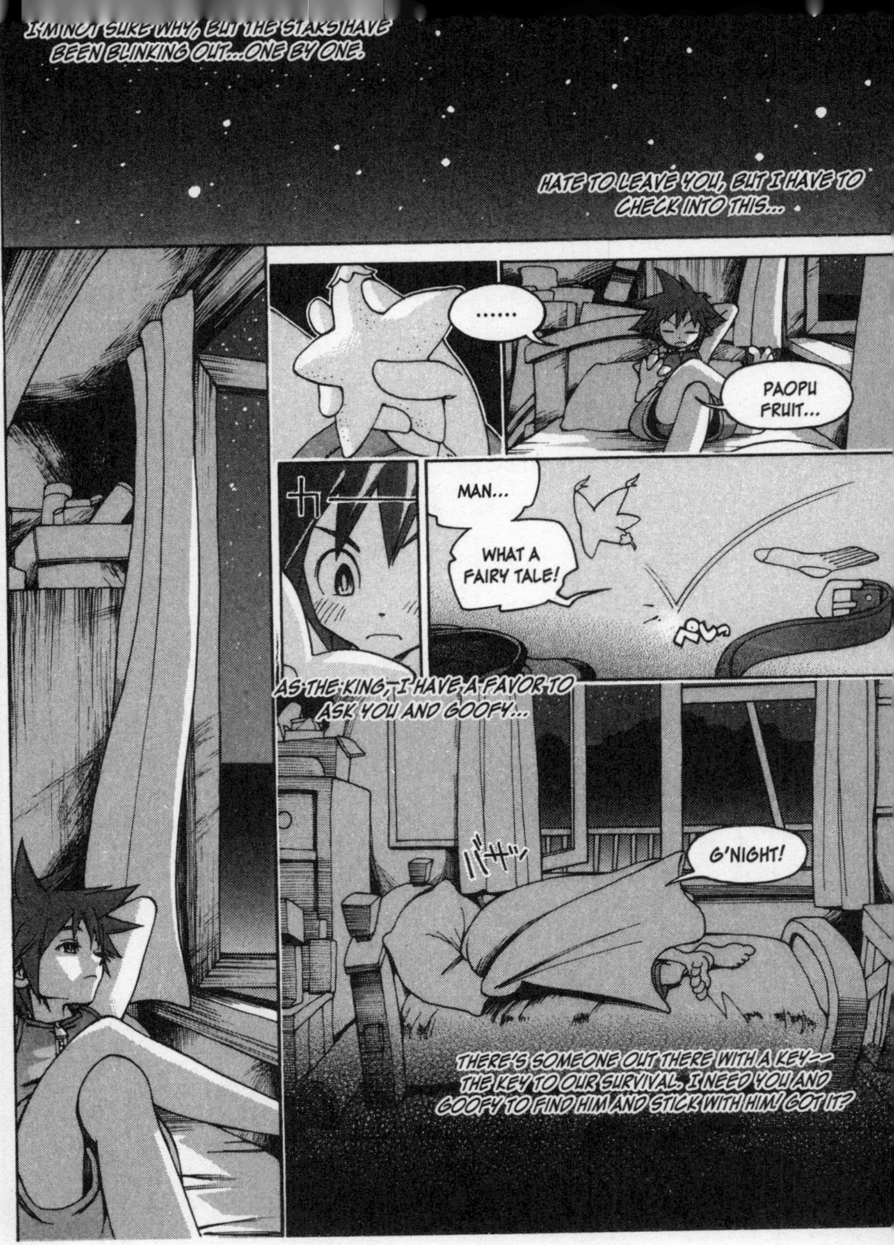
I'M NOT SURE WHY, BUT THE STARS HAVE BEEN BLINKING OUT...ONE BY ONE.
HATE TO LEAVE YOU, BUT I HAVE TO CHECK INTO THIS...
......
PAOPU FRUIT...
MAN...
WHAT A FAIRY TALE!
AS THE KING, I HAVE A FAVOR TO ASK YOU AND GOOFY...
G'NIGHT!
THERE'S SOMEONE OUT THERE WITH A KEY-- THE KEY TO OUR SURVIVAL. I NEED YOU AND GOOFY TO FIND HIM AND STICK WITH HIM! GOT IT?

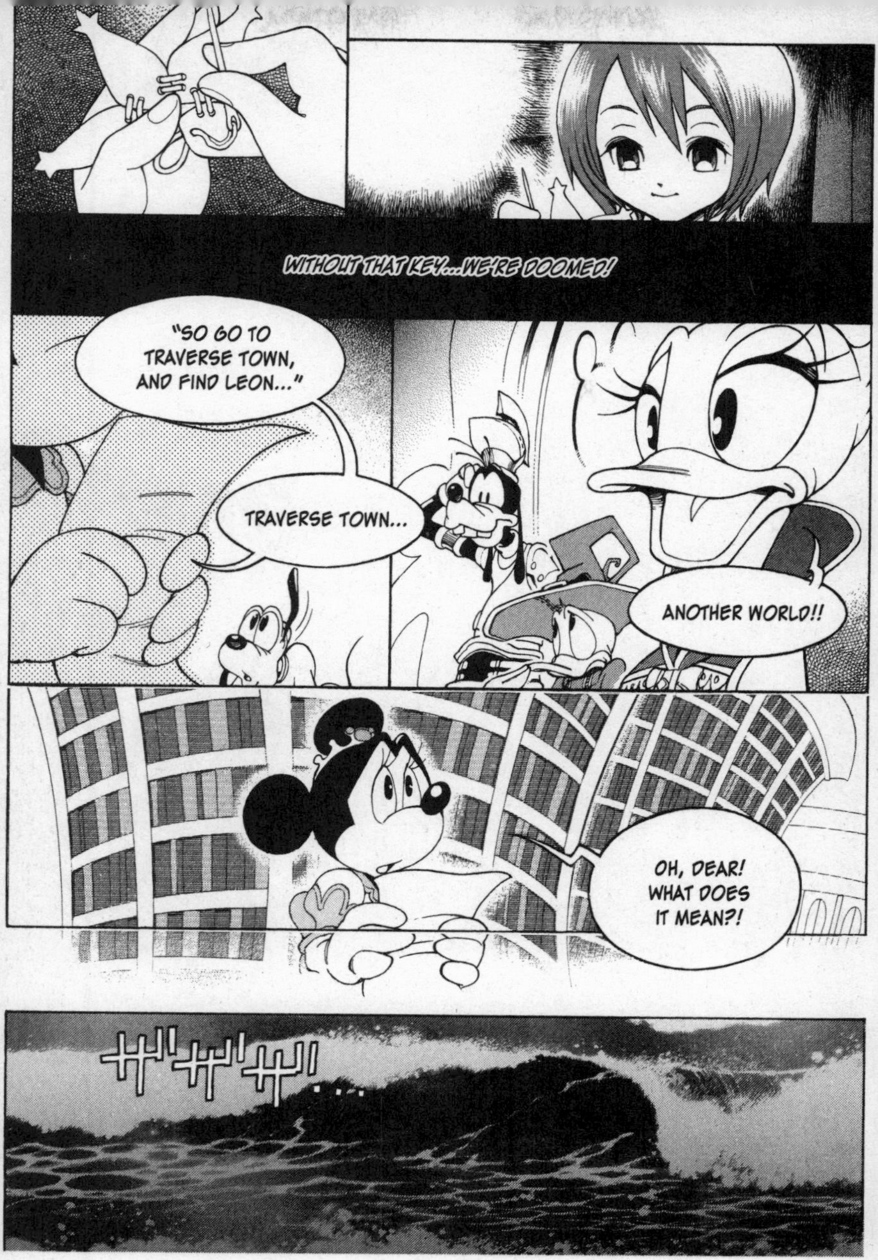
WITHOUT THAT KEY...WE'RE DOOMED!
"SO GO TO TRAVERSE TOWN, AND FIND LEON..."
TRAVERSE TOWN...
ANOTHER WORLD!!
OH, DEAR! WHAT DOES IT MEAN?!

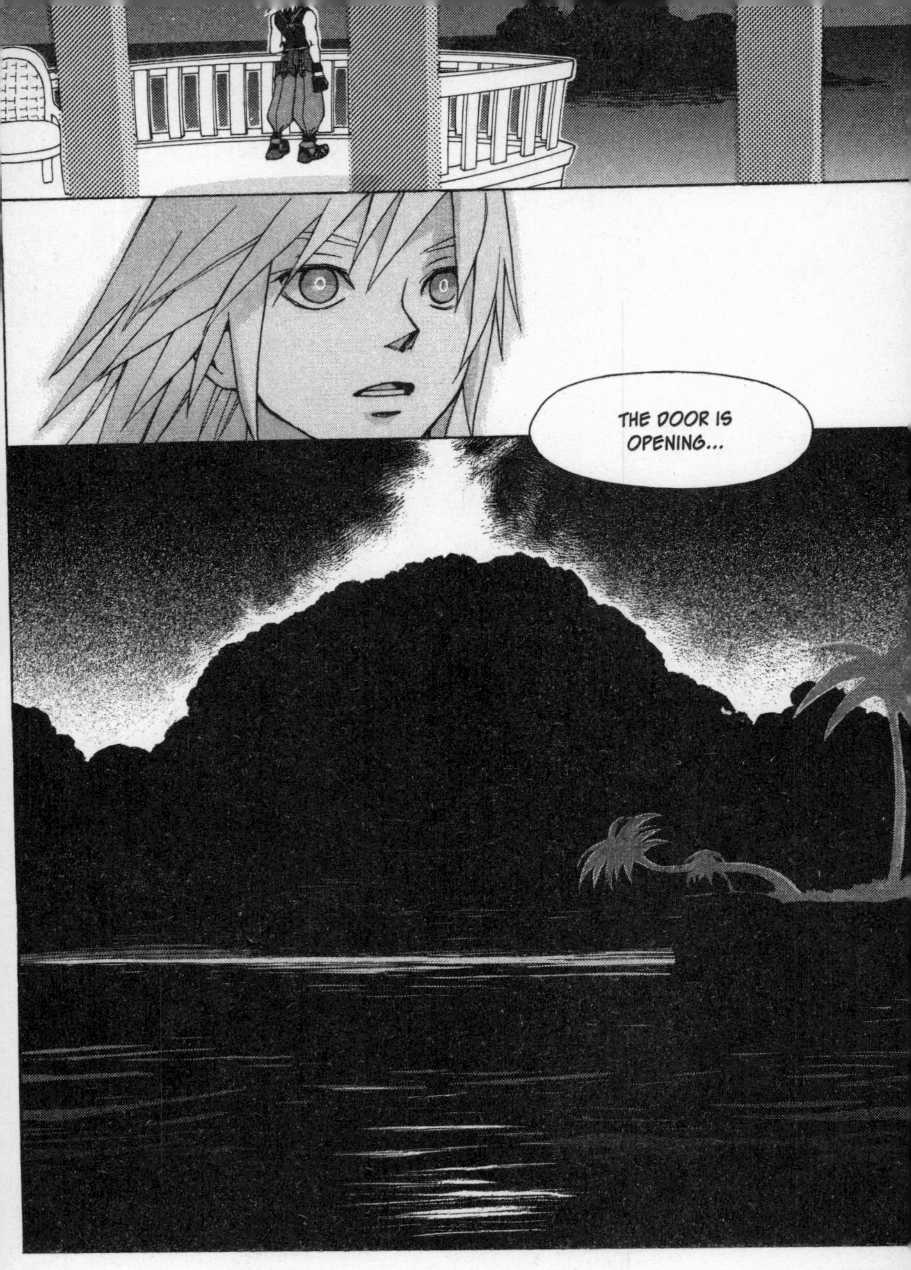
THE DOOR IS OPENING...

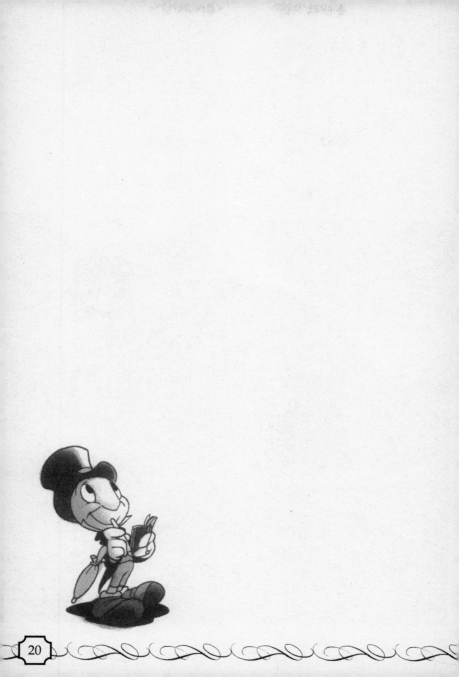

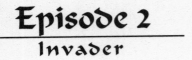

Episode 2
Invader

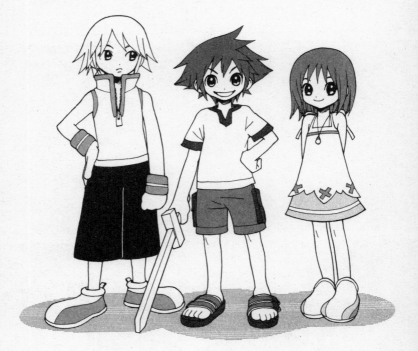

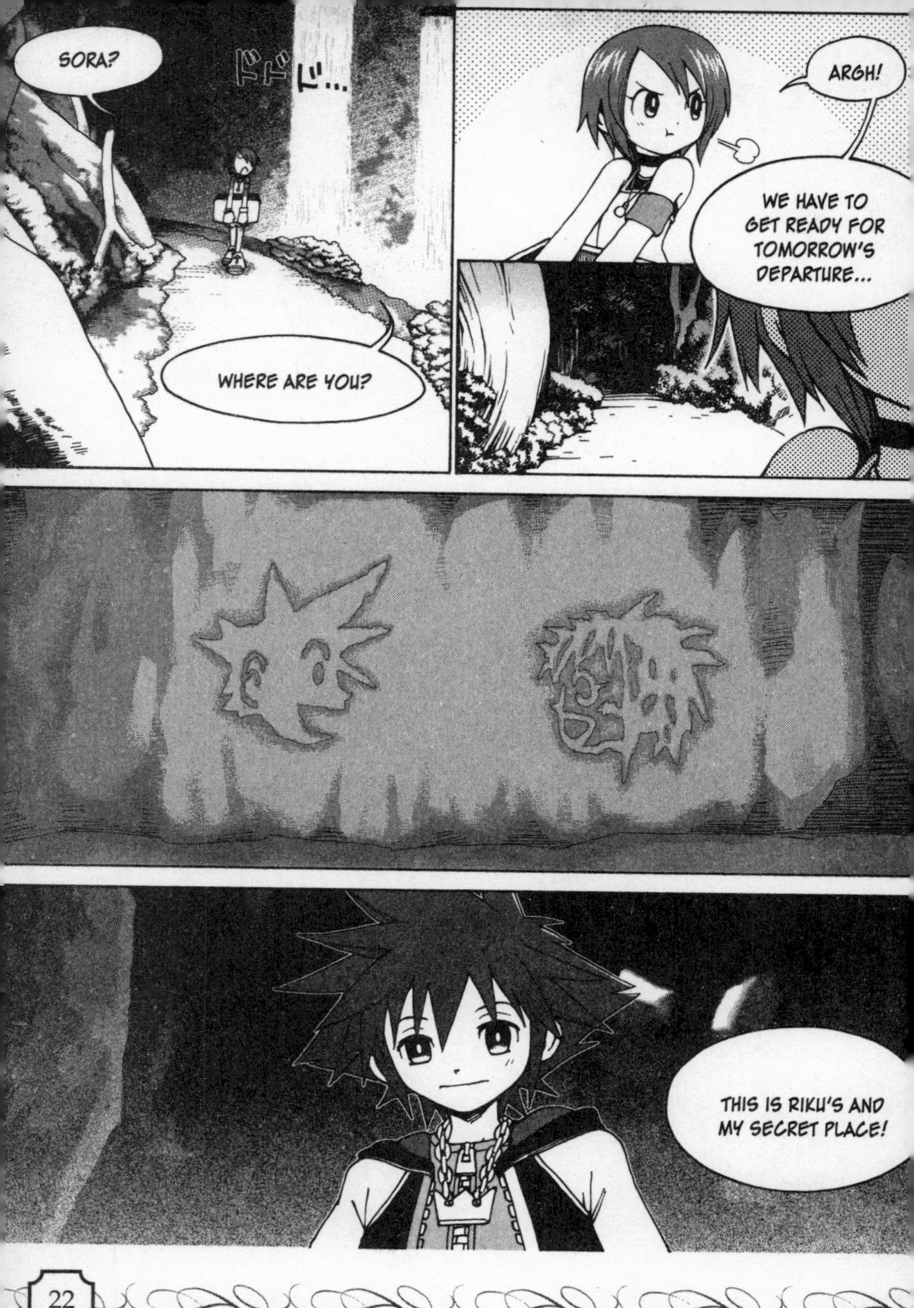
SORA?
ドドド...
WHERE ARE YOU?
ARGH!
WE HAVE TO GET READY FOR TOMORROW'S DEPARTURE...
THIS IS RIKU'S AND MY SECRET PLACE!

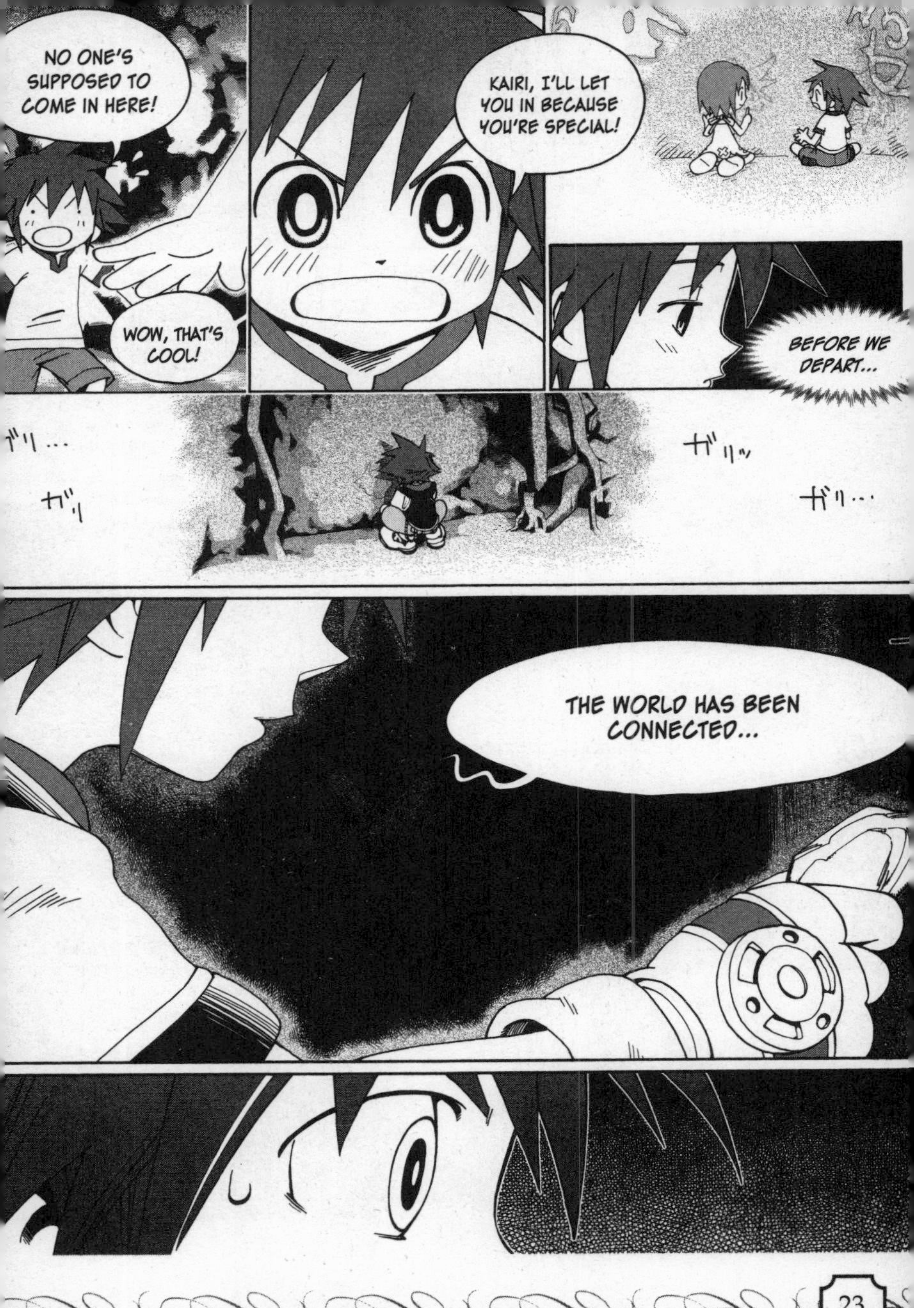
NO ONE'S SUPPOSED TO COME IN HERE!
WOW, THAT'S COOL!
KAIRI, I'LL LET YOU IN BECAUSE YOU'RE SPECIAL!
BEFORE WE DEPART...
ガリッ
ガリ…
THE WORLD HAS BEEN CONNECTED...

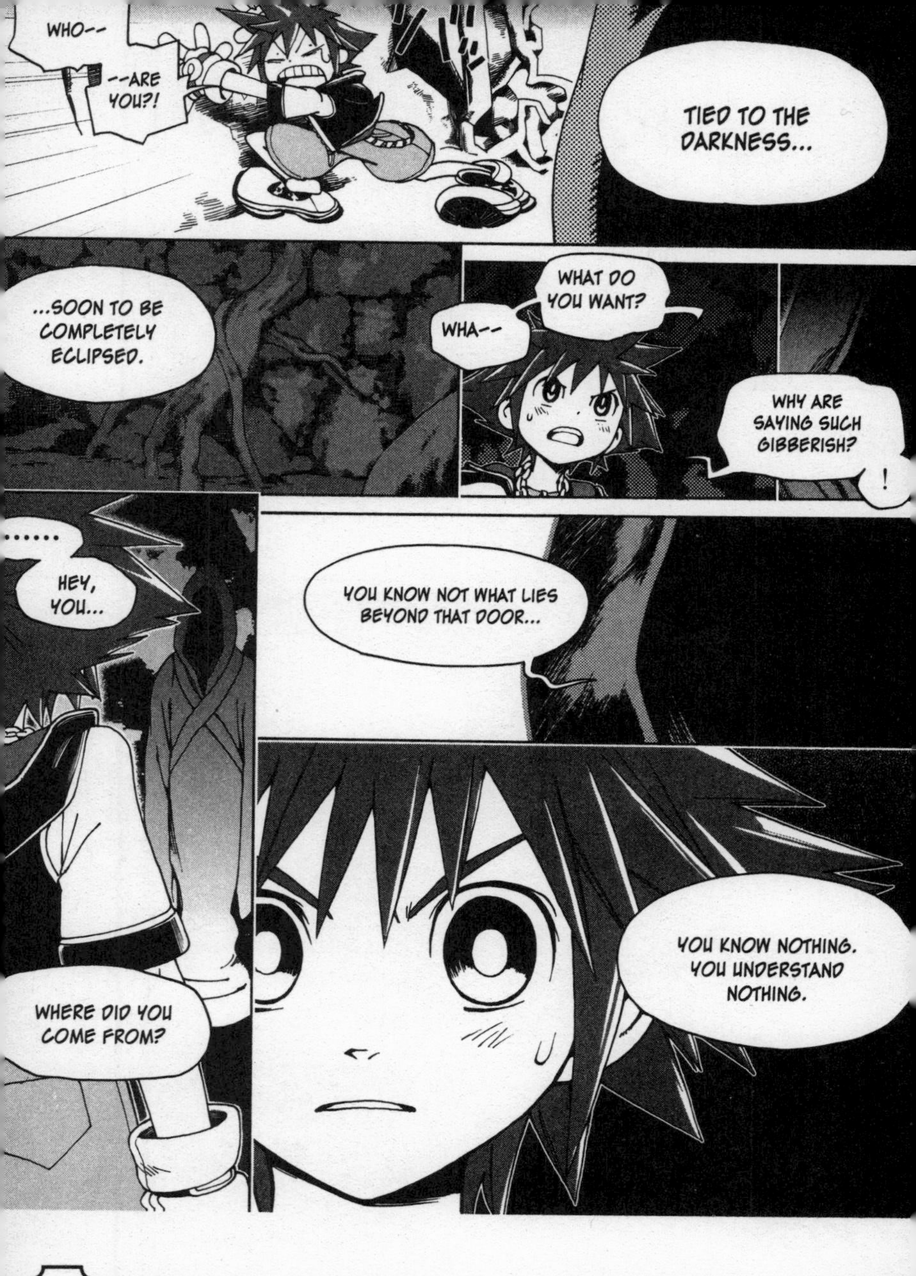
WHO--
--ARE YOU?!
TIED TO THE DARKNESS...
...SOON TO BE COMPLETELY ECLIPSED.
WHAT DO YOU WANT?
WHA--
WHY ARE SAYING SUCH GIBBERISH?
!
......
HEY, YOU...
WHERE DID YOU COME FROM?
YOU KNOW NOT WHAT LIES BEYOND THAT DOOR...
YOU KNOW NOTHING. YOU UNDERSTAND NOTHING.

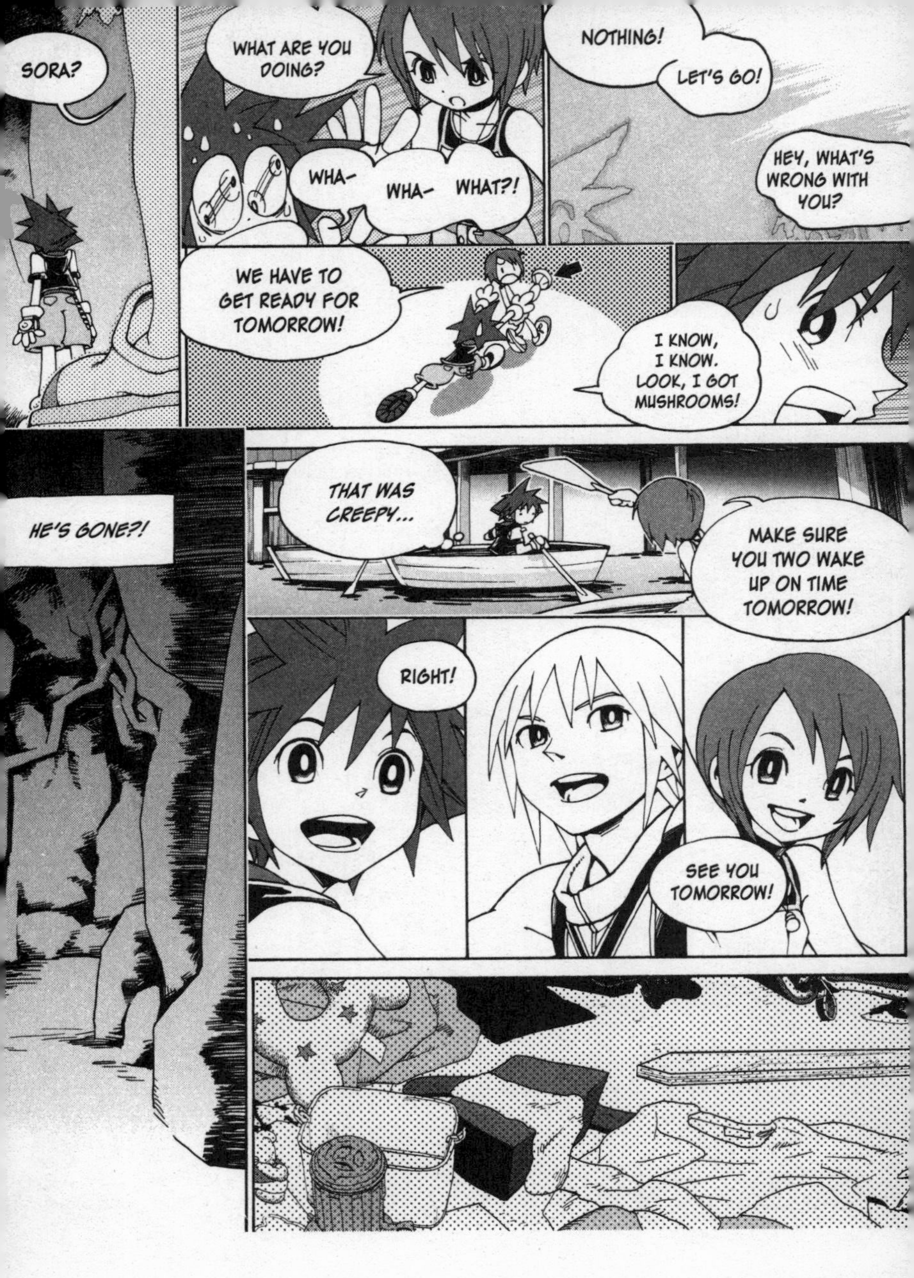
SORA?
WHAT ARE YOU DOING?
WHA- WHA- WHAT?!
NOTHING!
LET'S GO!
HEY, WHAT'S WRONG WITH YOU?
WE HAVE TO GET READY FOR TOMORROW!
I KNOW, I KNOW. LOOK, I GOT MUSHROOMS!
HE'S GONE?!
THAT WAS CREEPY...
MAKE SURE YOU TWO WAKE UP ON TIME TOMORROW!
RIGHT!
SEE YOU TOMORROW!

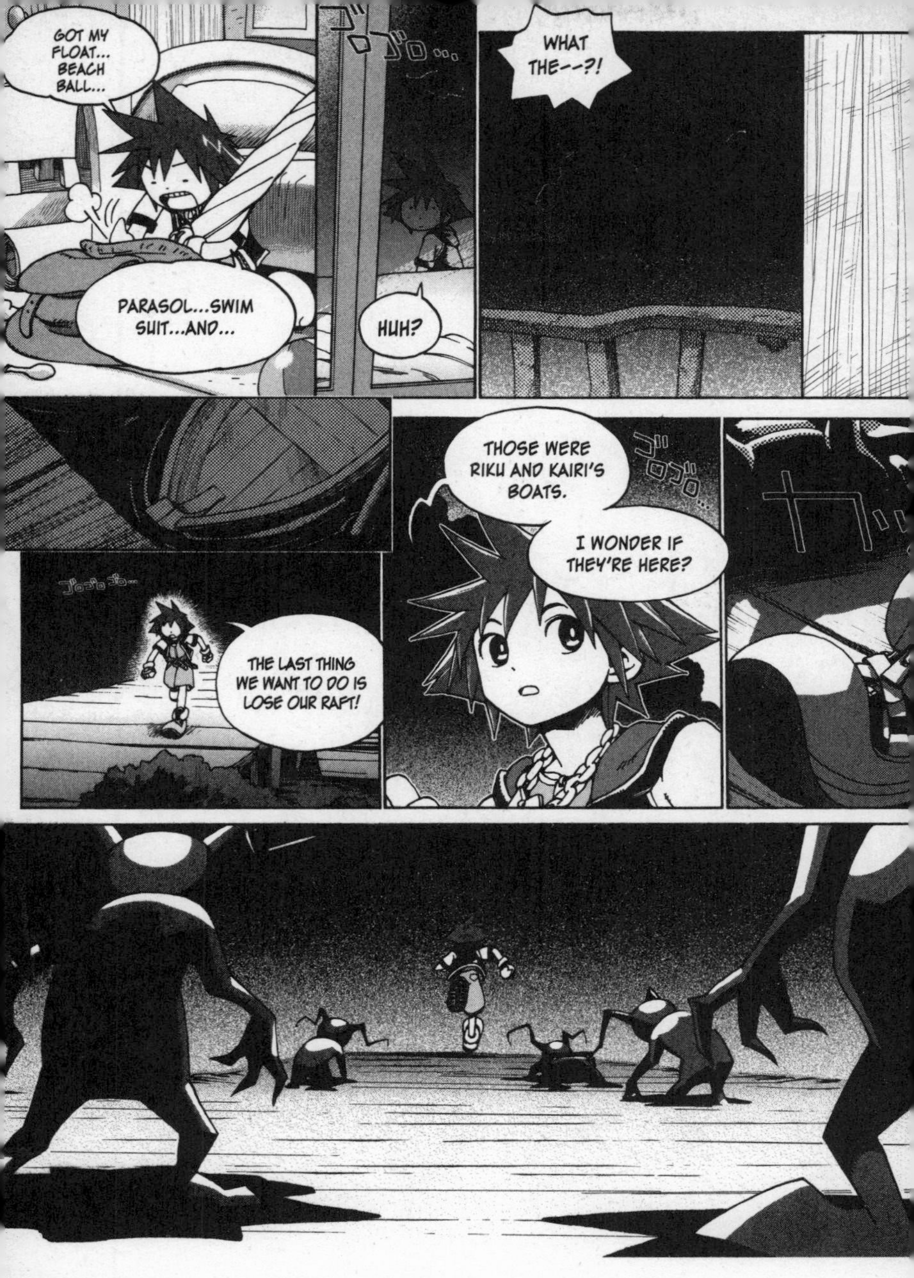
GOT MY FLOAT... BEACH BALL...
PARASOL...SWIM SUIT...AND...
HUH?
WHAT THE--?!
THE LAST THING WE WANT TO DO IS LOSE OUR RAFT!
THOSE WERE RIKU AND KAIRI'S BOATS.
I WONDER IF THEY'RE HERE?

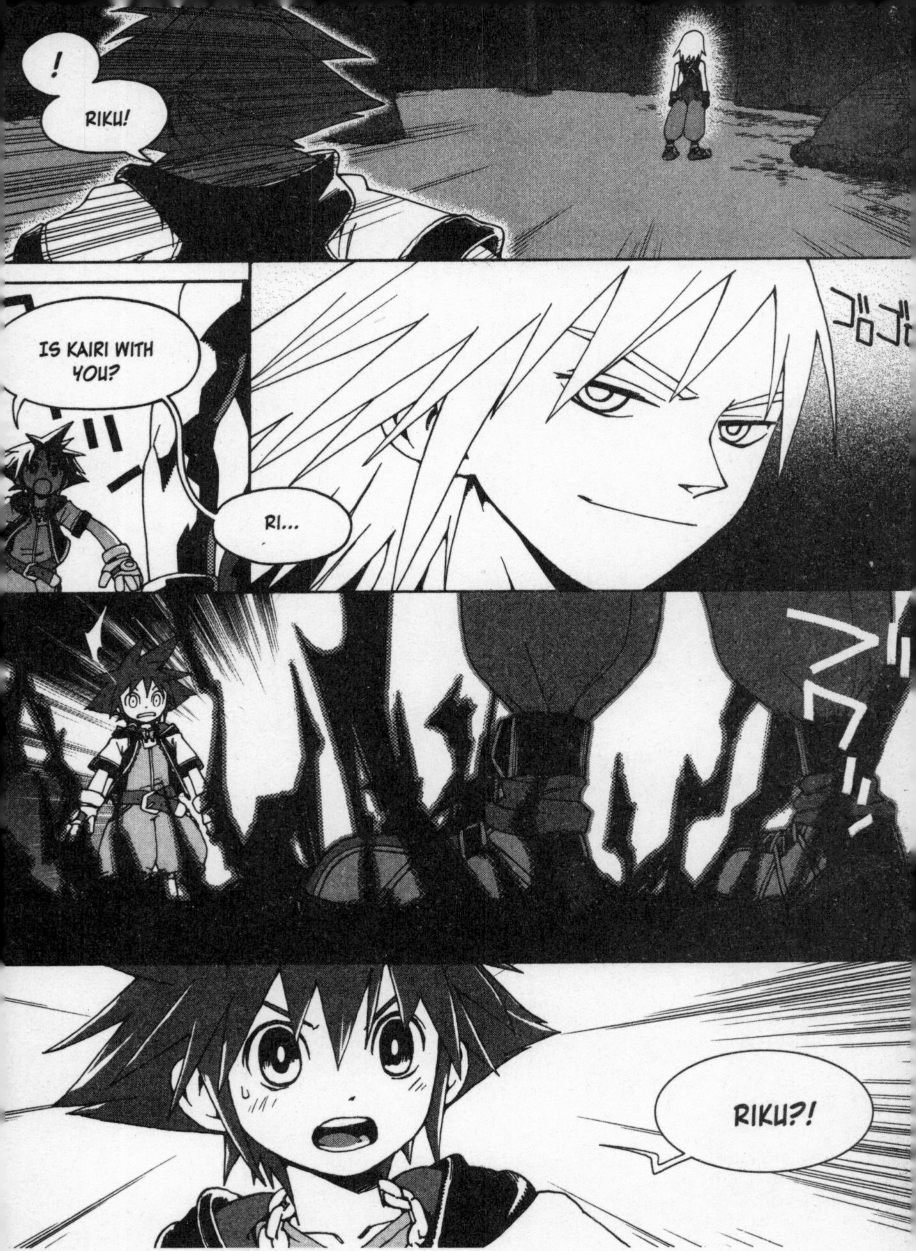
!
RIKU!
IS KAIRI WITH YOU?
RI...
ゴロゴロ
RIKU?!

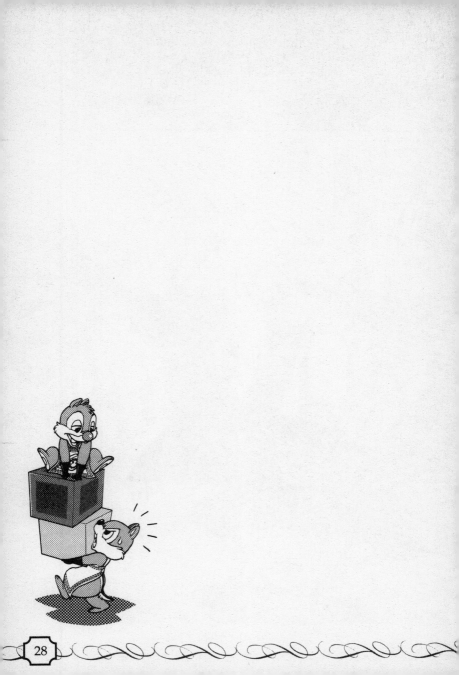

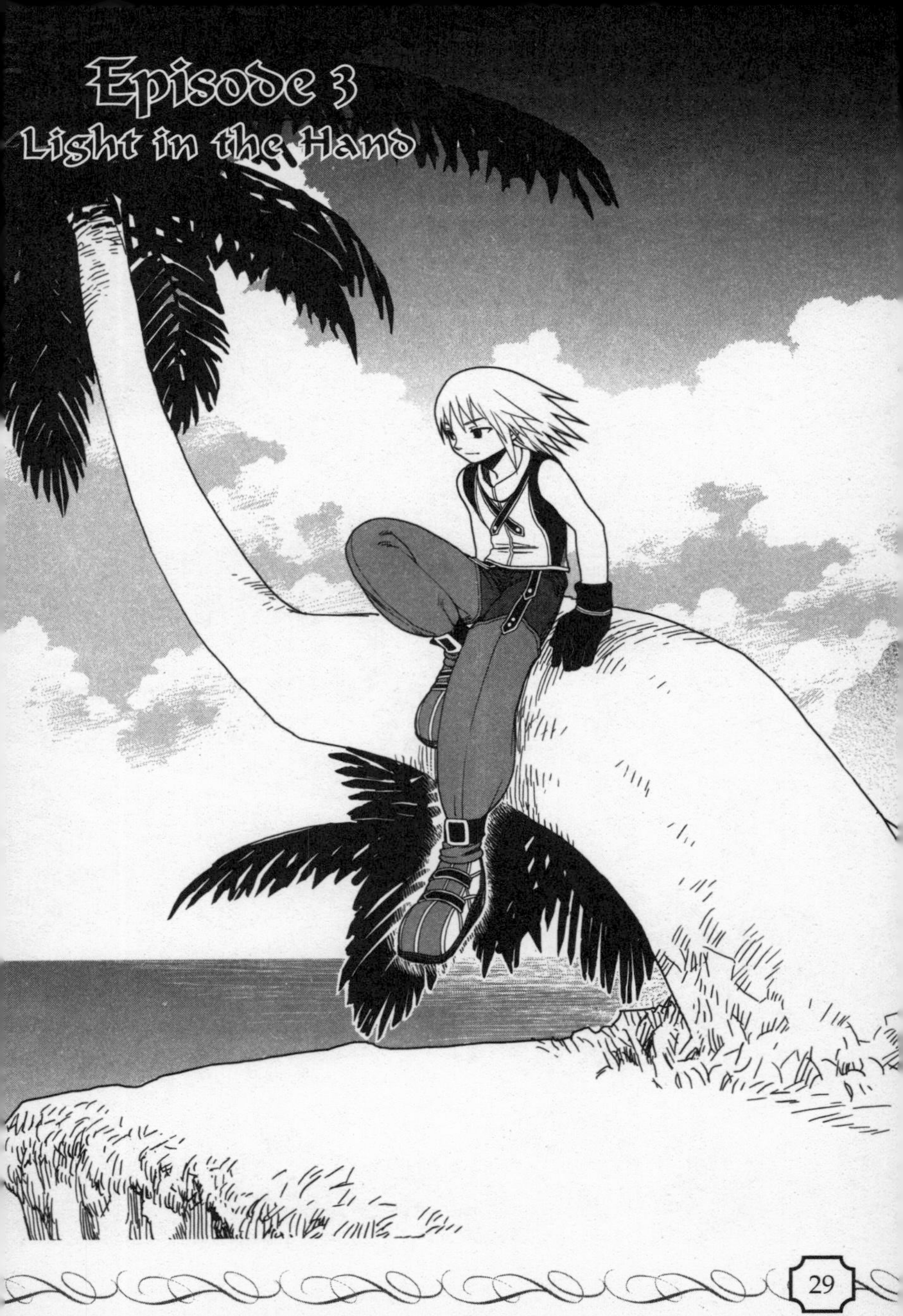
Episode 3
Light in the Hand

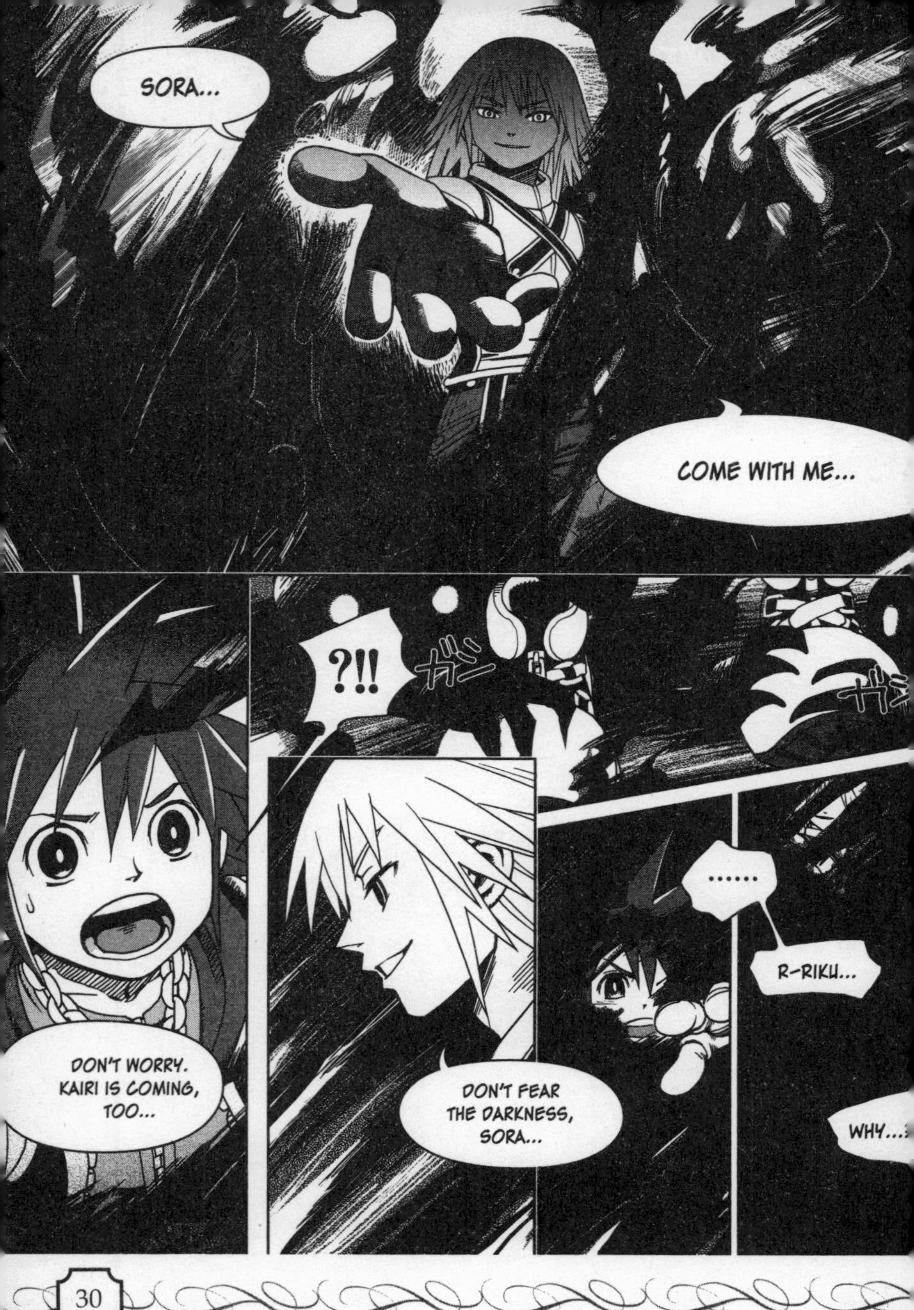
SORA...
COME WITH ME...
DON'T WORRY.
KAIRI IS COMING,
TOO...
?!!
DON'T FEAR
THE DARKNESS,
SORA...
......
R-RIKU...
WHY...

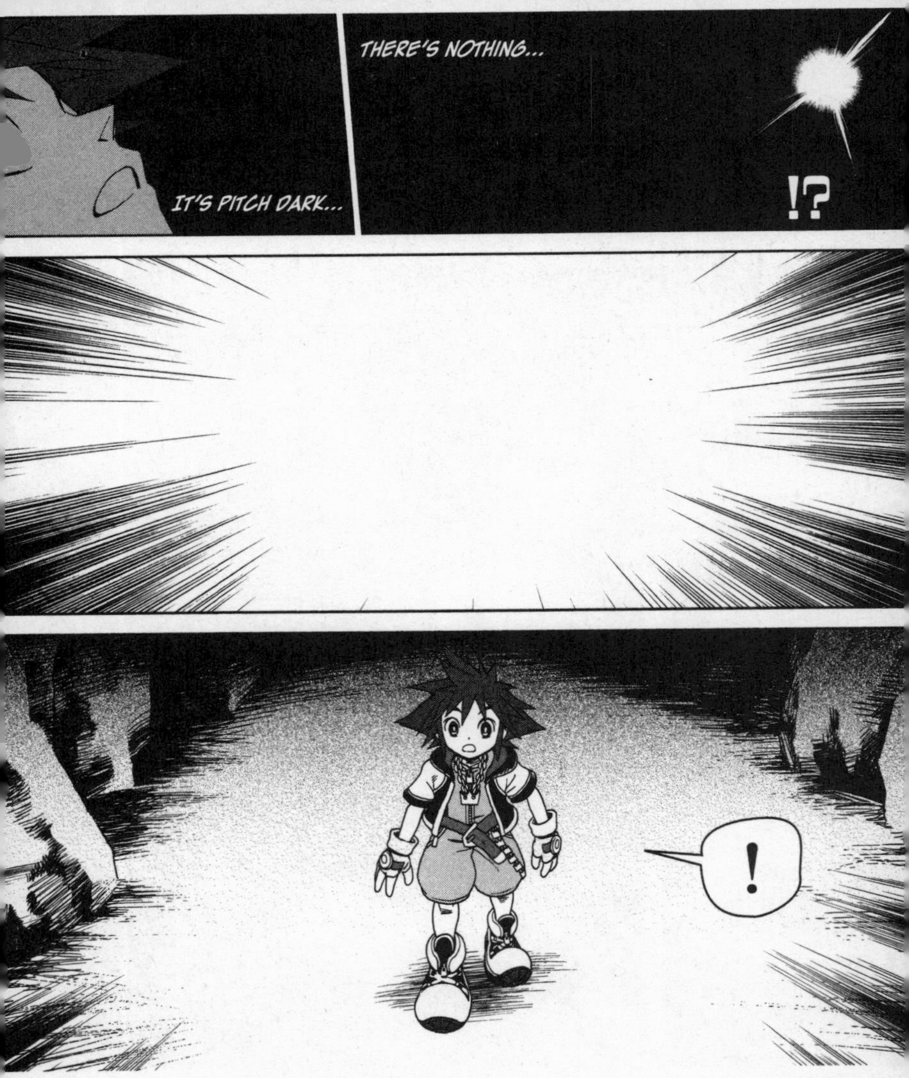
IT'S PITCH DARK...
THERE'S NOTHING...
!?
!

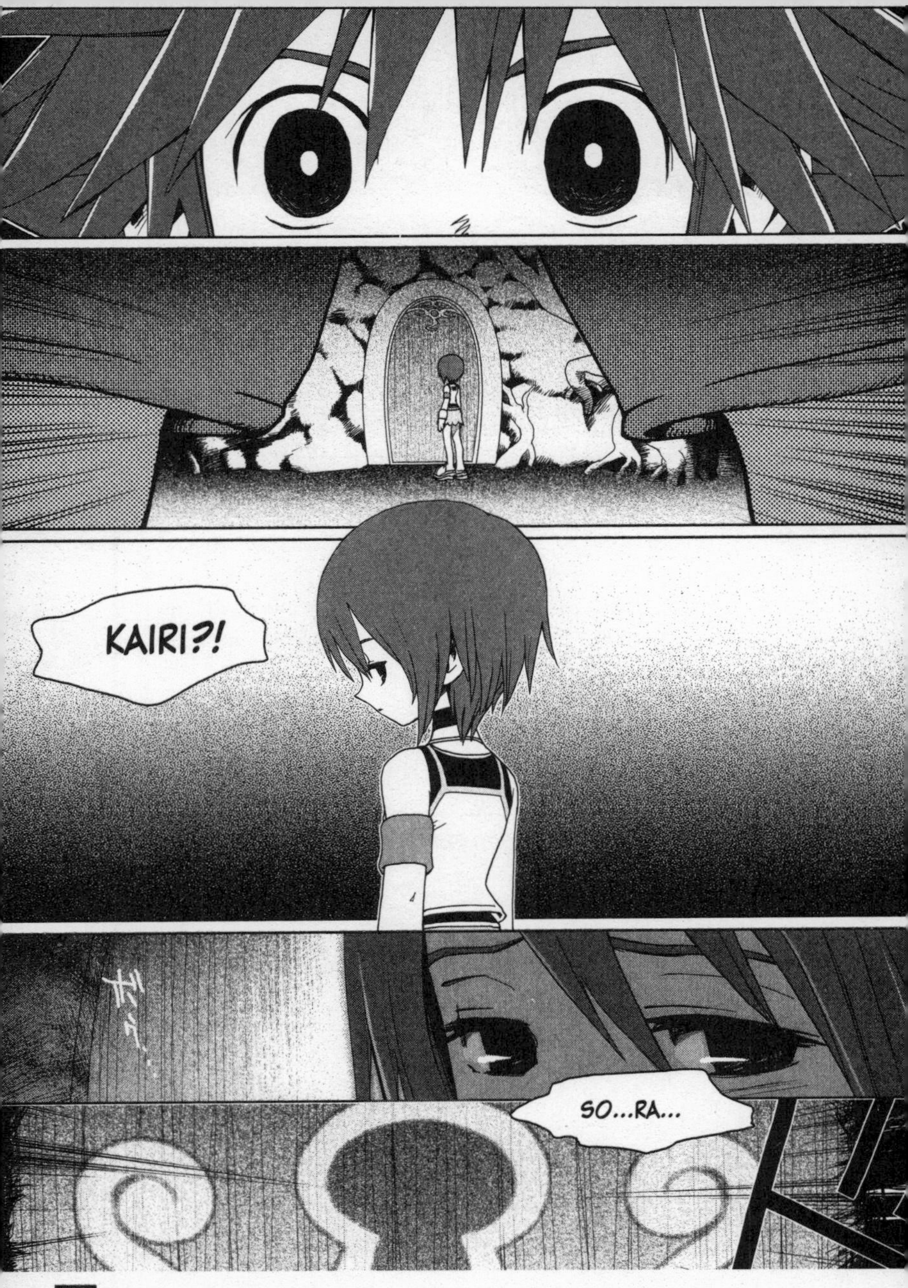
KAIRI?!
SO...RA...

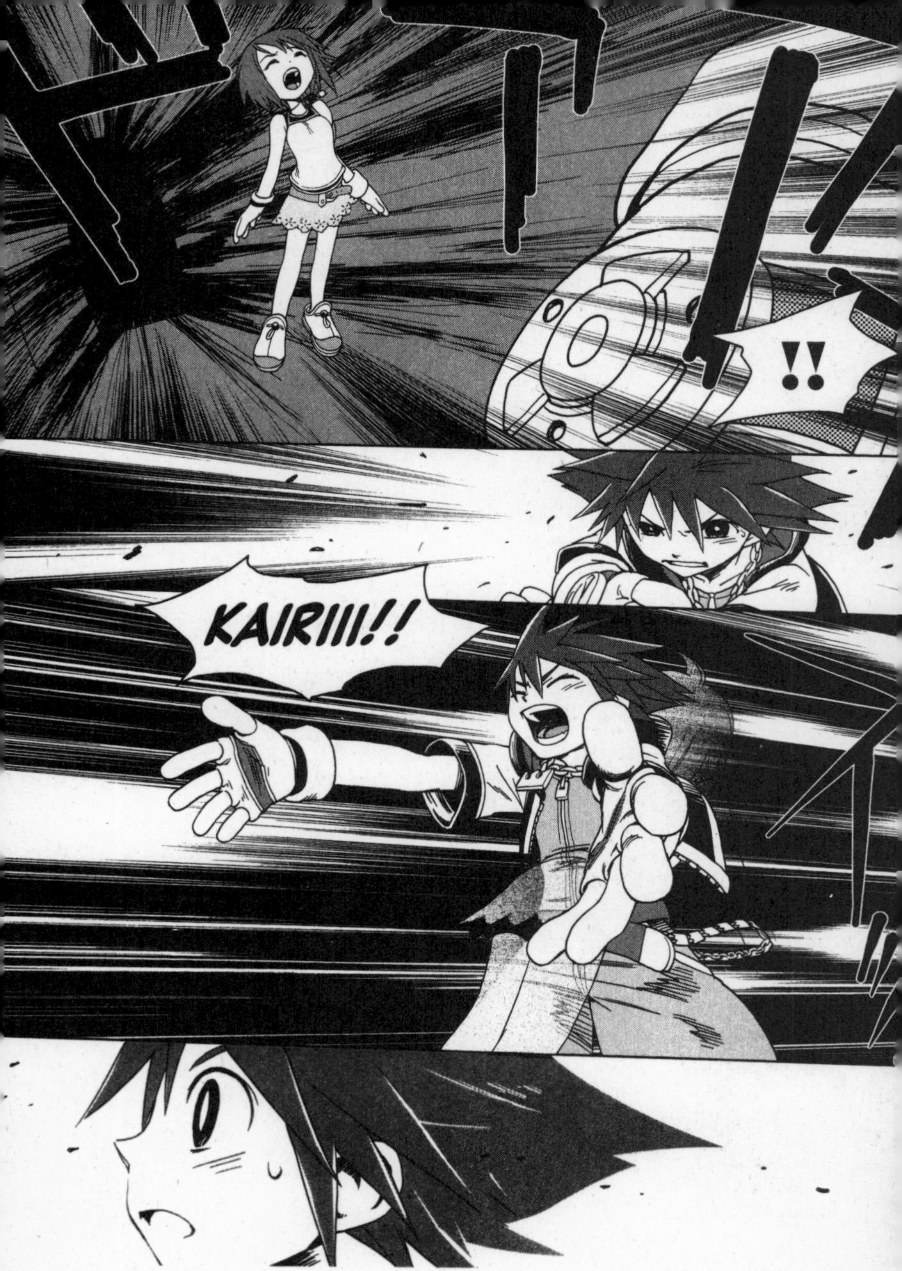
!!
KAIRIII!!

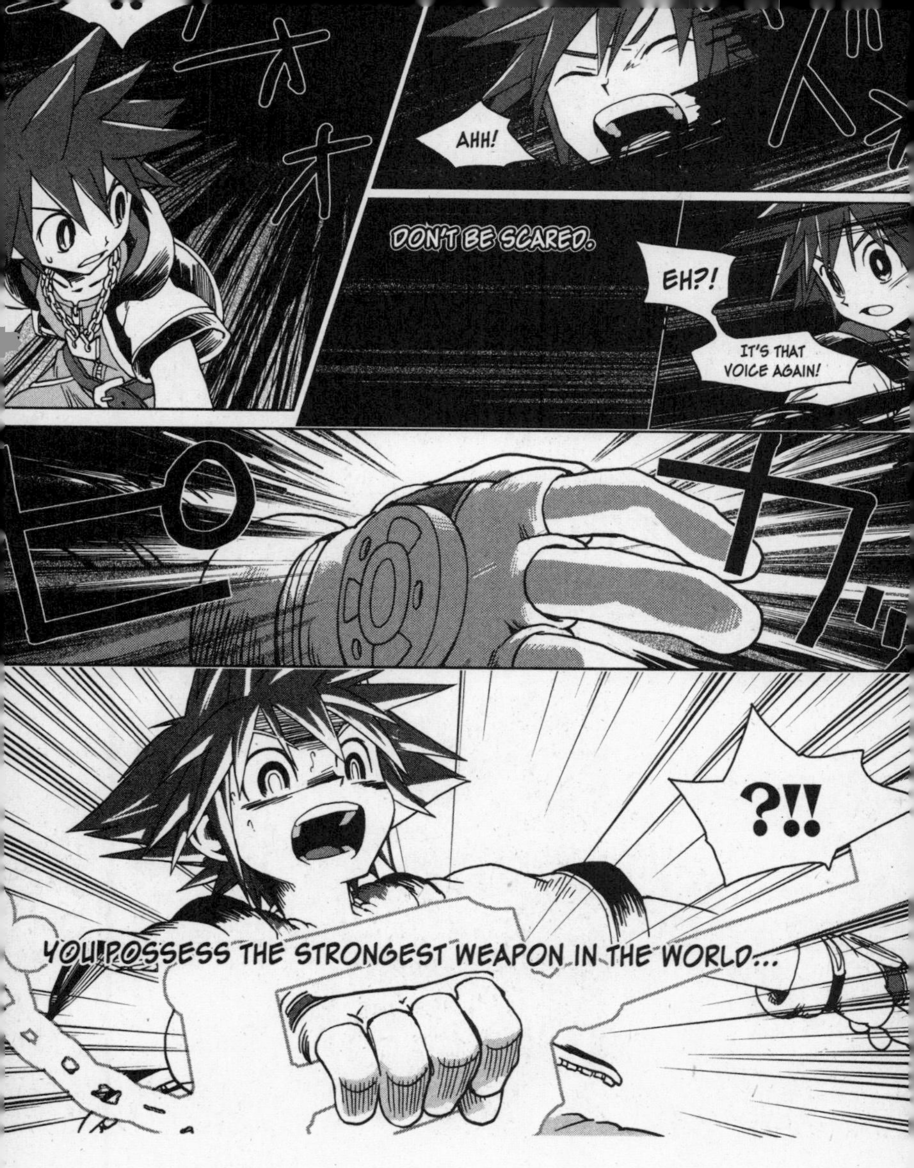
AHH!
DON'T BE SCARED.
EH?!
IT'S THAT VOICE AGAIN!
?!!
YOU POSSESS THE STRONGEST WEAPON IN THE WORLD...

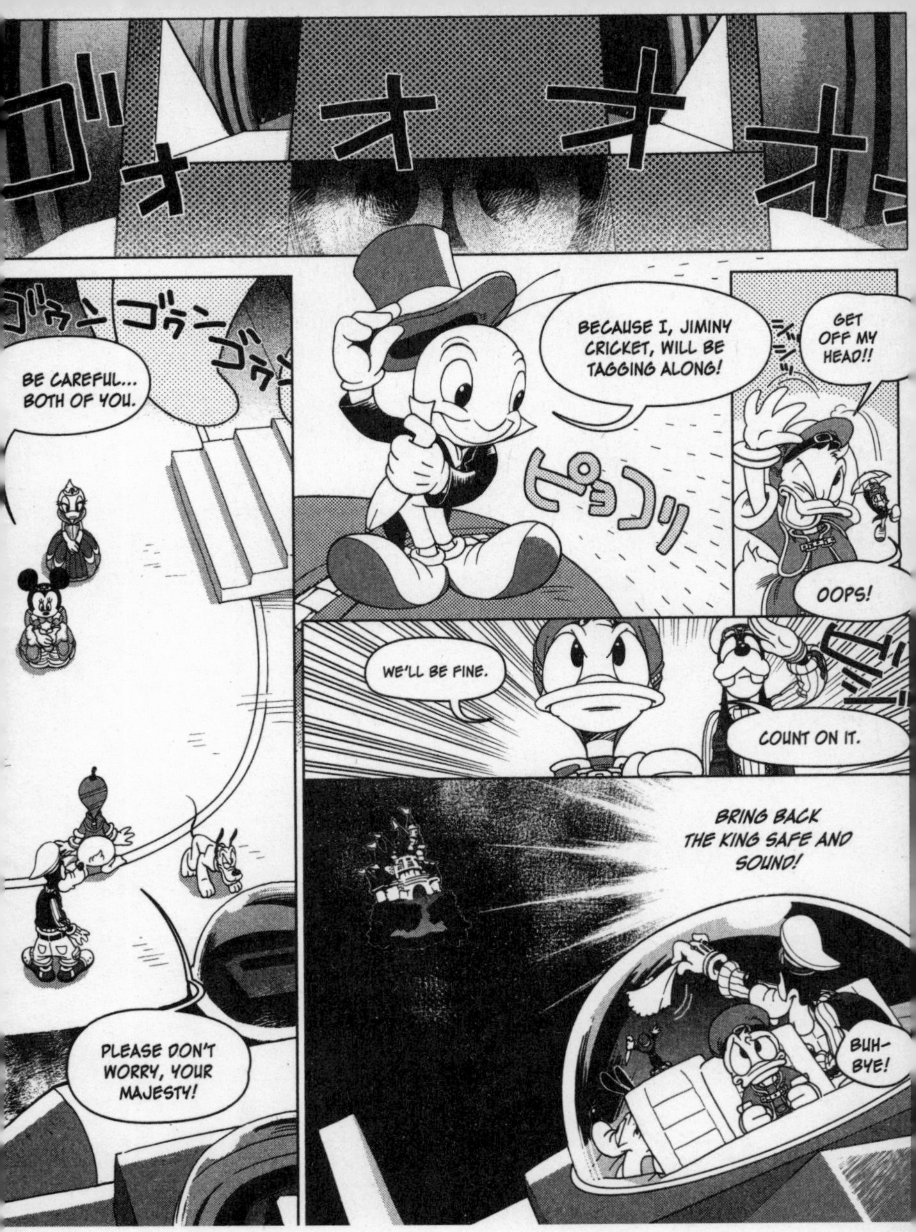
ゴォオオッ
ゴゥンゴゥンゴゥン
BE CAREFUL... BOTH OF YOU.
PLEASE DON'T WORRY, YOUR MAJESTY!
BECAUSE I, JIMINY CRICKET, WILL BE TAGGING ALONG!
ピョコリ
GET OFF MY HEAD!!
OOPS!
WE'LL BE FINE.
COUNT ON IT.
BRING BACK THE KING SAFE AND SOUND!
BUH-BYE!

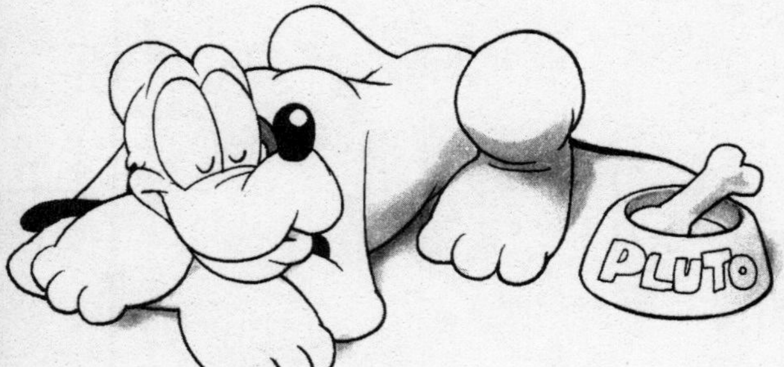
PLUTO

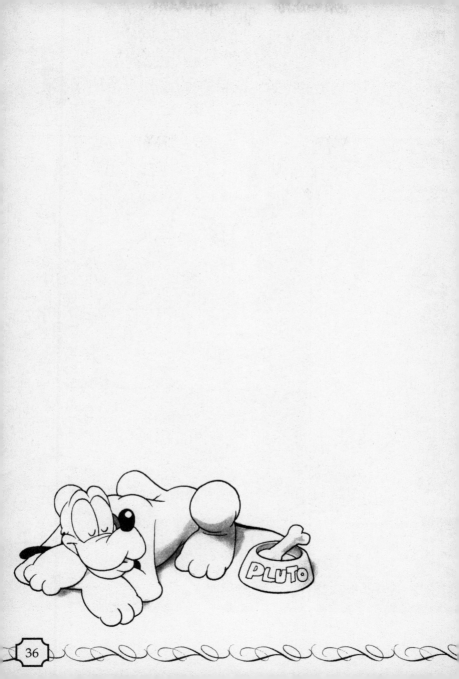

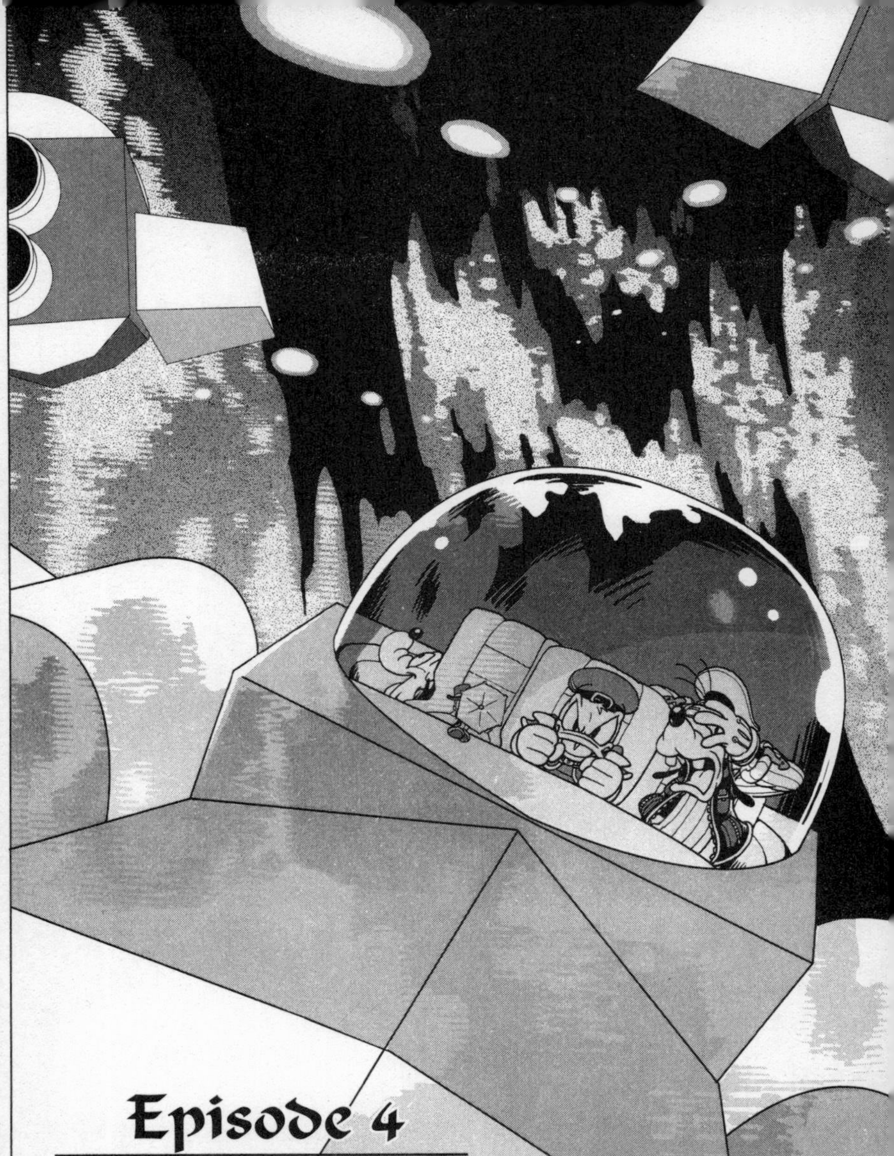

Episode 4

Giant Shadow

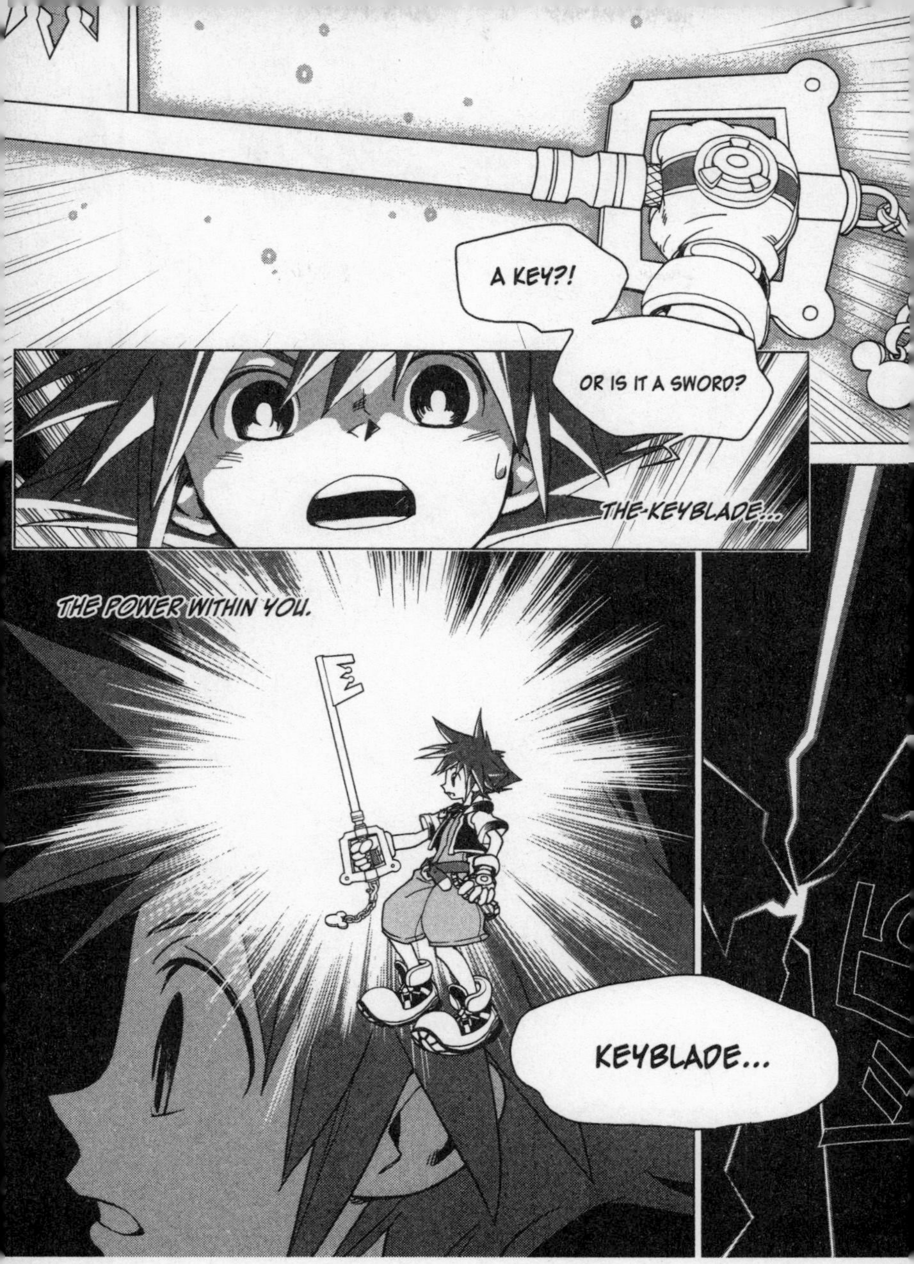
A KEY?!
OR IS IT A SWORD?
THE-KEYBLADE...
THE POWER WITHIN YOU.
KEYBLADE...

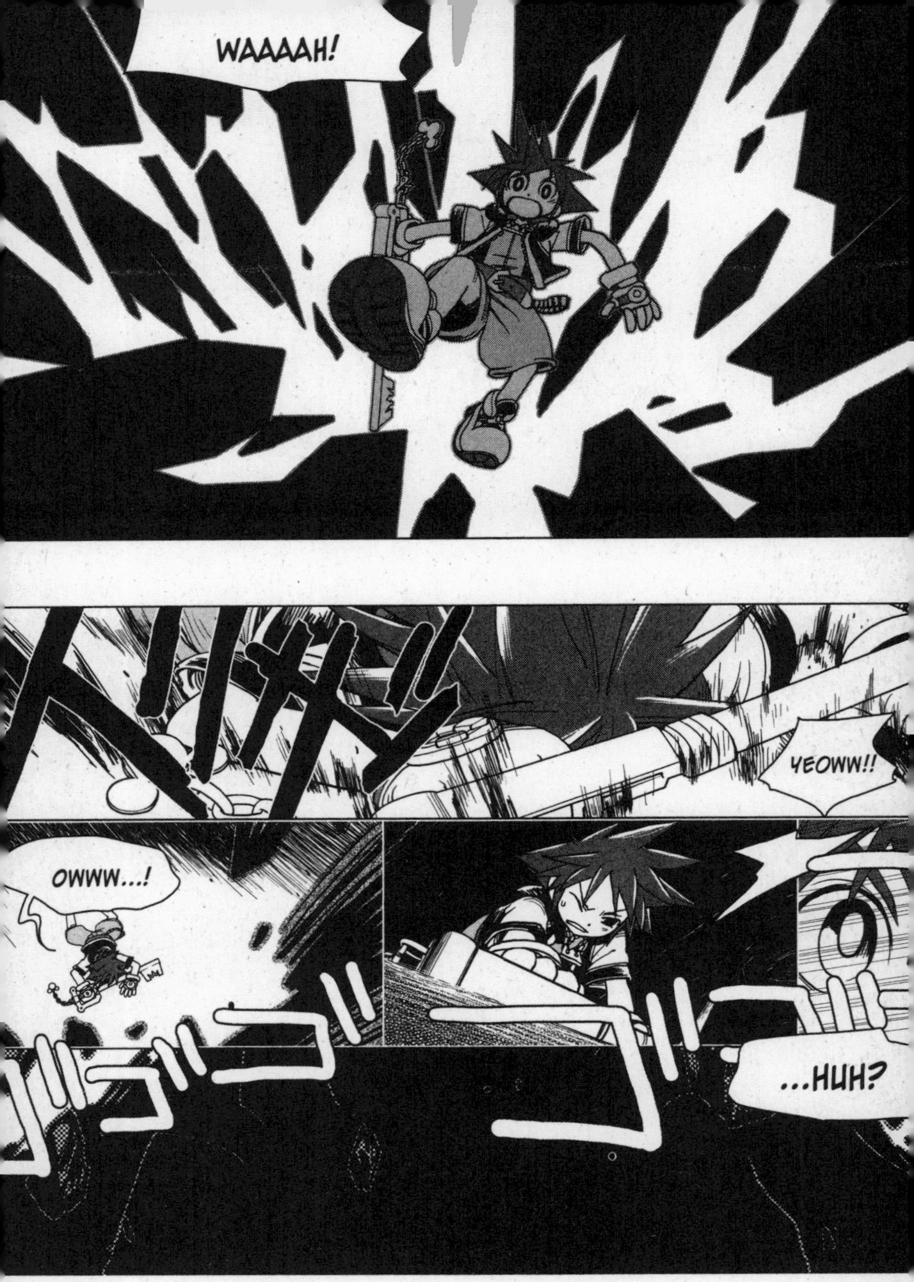
WAAAAH!
YEOWW!!
OWWW...!
...HUH?

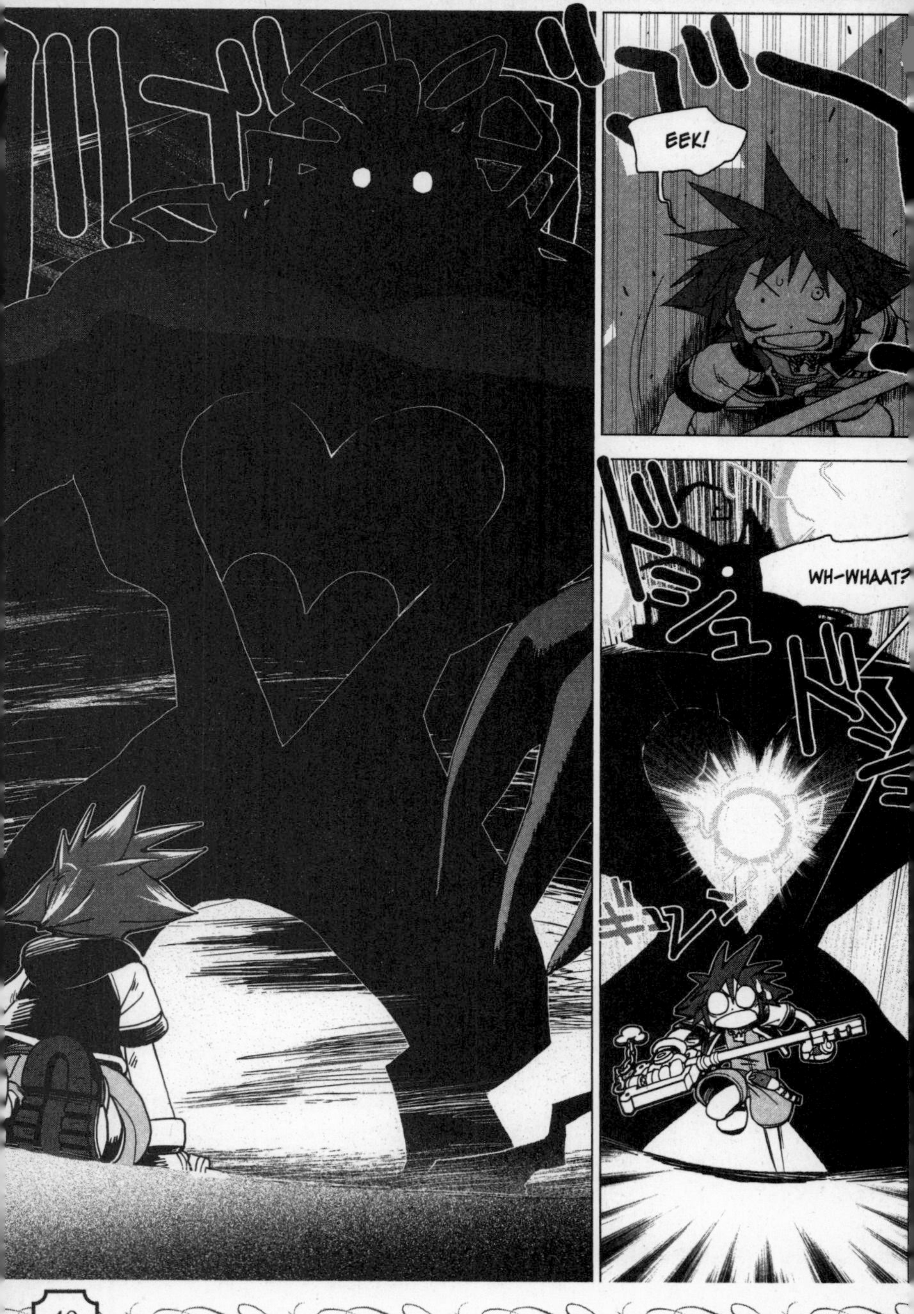
EEK!
WH-WHAAT?

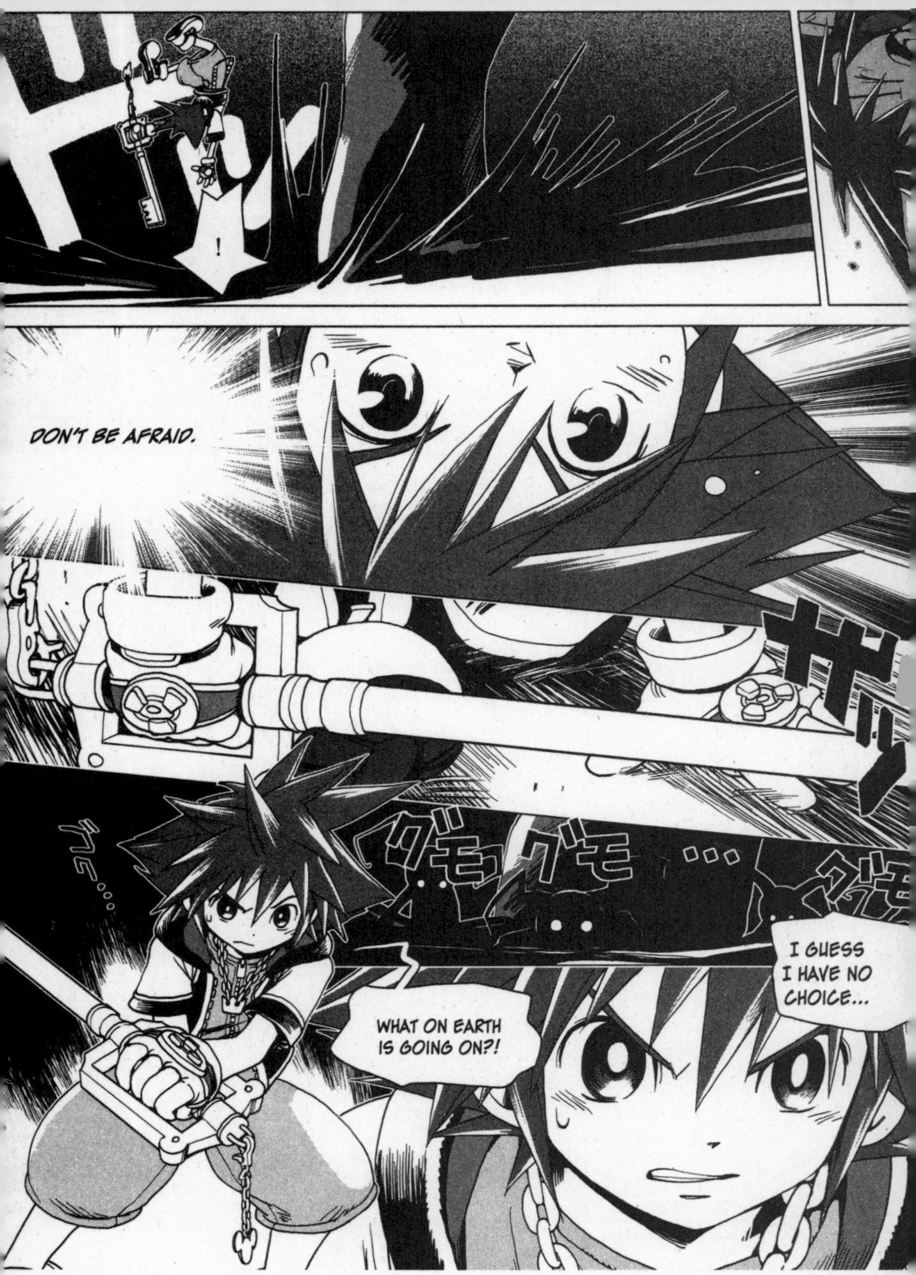
!
DON'T BE AFRAID.
ザッ
WHAT ON EARTH IS GOING ON?!
I GUESS I HAVE NO CHOICE...

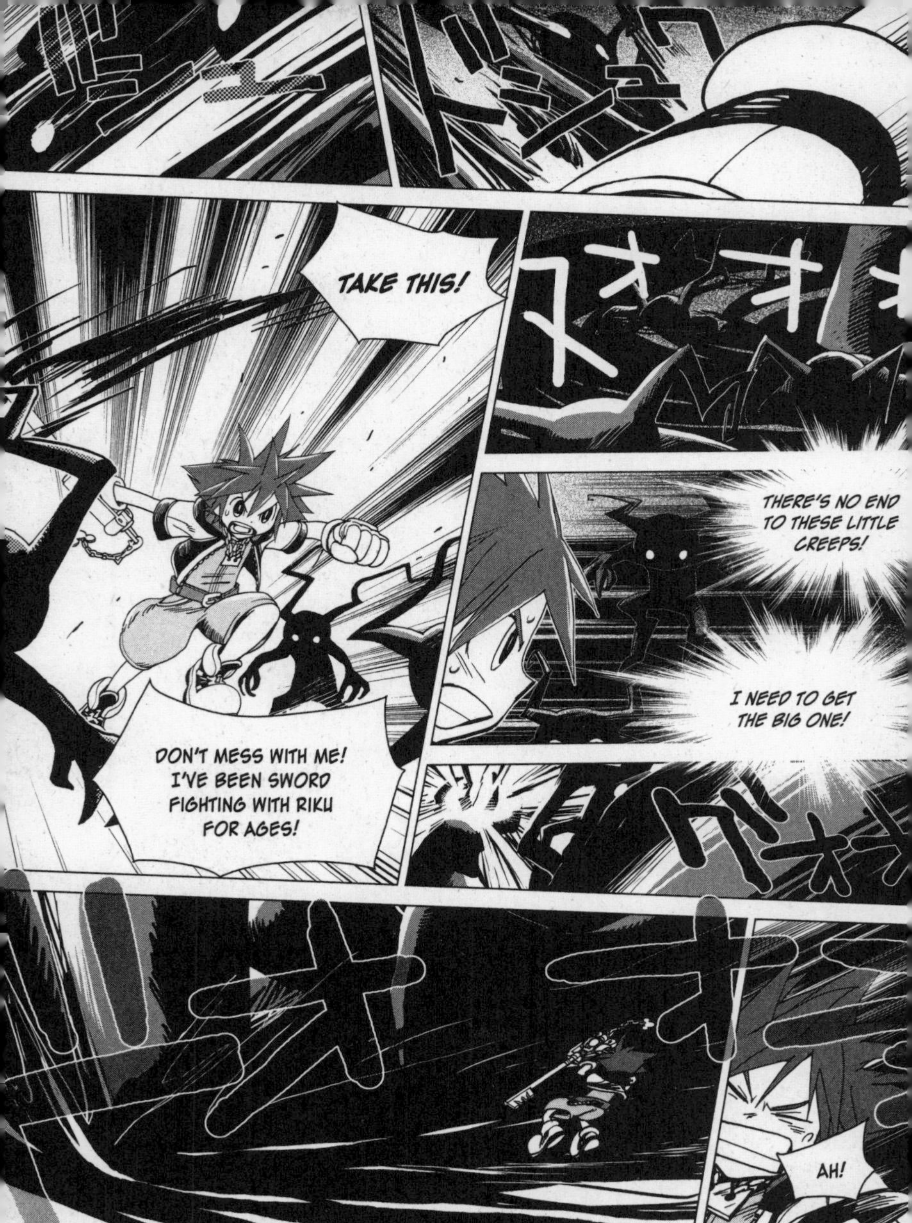
TAKE THIS!
DON'T MESS WITH ME! I'VE BEEN SWORD FIGHTING WITH RIKU FOR AGES!
THERE'S NO END TO THESE LITTLE CREEPS!
I NEED TO GET THE BIG ONE!
AH!

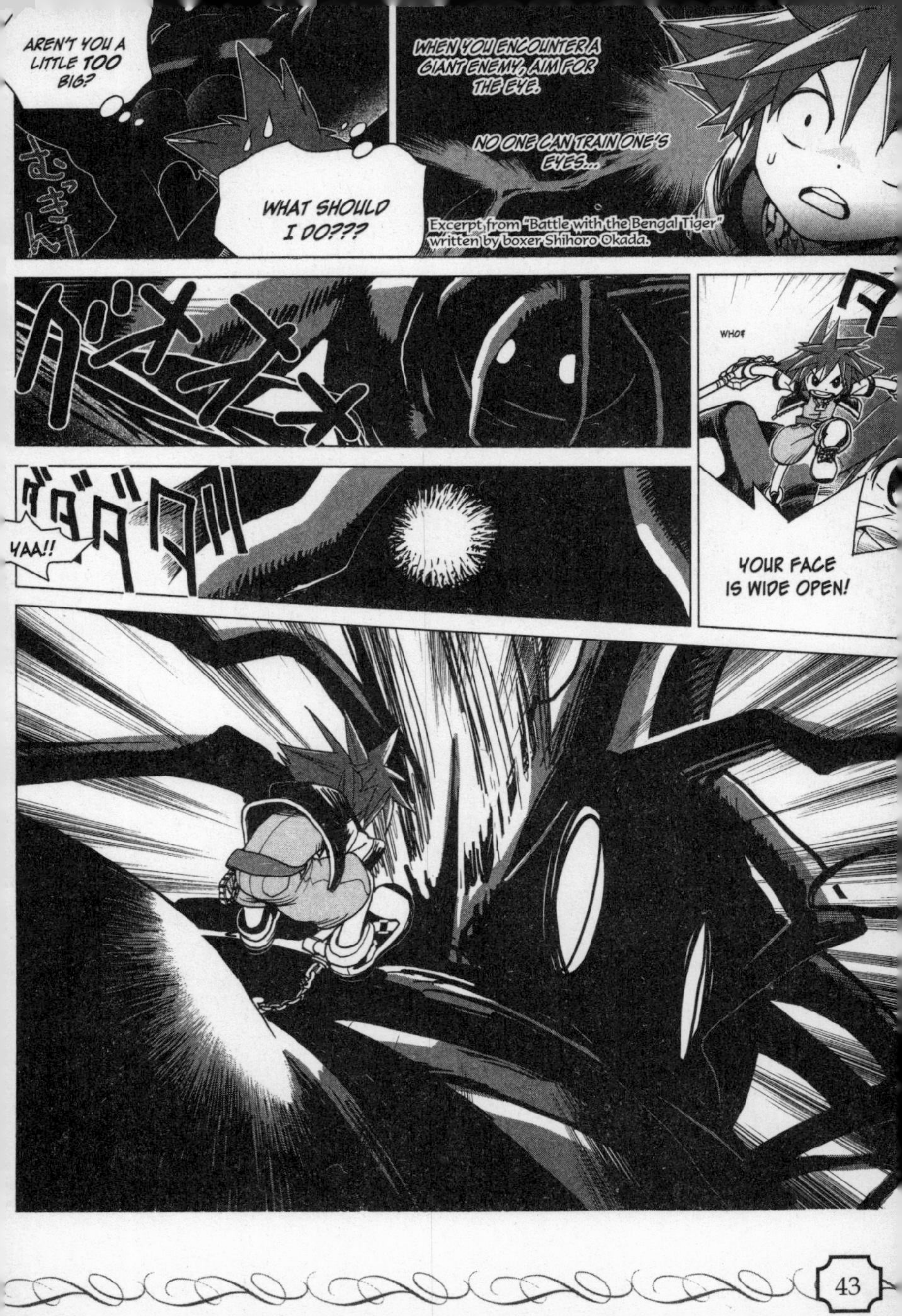
WHEN YOU ENCOUNTER A GIANT ENEMY, AIM FOR THE EYE.
NO ONE CAN TRAIN ONE'S EYES...
Excerpt from "Battle with the Bengal Tiger" written by boxer Shihoro Okada.
AREN'T YOU A LITTLE TOO BIG?
WHAT SHOULD I DO???
WHO?
YOUR FACE IS WIDE OPEN!
ガオオー
YAA!!

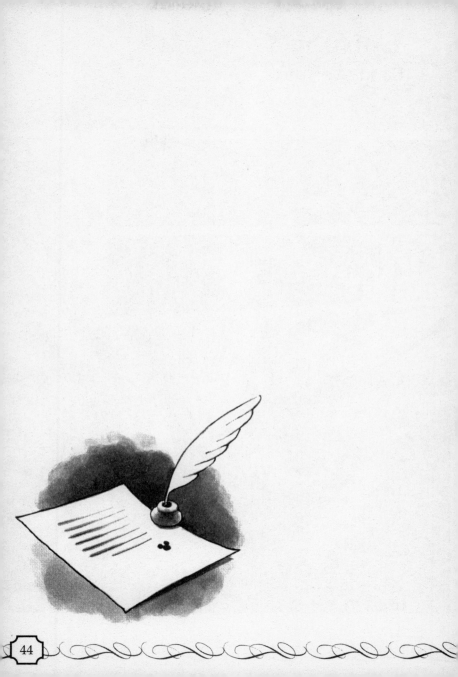

Episode 5

Cast Ashore

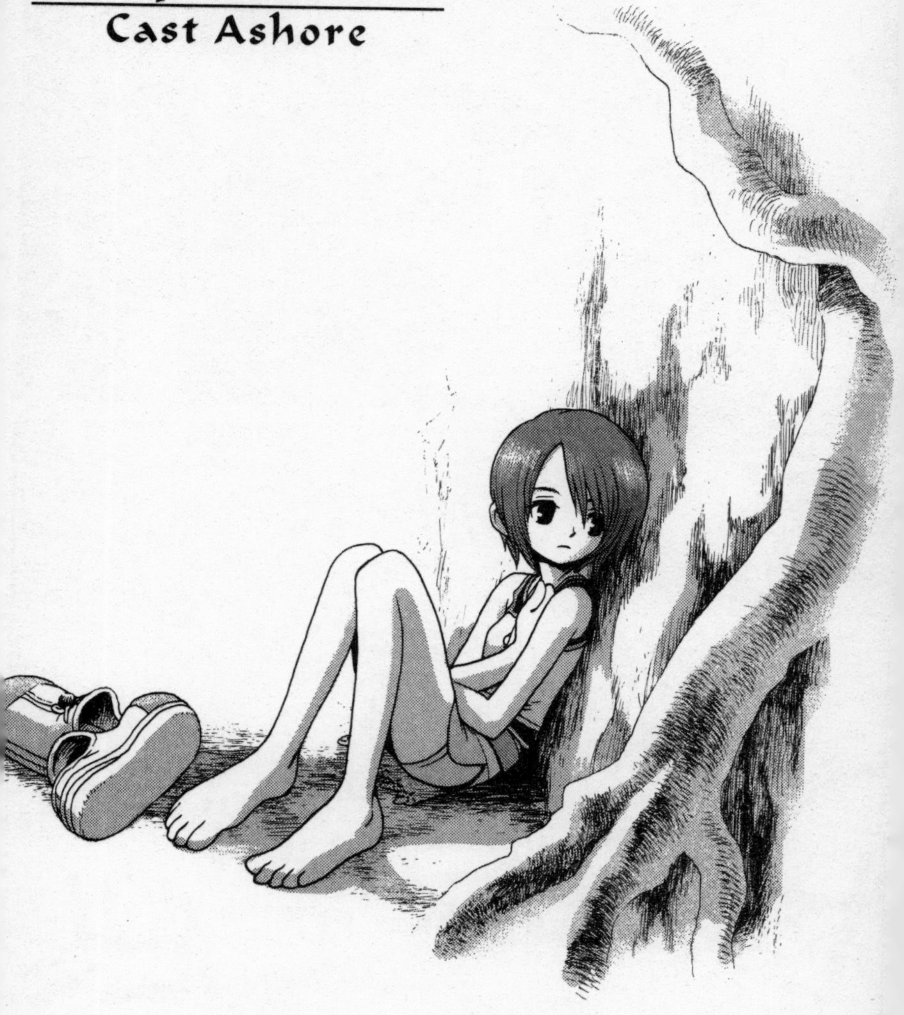

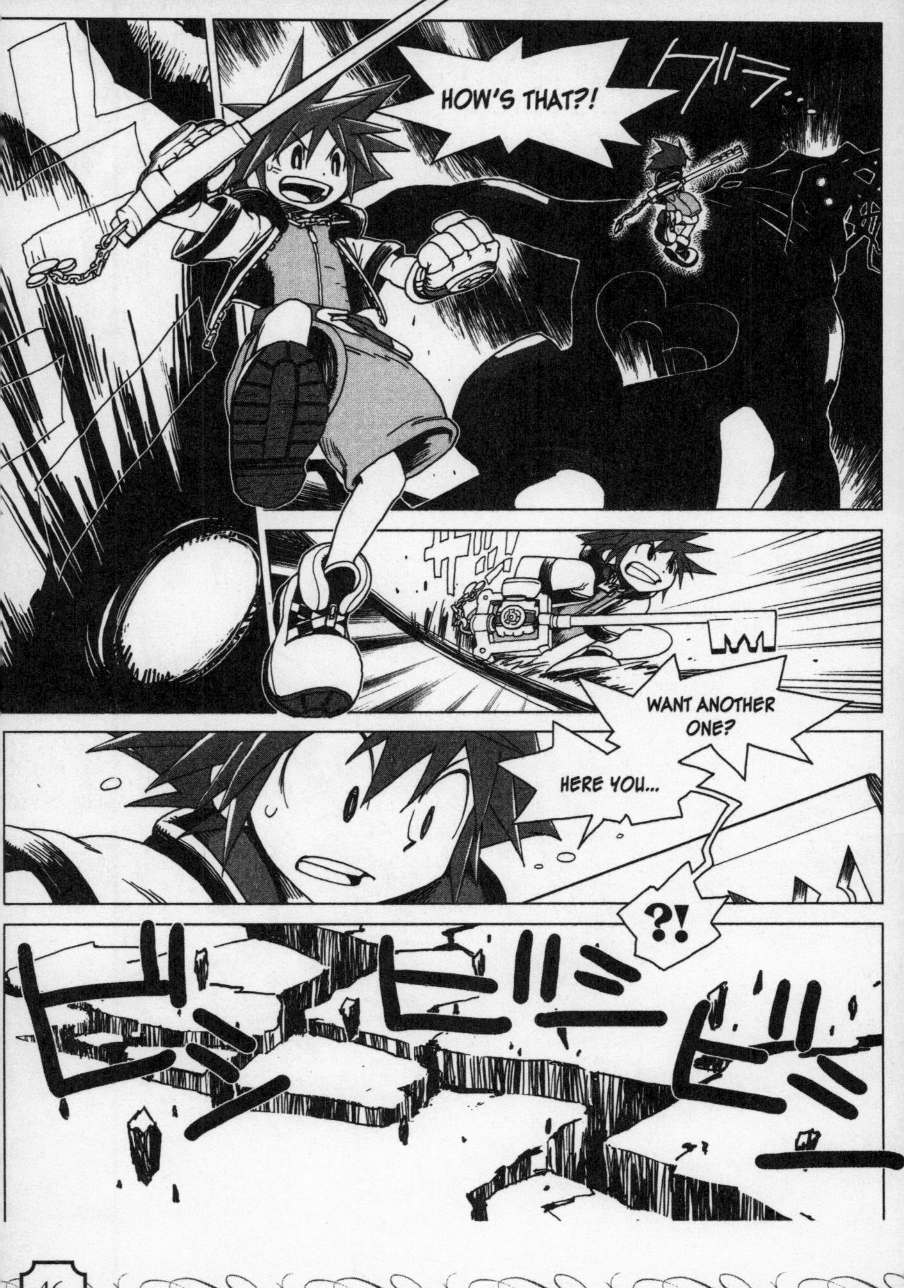
HOW'S THAT?!
WANT ANOTHER ONE?
HERE YOU...
?!

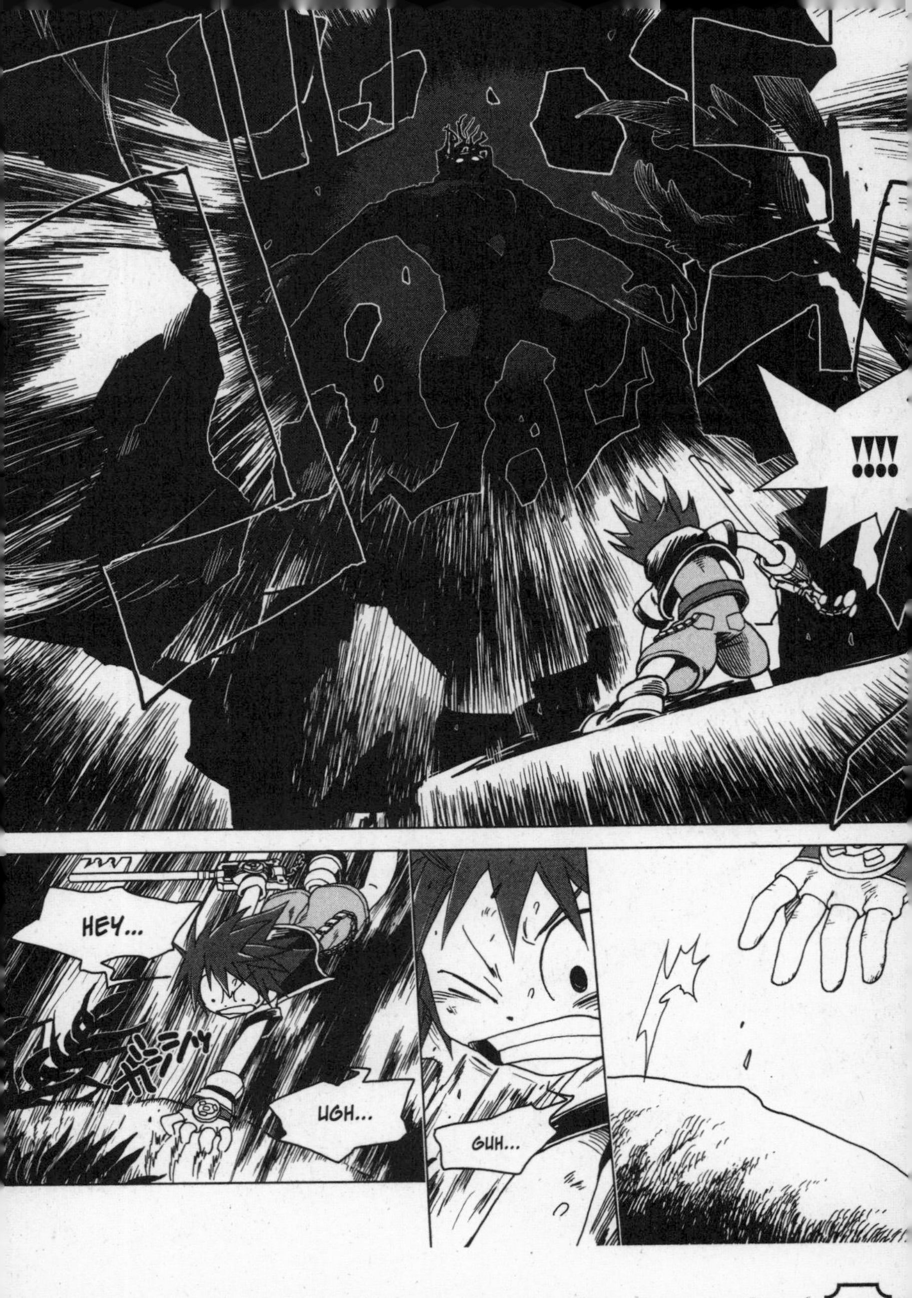

!!!!
HEY...
UGH...
GUH...

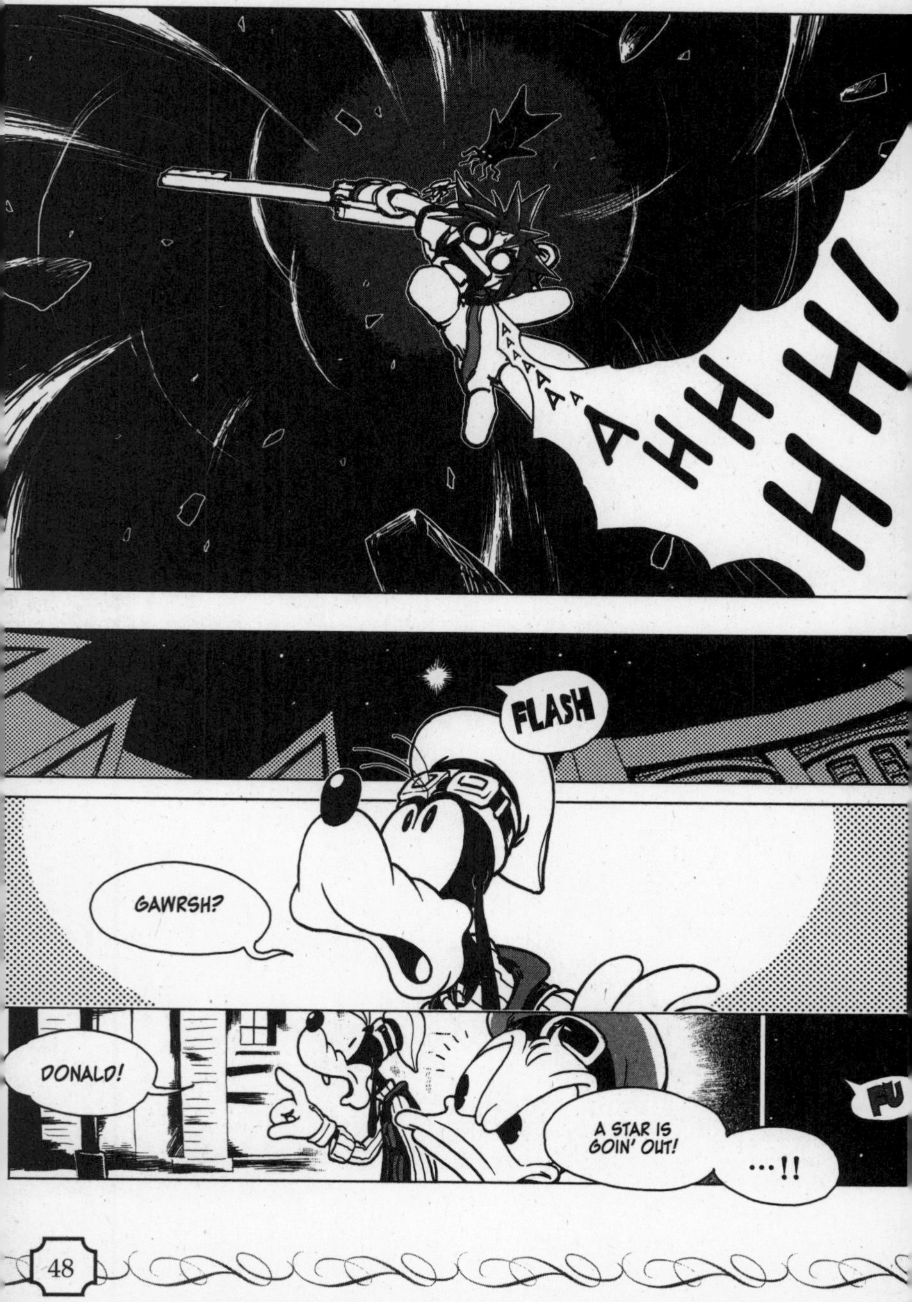
AAAAAAAAAAHHHH!
FLASH
GAWRSH?
DONALD!
A STAR IS GOIN' OUT!
...!!
FU

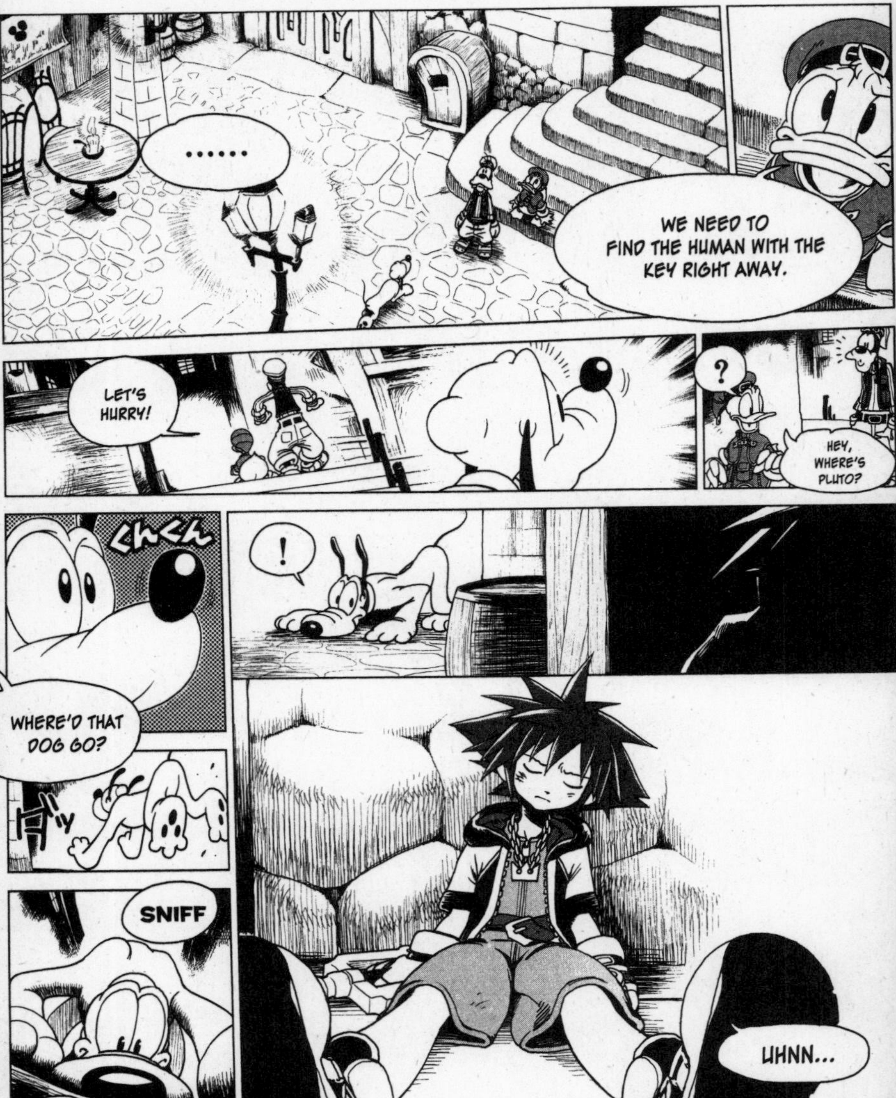
......
WE NEED TO FIND THE HUMAN WITH THE KEY RIGHT AWAY.
LET'S HURRY!
?
HEY, WHERE'S PLUTO?
くんくん
WHERE'D THAT DOG GO?
SNIFF
SNIFF
!
UHNN...

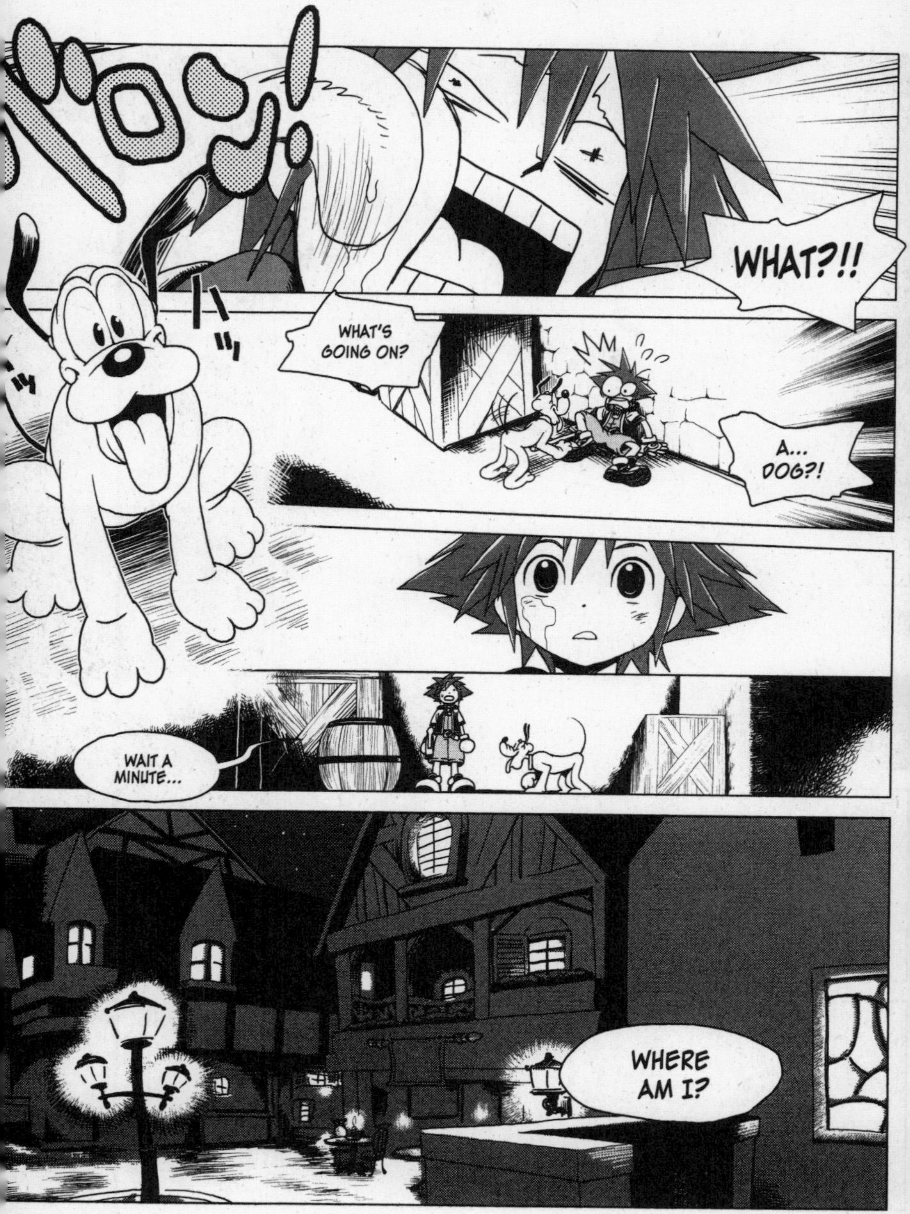
WHAT?!!
WHAT'S GOING ON?
A... DOG?!
WAIT A MINUTE...
WHERE AM I?

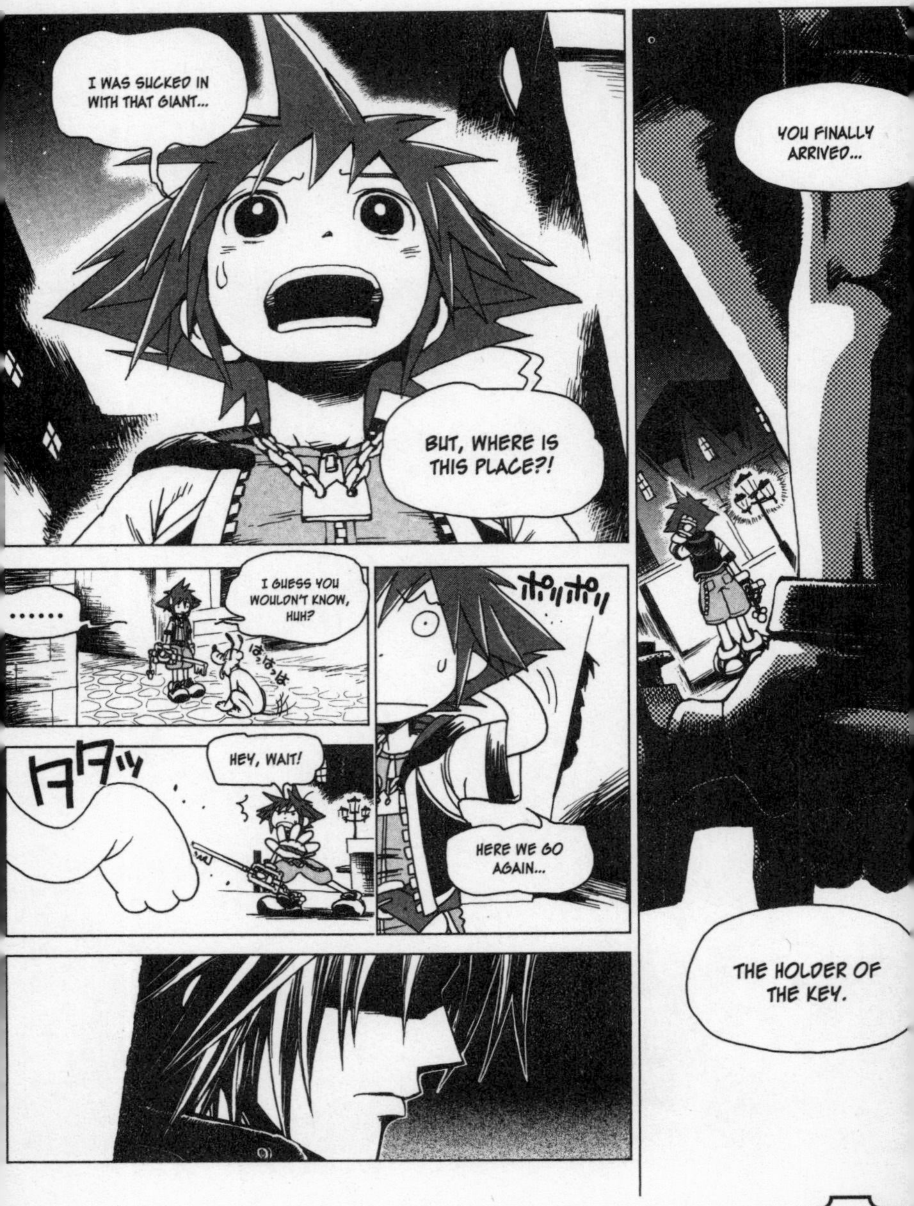

I WAS SUCKED IN WITH THAT GIANT...
BUT, WHERE IS THIS PLACE?!
......
I GUESS YOU WOULDN'T KNOW, HUH?
はっはっは
タタッ
HEY, WAIT!
ポリポリ
HERE WE GO AGAIN...
YOU FINALLY ARRIVED...
THE HOLDER OF THE KEY.

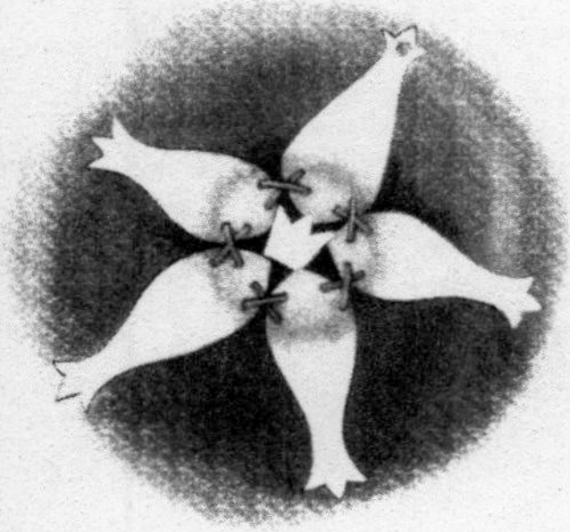

Episode 6
"Traverse Town"

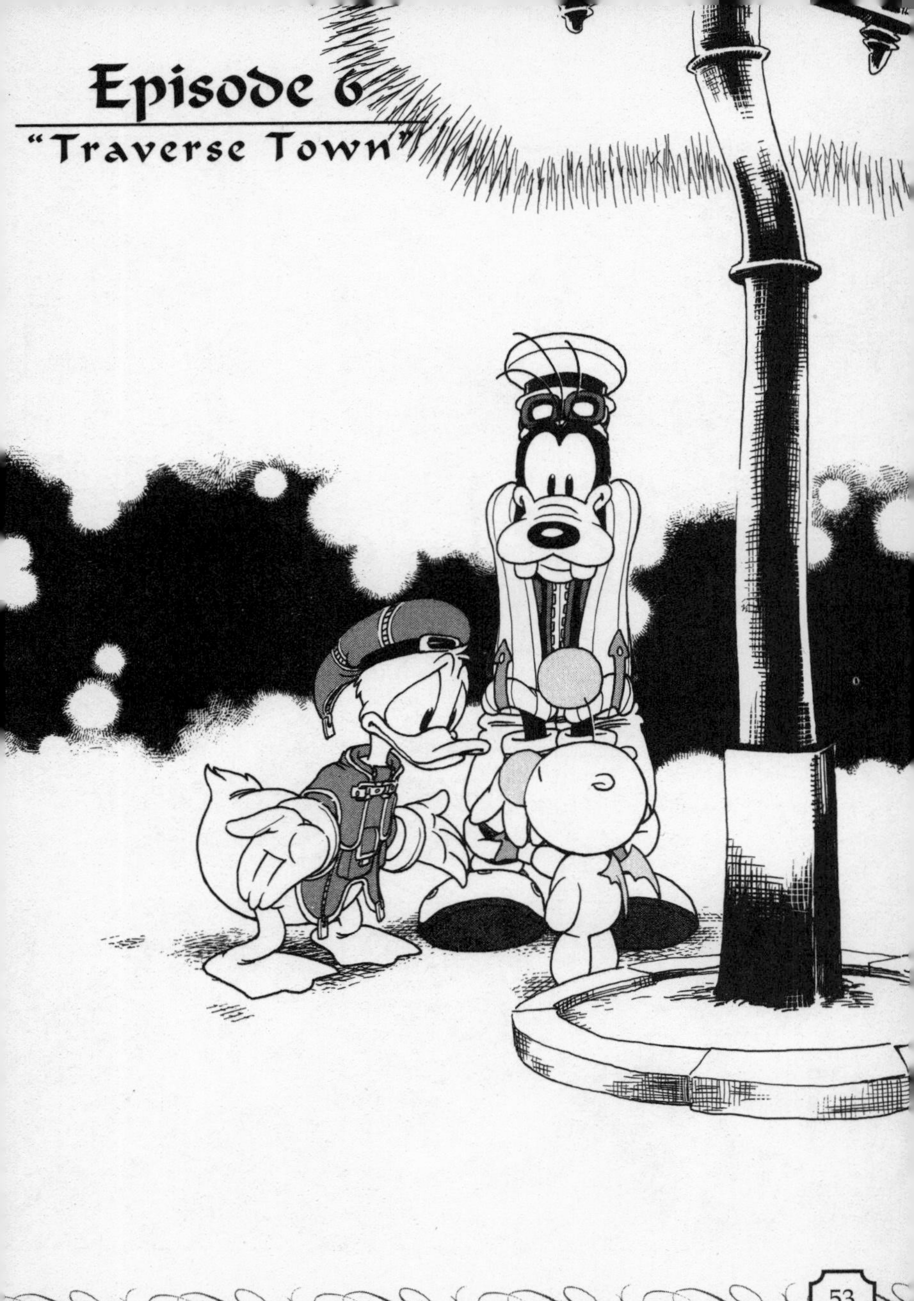

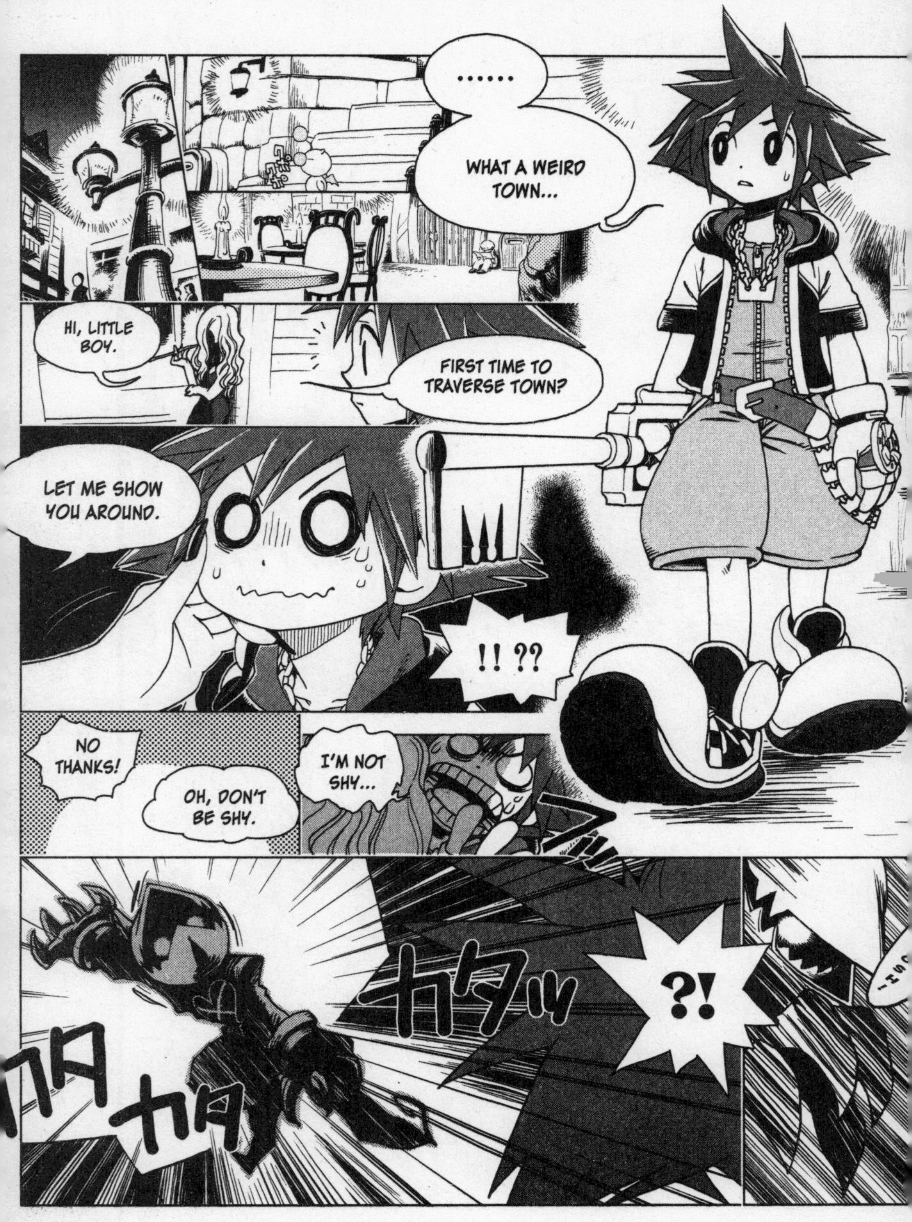

......
WHAT A WEIRD TOWN...
HI, LITTLE BOY.
FIRST TIME TO TRAVERSE TOWN?
LET ME SHOW YOU AROUND.
!! ??
NO THANKS!
OH, DON'T BE SHY.
I'M NOT SHY...
カタ
カタ
カタッ
?!

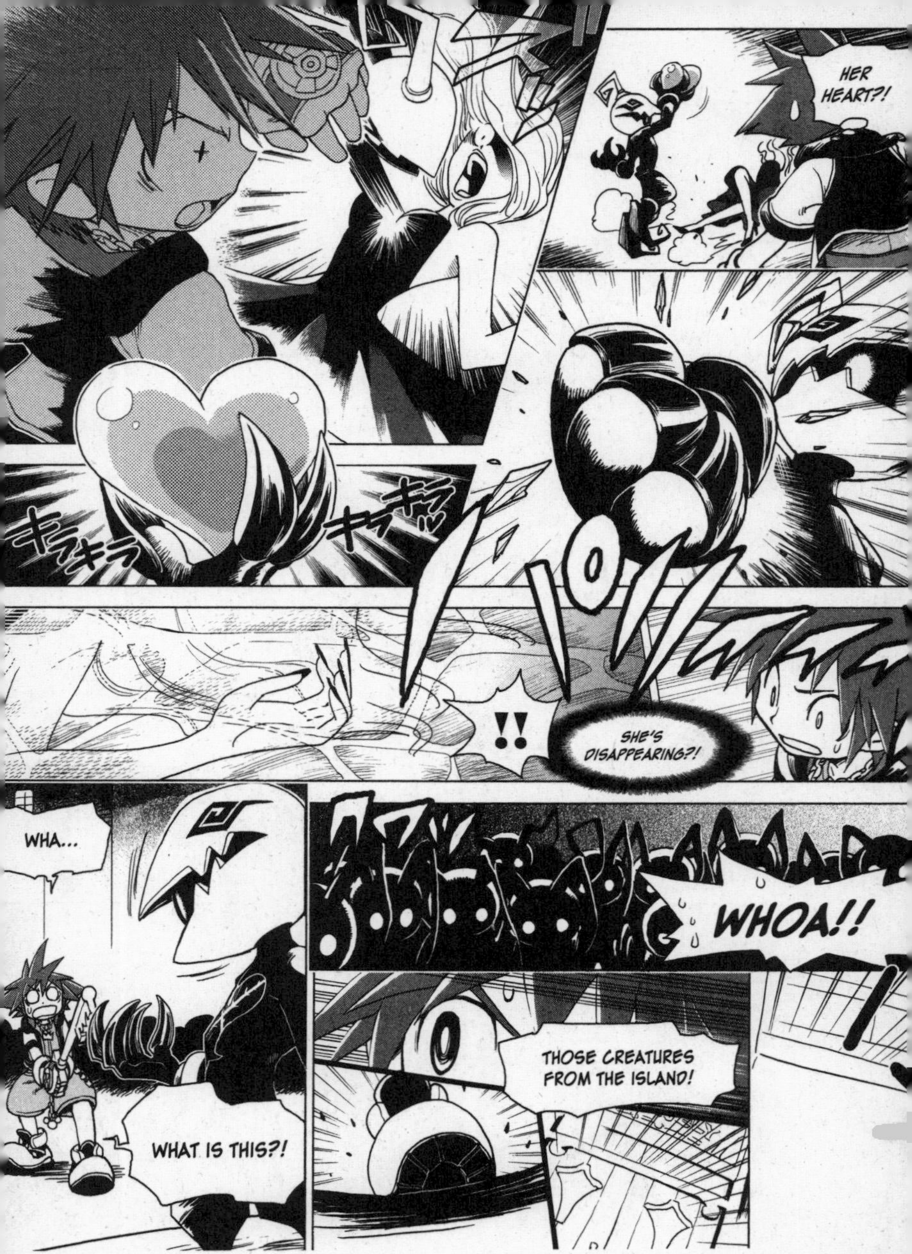
HER HEART?!
キラキラ
キラキラ
!!
SHE'S DISAPPEARING?!
WHOA!!
THOSE CREATURES FROM THE ISLAND!
WHA...
WHAT IS THIS?!

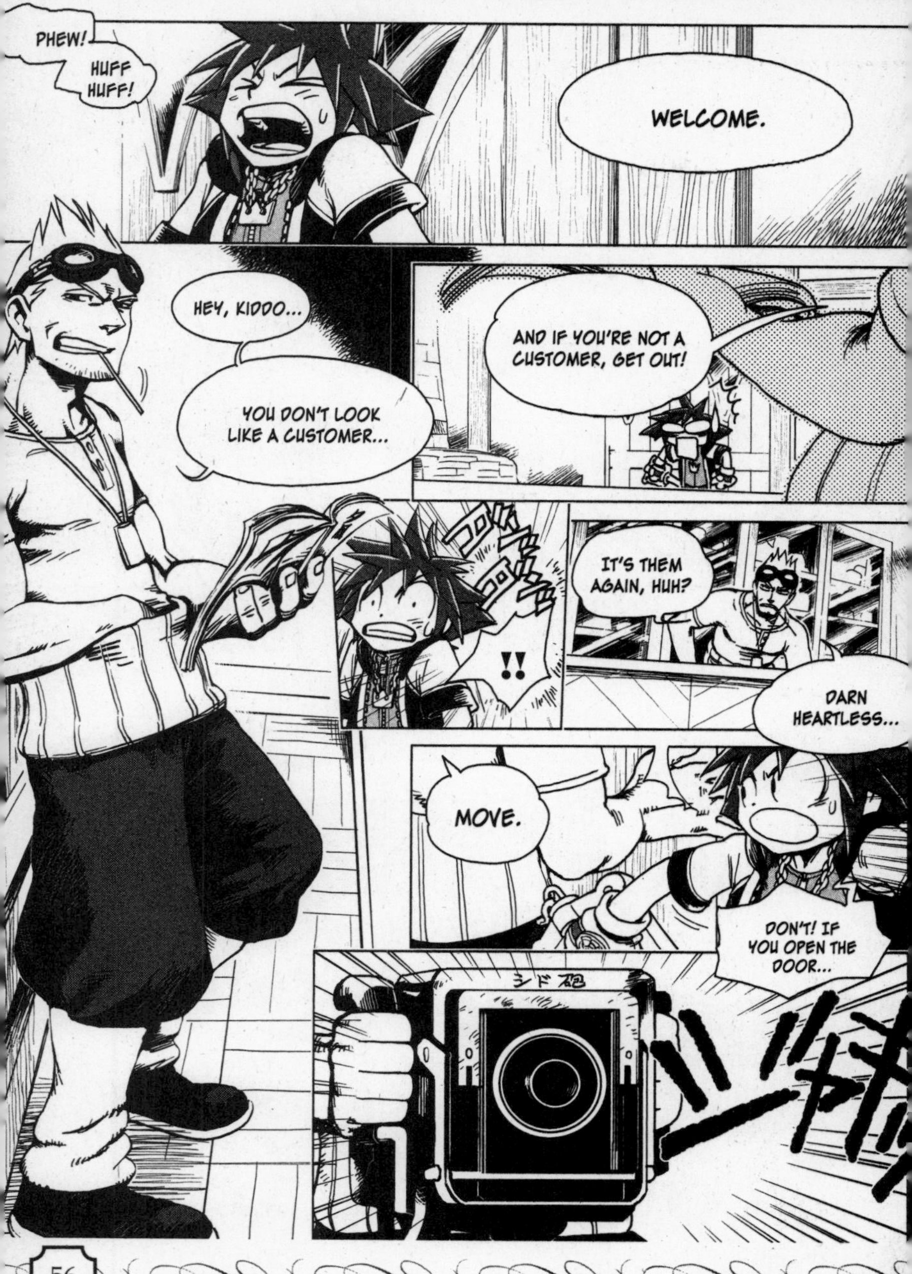
PHEW!
HUFF HUFF!
WELCOME.
HEY, KIDDO...
YOU DON'T LOOK LIKE A CUSTOMER...
AND IF YOU'RE NOT A CUSTOMER, GET OUT!
!!
IT'S THEM AGAIN, HUH?
DARN HEARTLESS...
MOVE.
DON'T! IF YOU OPEN THE DOOR...
シド砲

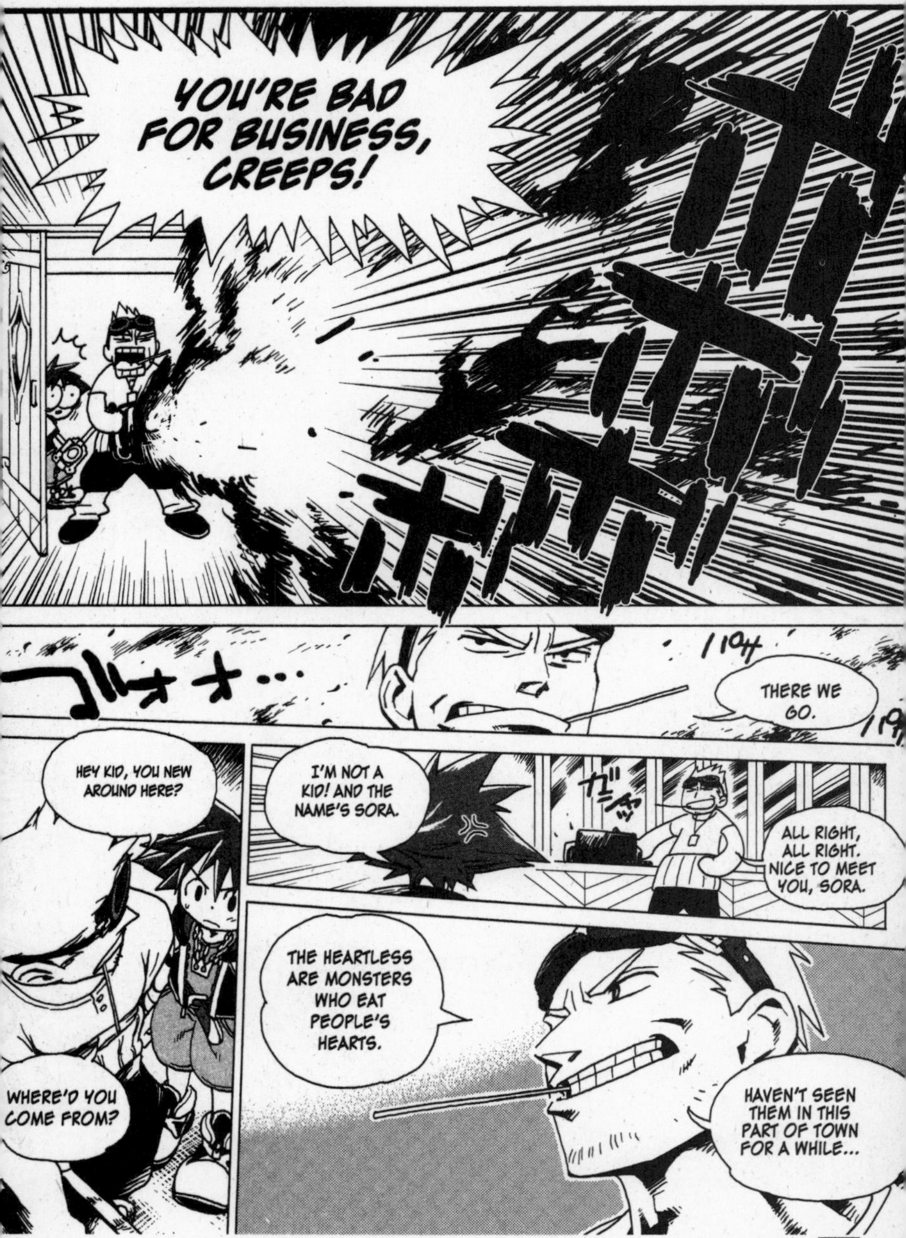
YOU'RE BAD FOR BUSINESS, CREEPS!
THERE WE GO.
HEY KID, YOU NEW AROUND HERE?
WHERE'D YOU COME FROM?
I'M NOT A KID! AND THE NAME'S SORA.
ALL RIGHT, ALL RIGHT. NICE TO MEET YOU, SORA.
THE HEARTLESS ARE MONSTERS WHO EAT PEOPLE'S HEARTS.
HAVEN'T SEEN THEM IN THIS PART OF TOWN FOR A WHILE...

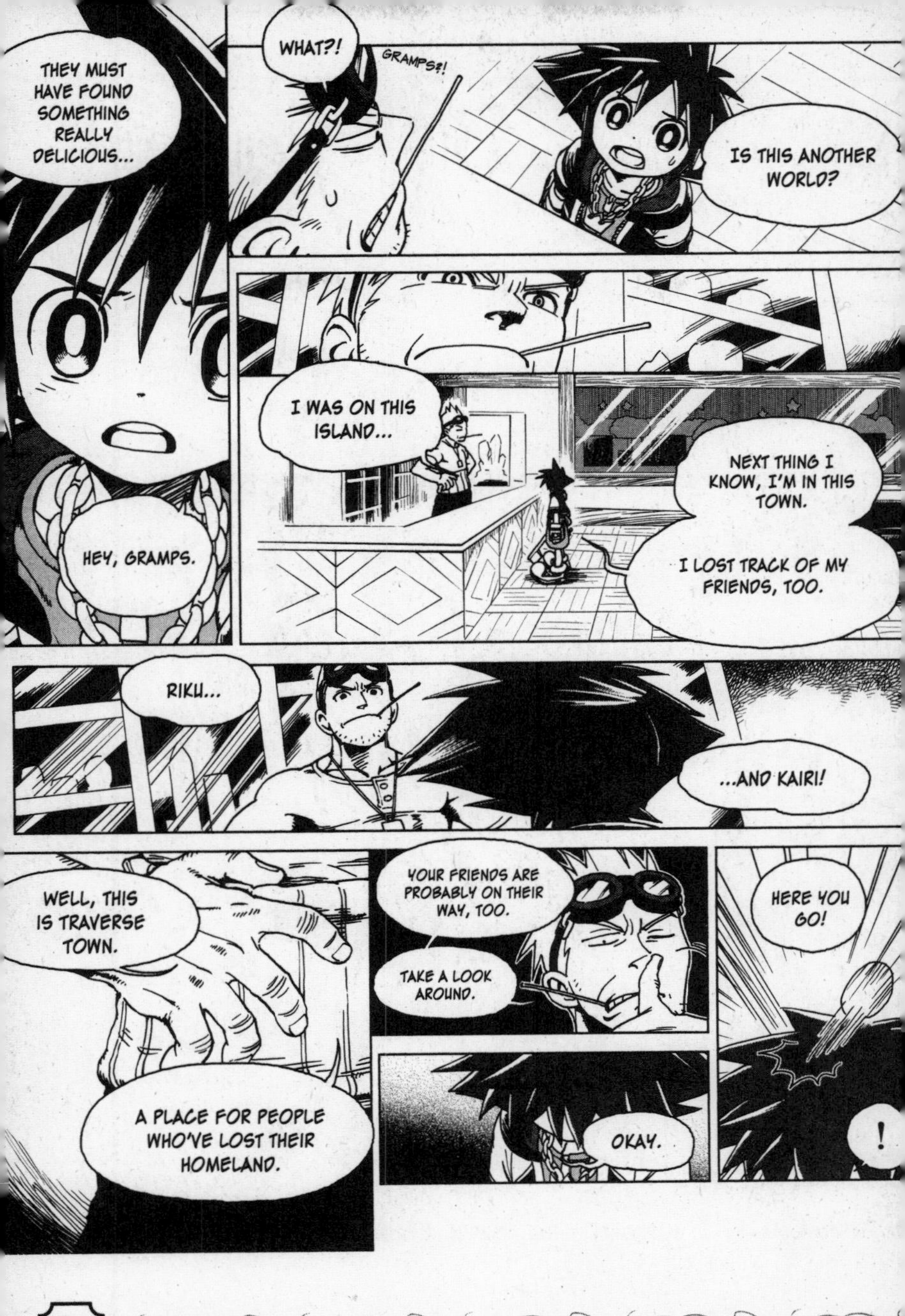
THEY MUST HAVE FOUND SOMETHING REALLY DELICIOUS...
HEY, GRAMPS.
WHAT?!
GRAMPS?!
IS THIS ANOTHER WORLD?
I WAS ON THIS ISLAND...
NEXT THING I KNOW, I'M IN THIS TOWN.
I LOST TRACK OF MY FRIENDS, TOO.
RIKU...
...AND KAIRI!
WELL, THIS IS TRAVERSE TOWN.
A PLACE FOR PEOPLE WHO'VE LOST THEIR HOMELAND.
YOUR FRIENDS ARE PROBABLY ON THEIR WAY, TOO.
TAKE A LOOK AROUND.
OKAY.
HERE YOU GO!
!

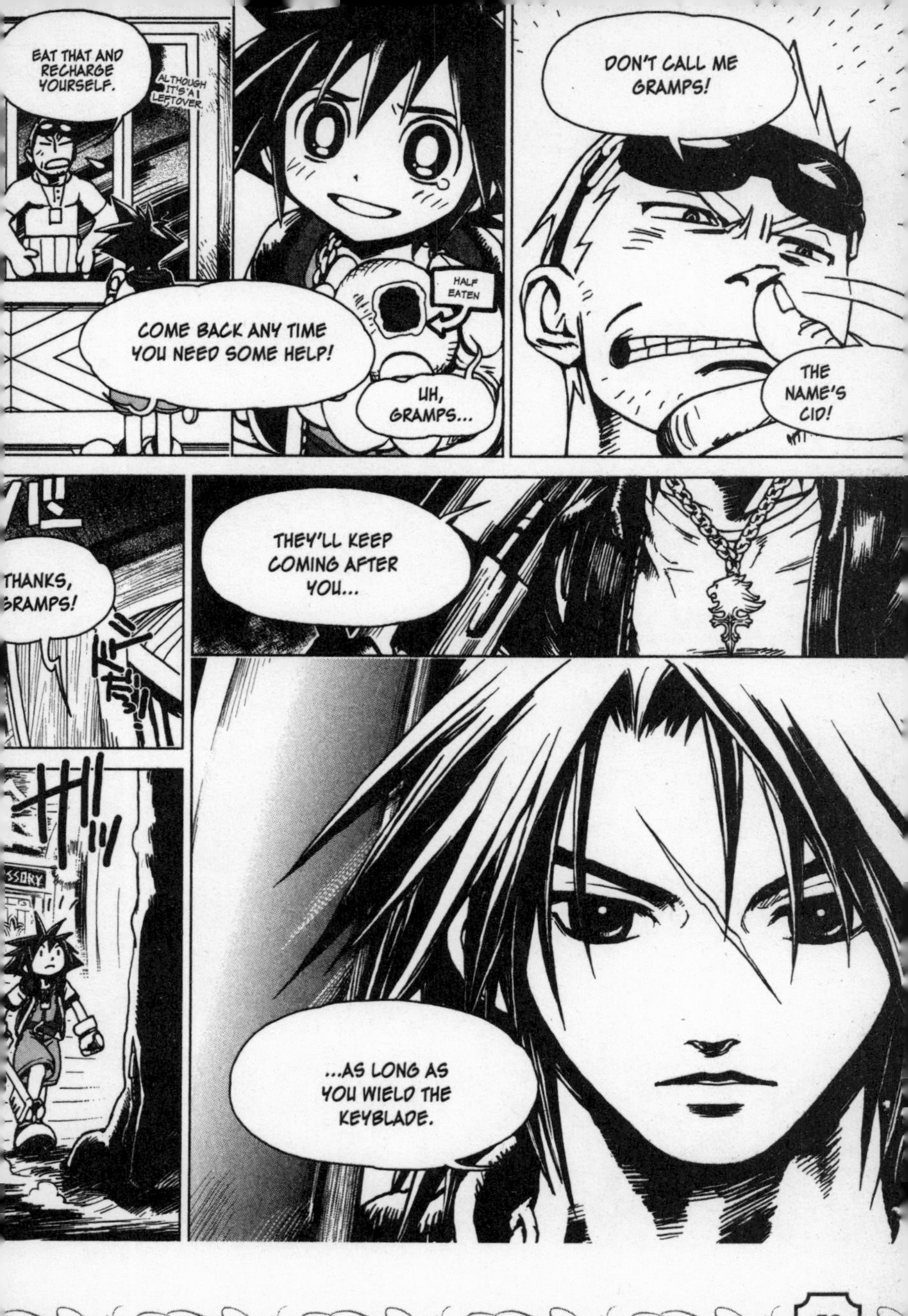
EAT THAT AND RECHARGE YOURSELF.
ALTHOUGH IT'S A LEFTOVER.
COME BACK ANY TIME YOU NEED SOME HELP!
HALF EATEN
UH, GRAMPS...
DON'T CALL ME GRAMPS!
THE NAME'S CID!
THANKS, GRAMPS!
THEY'LL KEEP COMING AFTER YOU...
...AS LONG AS YOU WIELD THE KEYBLADE.

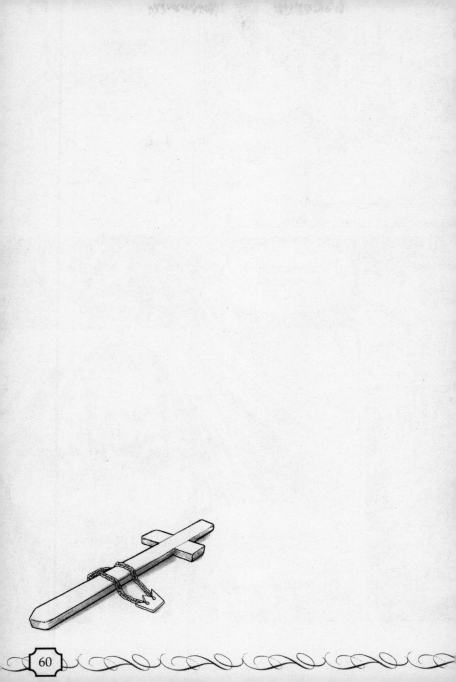

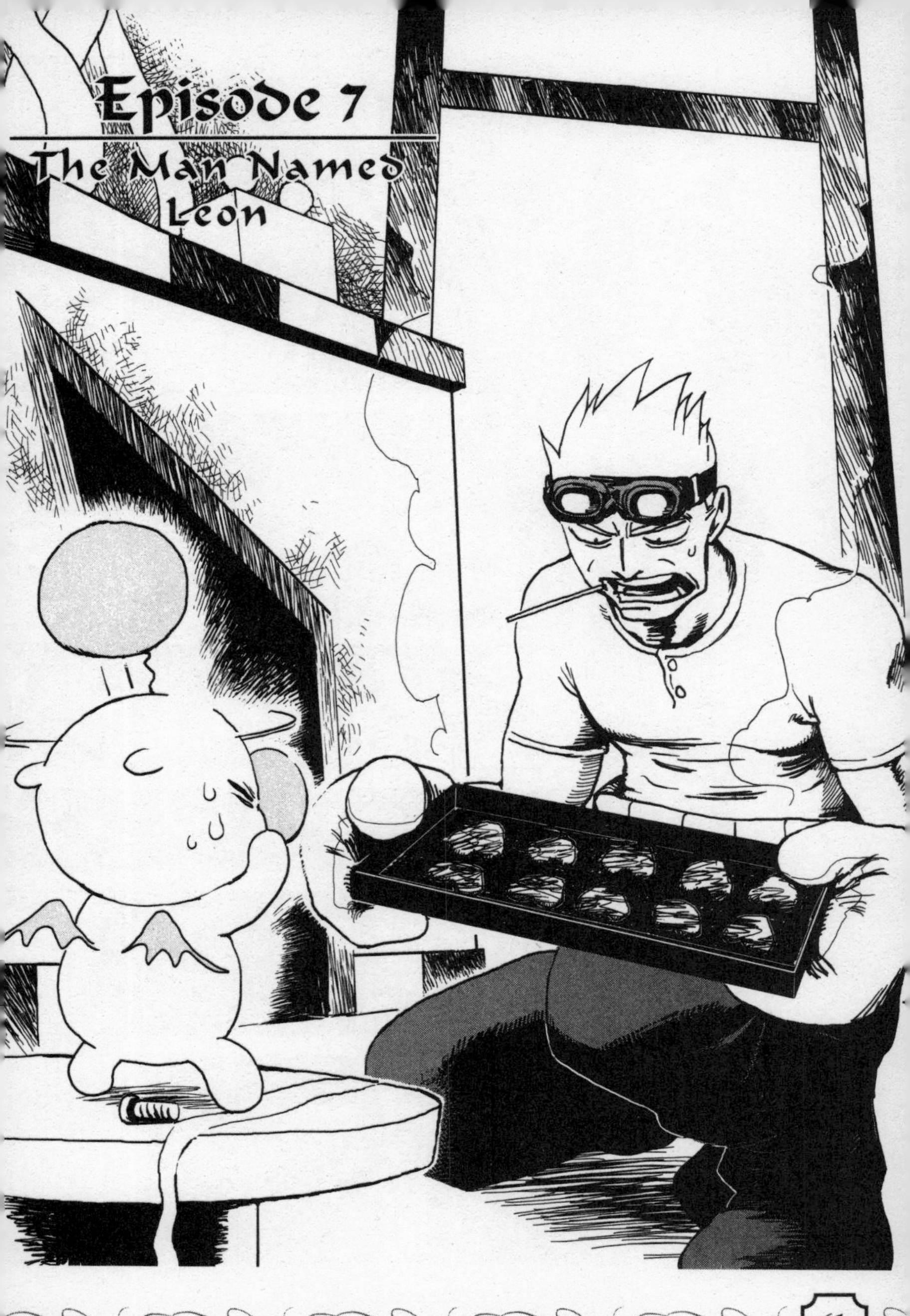
Episode 7
The Man Named Leon

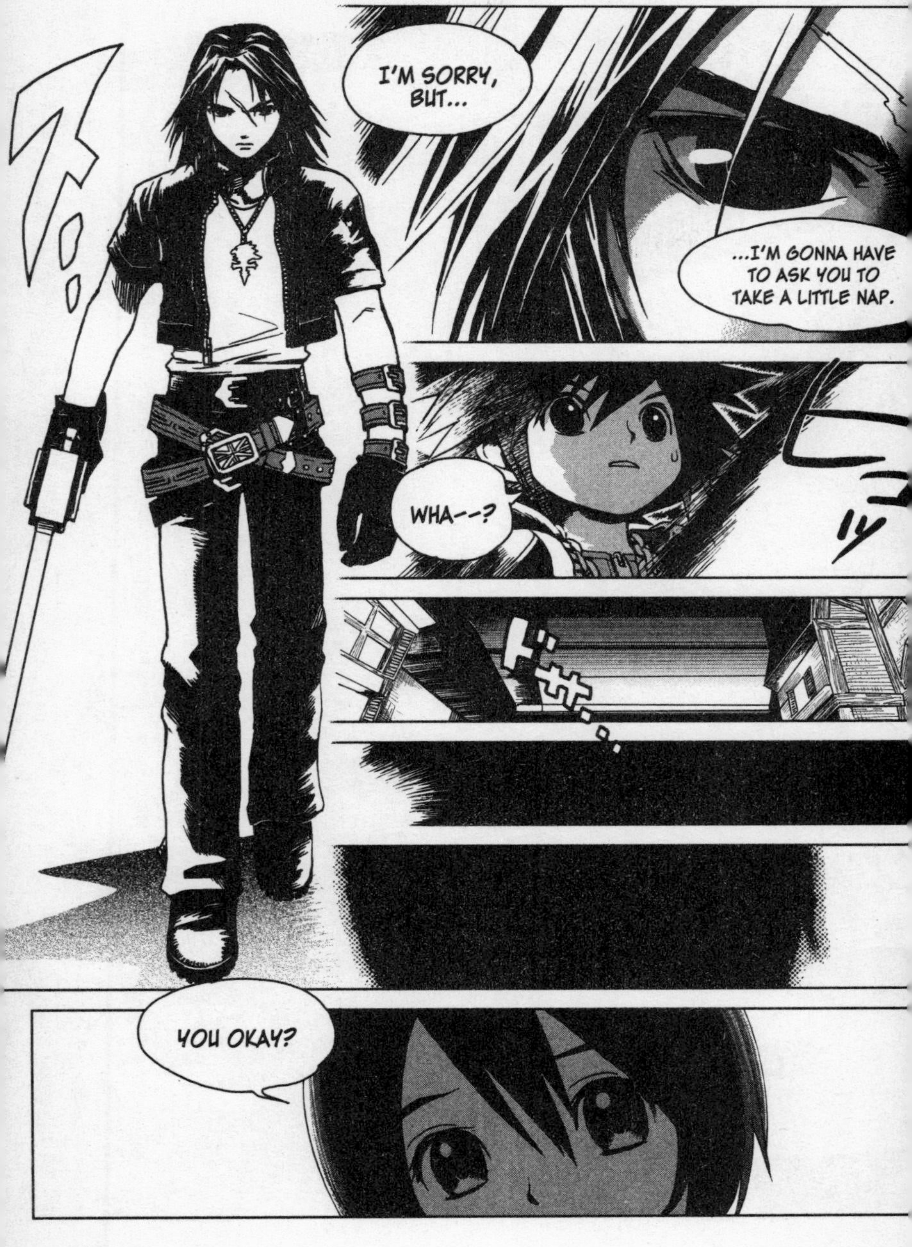
I'M SORRY, BUT...
...I'M GONNA HAVE TO ASK YOU TO TAKE A LITTLE NAP.
WHA--?
YOU OKAY?

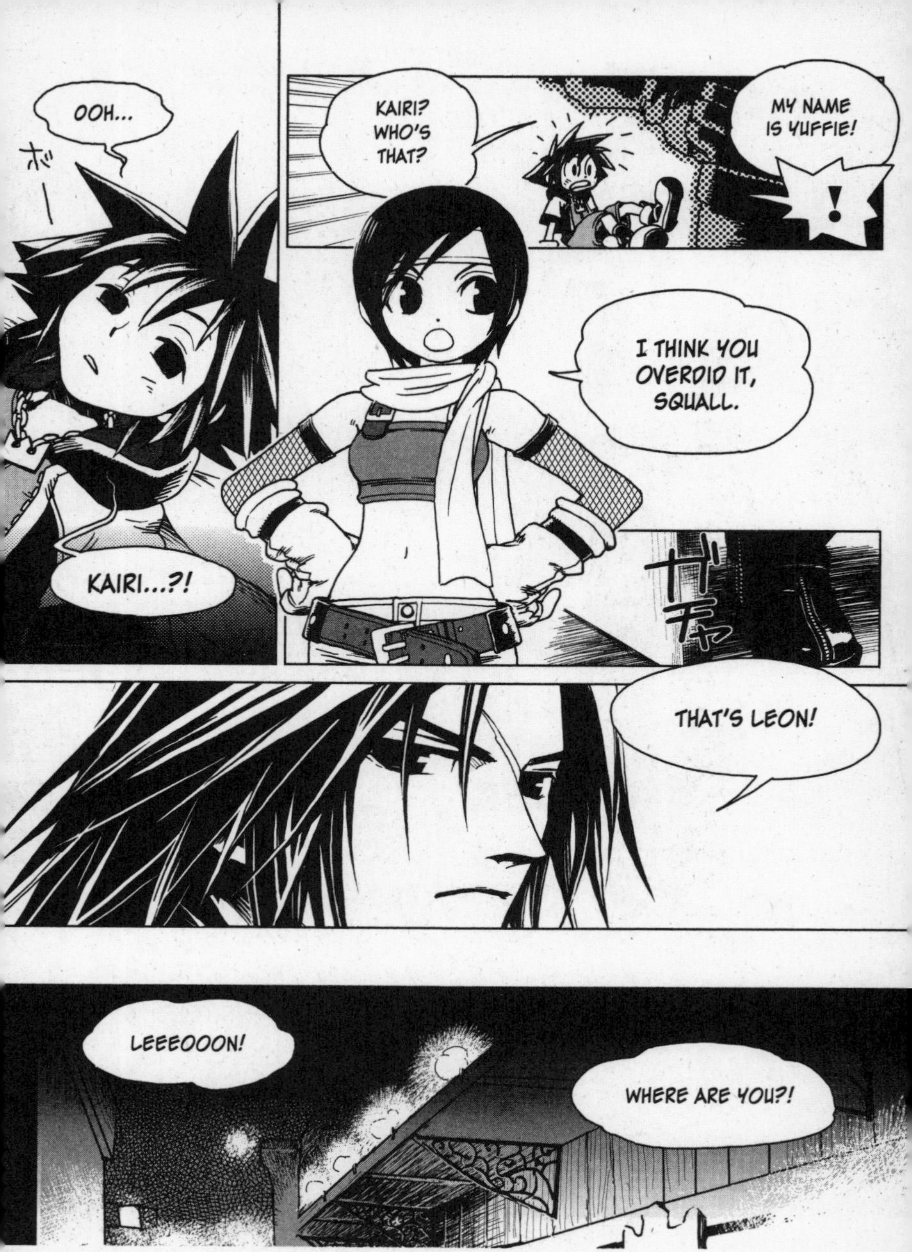
OOH...
ボー
KAIRI...?!
KAIRI? WHO'S THAT?
MY NAME IS YUFFIE!
!
I THINK YOU OVERDID IT, SQUALL.
ガチャ
THAT'S LEON!
LEEEOOON!
WHERE ARE YOU?!

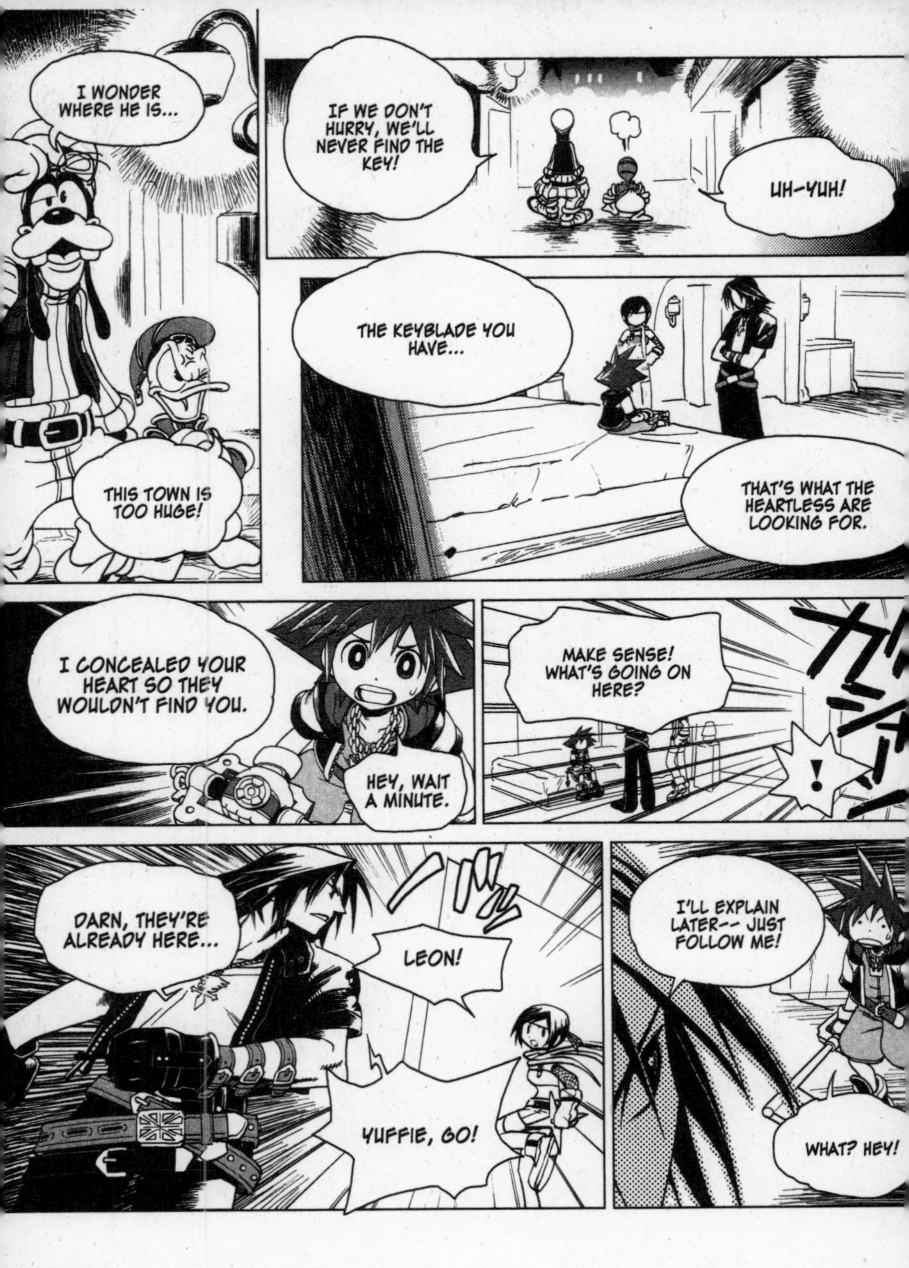
I WONDER WHERE HE IS...
THIS TOWN IS TOO HUGE!
IF WE DON'T HURRY, WE'LL NEVER FIND THE KEY!
UH-YUH!
THE KEYBLADE YOU HAVE...
THAT'S WHAT THE HEARTLESS ARE LOOKING FOR.
I CONCEALED YOUR HEART SO THEY WOULDN'T FIND YOU.
HEY, WAIT A MINUTE.
MAKE SENSE! WHAT'S GOING ON HERE?
!
DARN, THEY'RE ALREADY HERE...
LEON!
YUFFIE, GO!
I'LL EXPLAIN LATER-- JUST FOLLOW ME!
WHAT? HEY!

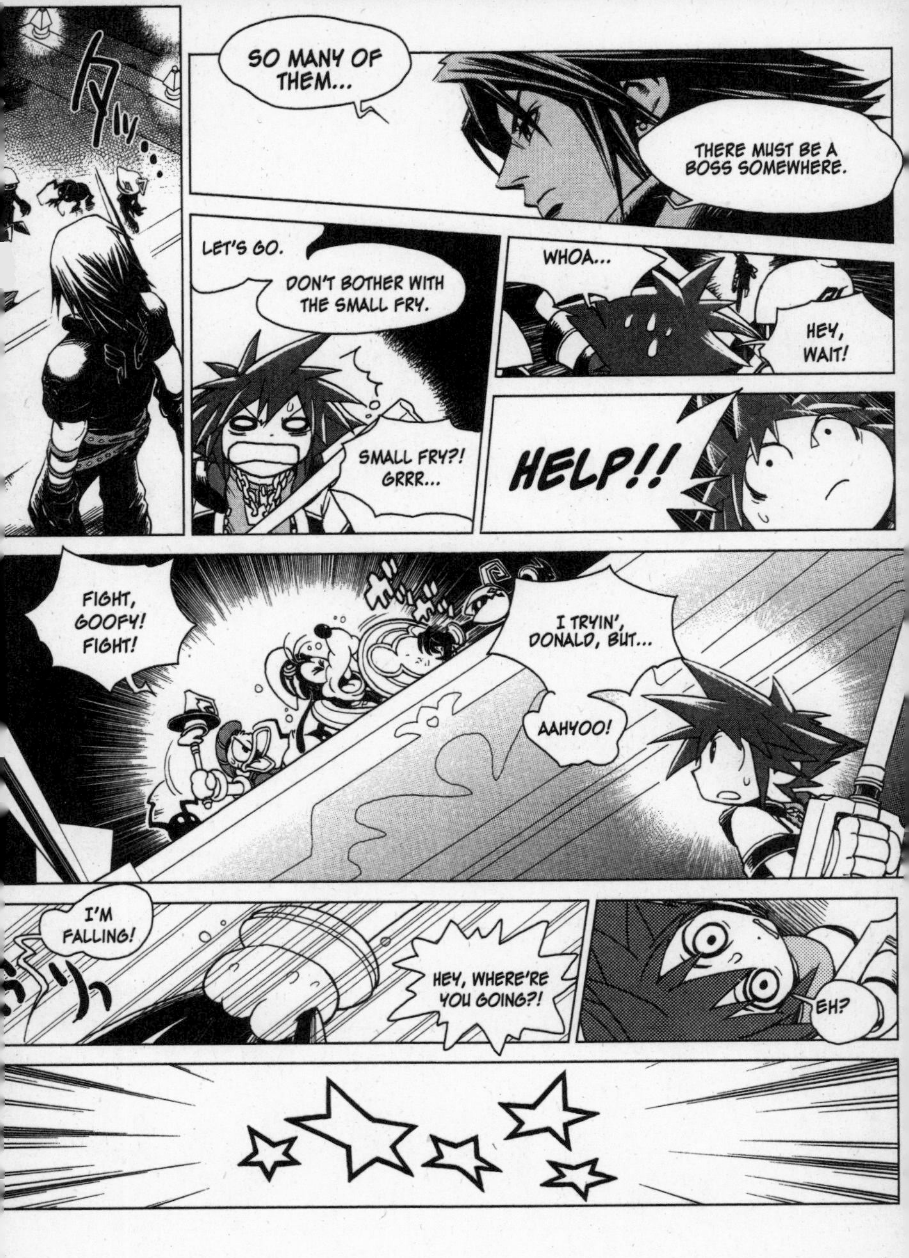

SO MANY OF THEM...
THERE MUST BE A BOSS SOMEWHERE.
LET'S GO.
DON'T BOTHER WITH THE SMALL FRY.
SMALL FRY?! GRRR...
WHOA...
HEY, WAIT!
HELP!!
FIGHT, GOOFY! FIGHT!
I TRYIN', DONALD, BUT...
AAHYOO!
I'M FALLING!
HEY, WHERE'RE YOU GOING?!
EH?

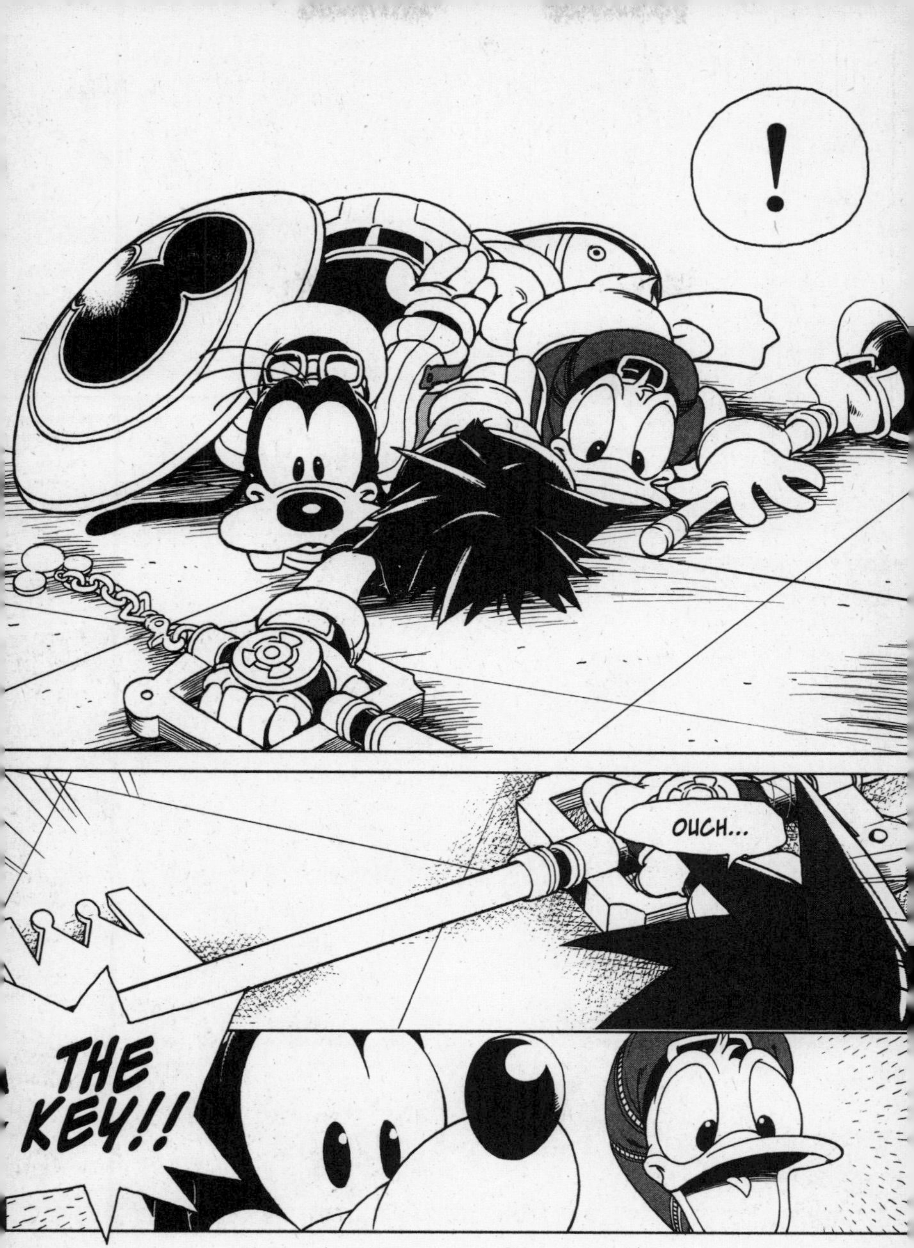
!
OUCH...
THE KEY!!

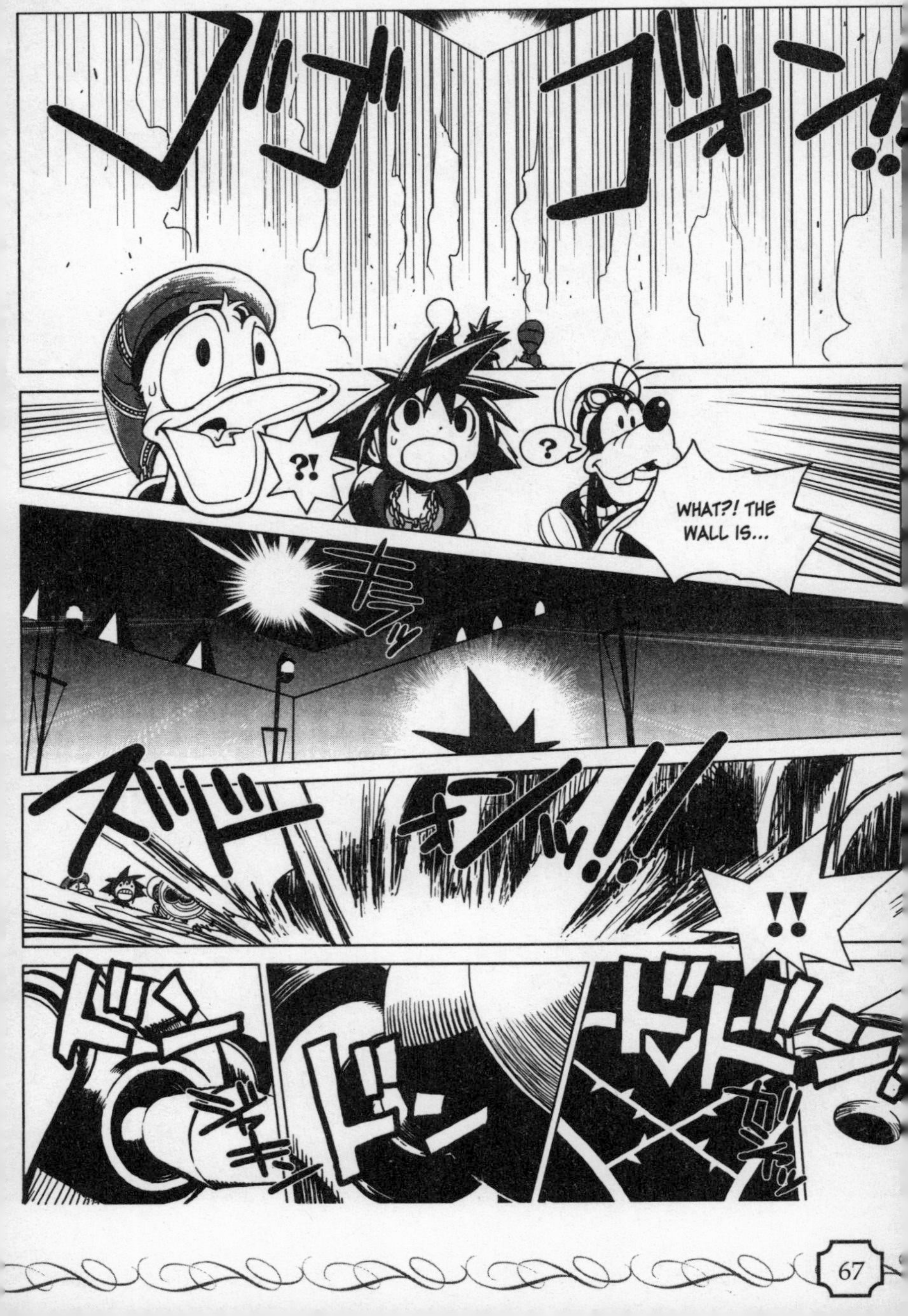
?!
?
WHAT?! THE WALL IS...
!!

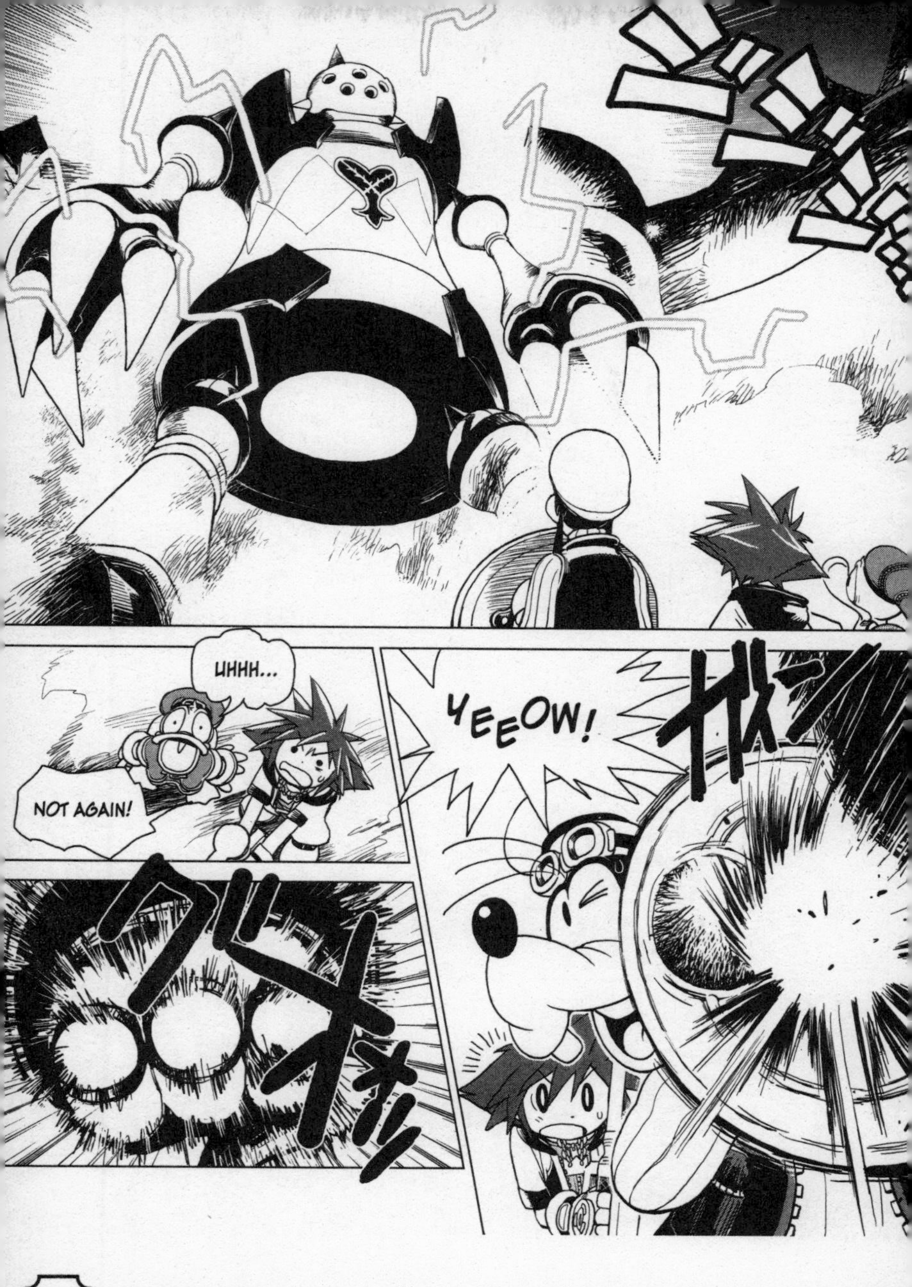
UHHH...
NOT AGAIN!
YEEEOW!

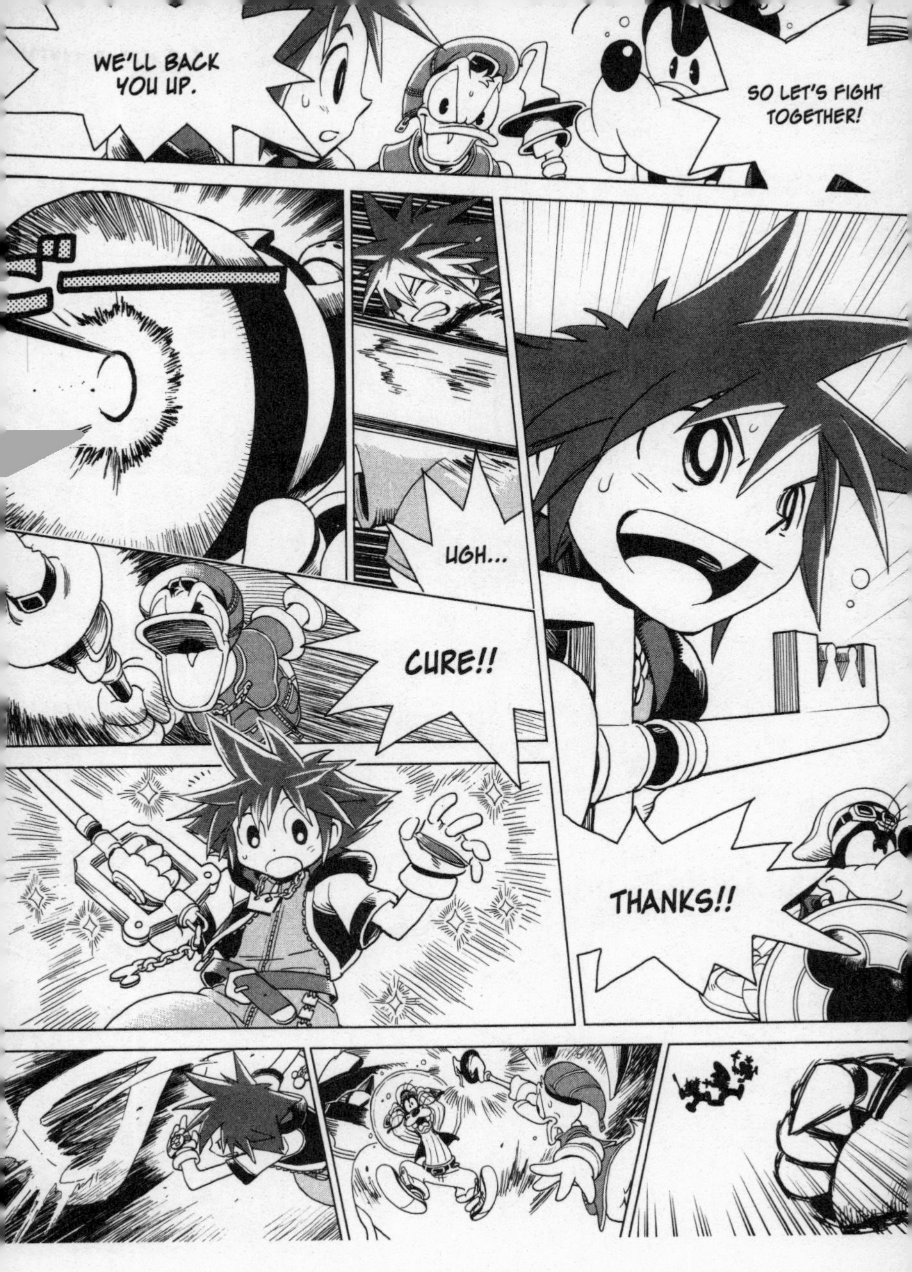
WE'LL BACK YOU UP.
SO LET'S FIGHT TOGETHER!
UGH...
CURE!!
THANKS!!

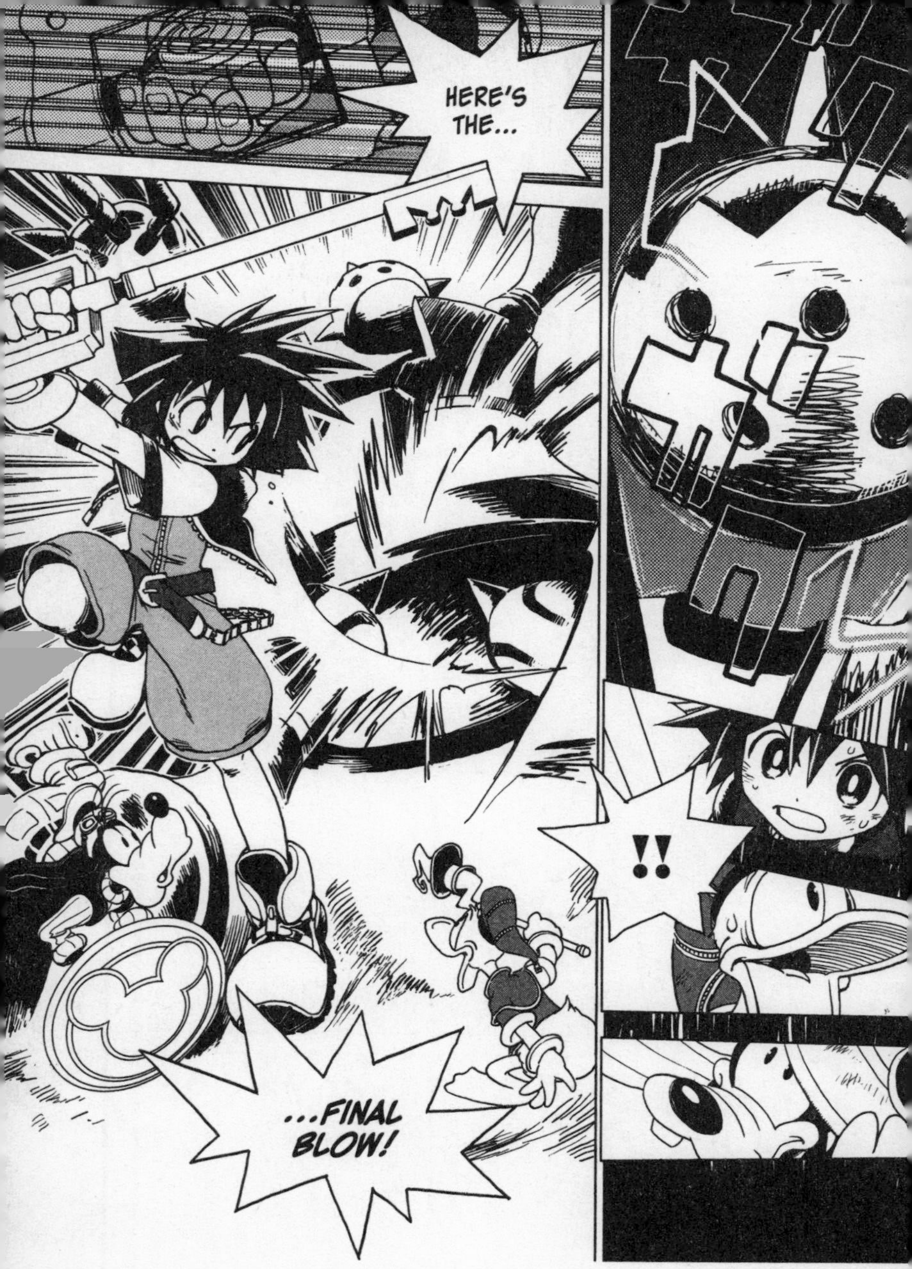
HERE'S THE...
...FINAL BLOW!
!!

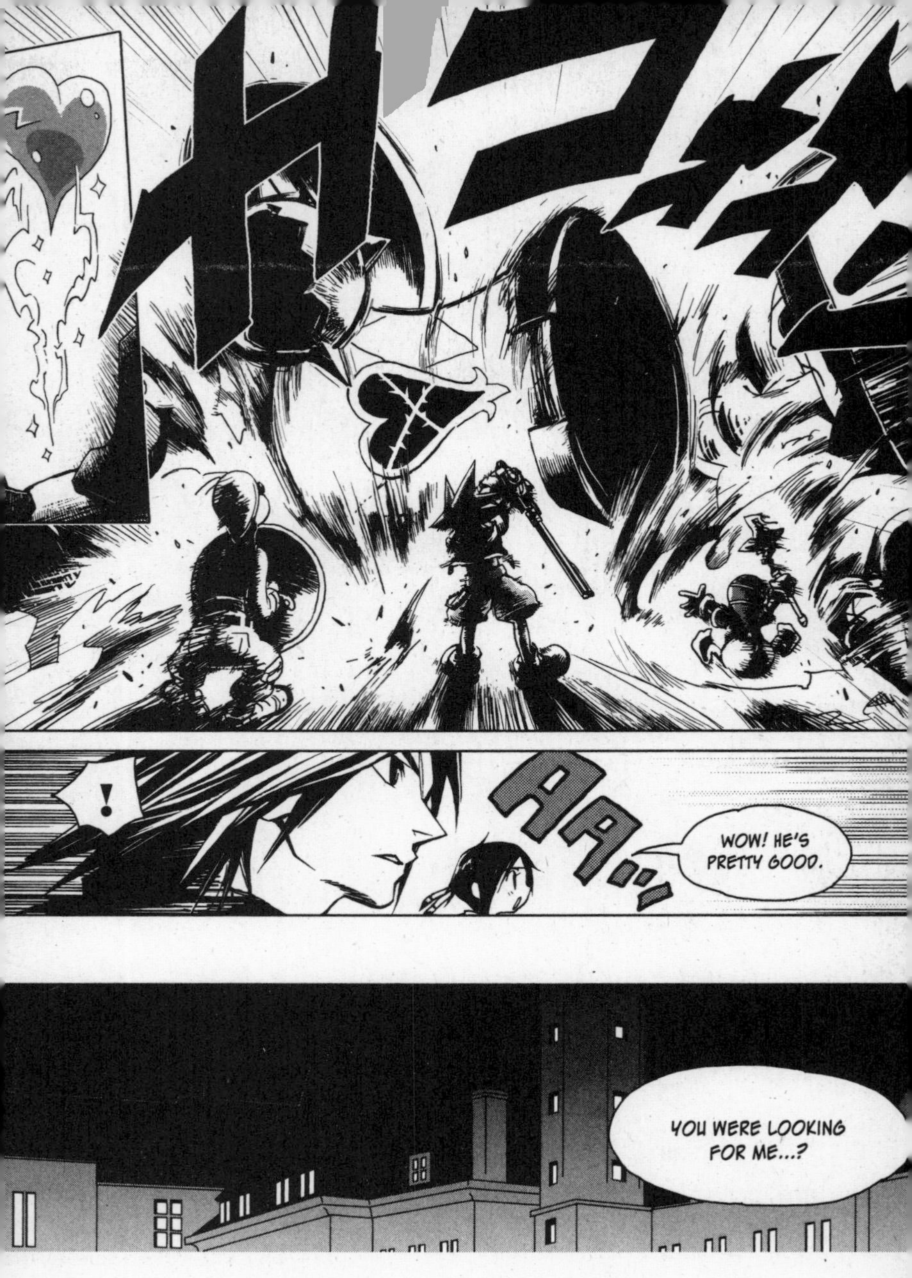
!
WOW! HE'S PRETTY GOOD.
YOU WERE LOOKING FOR ME...?

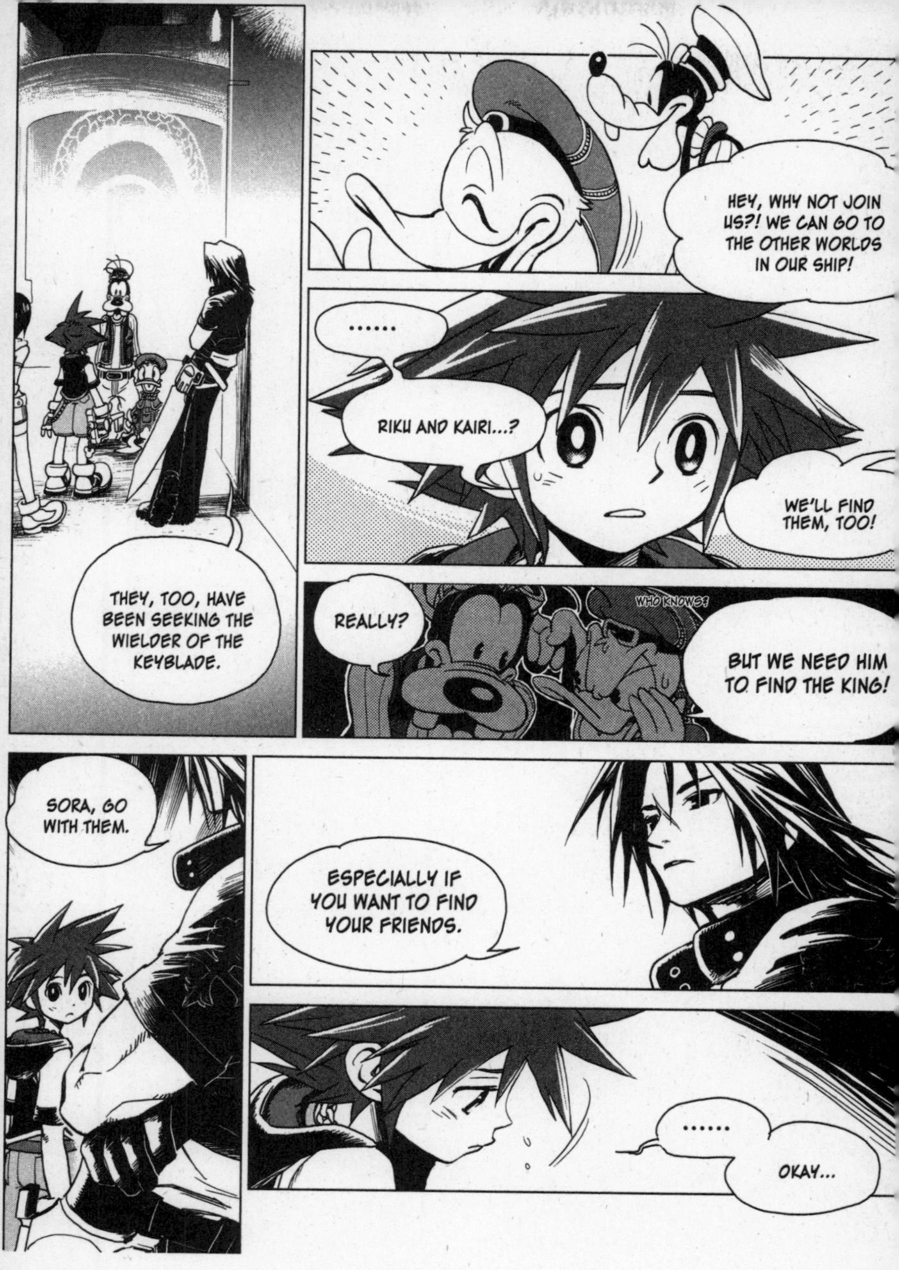
THEY, TOO, HAVE BEEN SEEKING THE WIELDER OF THE KEYBLADE.
HEY, WHY NOT JOIN US?! WE CAN GO TO THE OTHER WORLDS IN OUR SHIP!
......
RIKU AND KAIRI...?
WE'LL FIND THEM, TOO!
REALLY?
WHO KNOWS?
BUT WE NEED HIM TO FIND THE KING!
SORA, GO WITH THEM.
ESPECIALLY IF YOU WANT TO FIND YOUR FRIENDS.
......
OKAY...

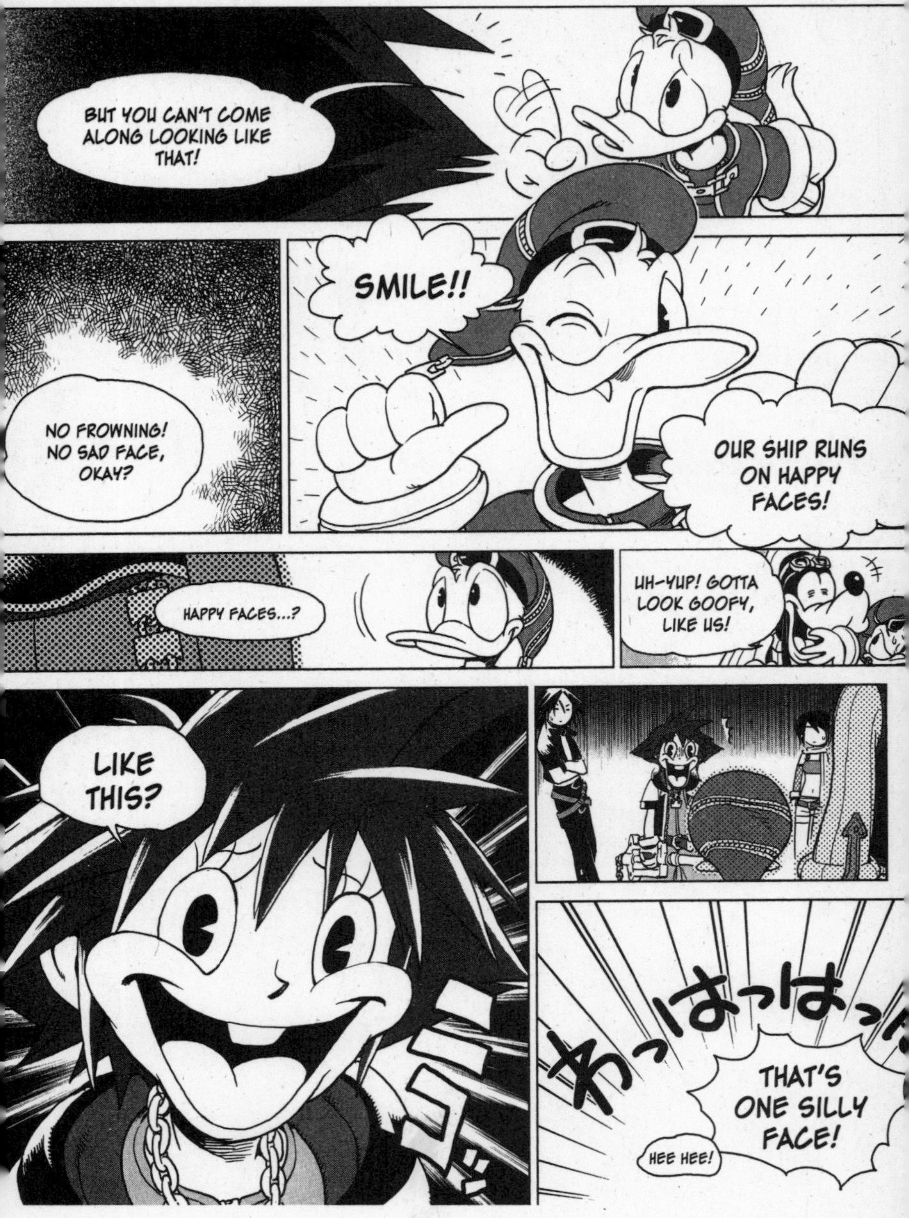

BUT YOU CAN'T COME ALONG LOOKING LIKE THAT!
NO FROWNING! NO SAD FACE, OKAY?
SMILE!!
OUR SHIP RUNS ON HAPPY FACES!
HAPPY FACES...?
UH-YUP! GOTTA LOOK GOOFY, LIKE US!
LIKE THIS?
わっはっはっ
THAT'S ONE SILLY FACE!
HEE HEE!

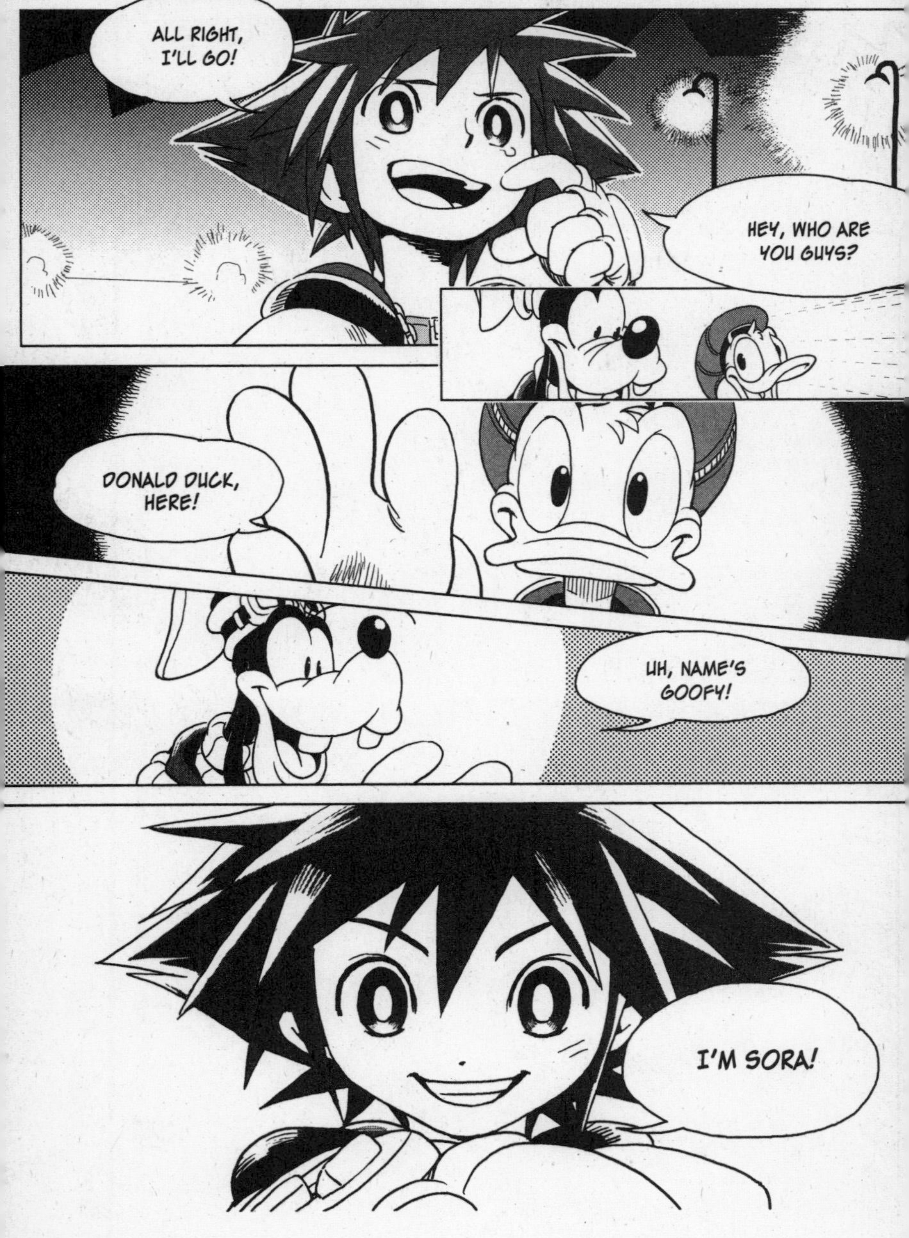
ALL RIGHT, I'LL GO!
HEY, WHO ARE YOU GUYS?
DONALD DUCK, HERE!
UH, NAME'S GOOFY!
I'M SORA!

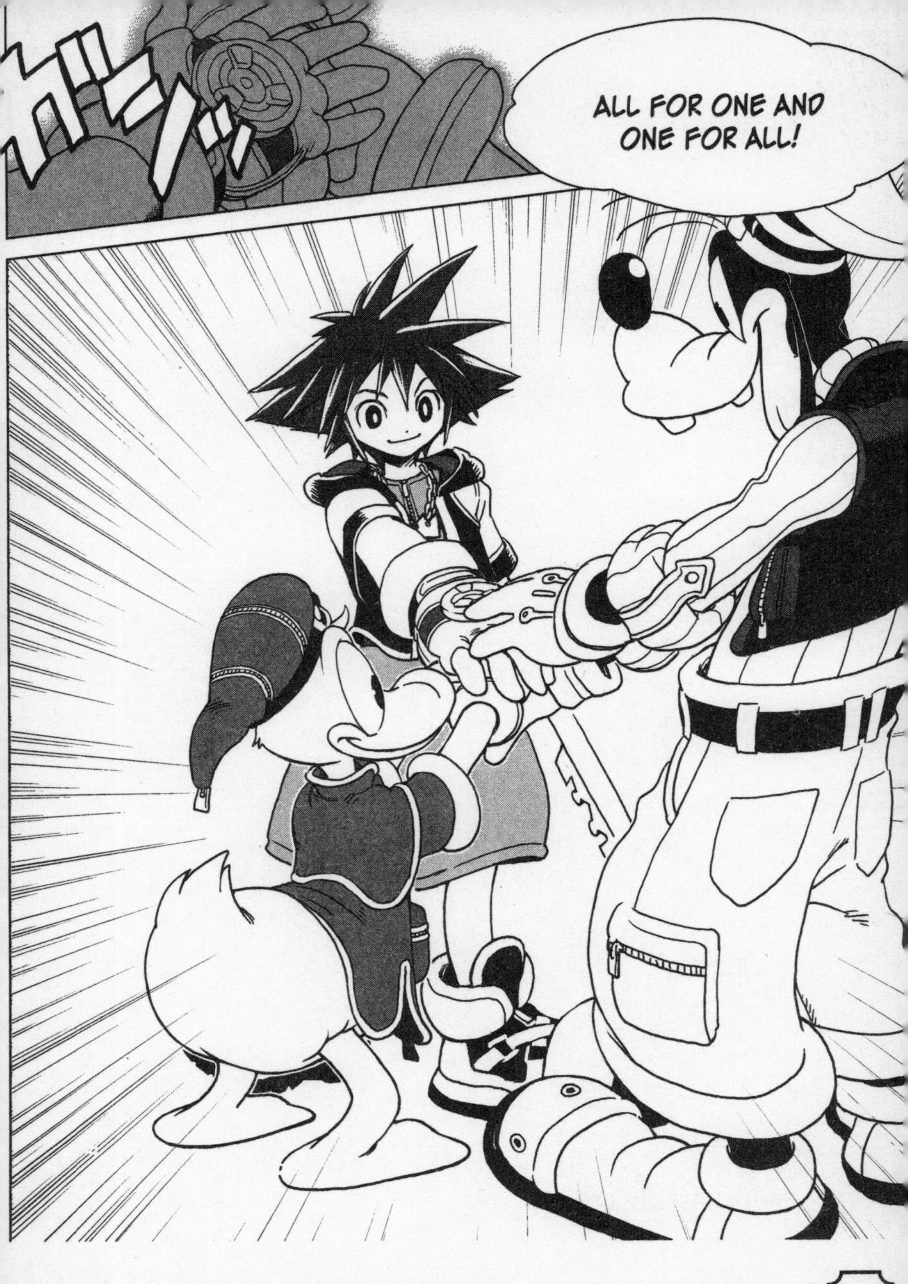
ALL FOR ONE AND ONE FOR ALL!

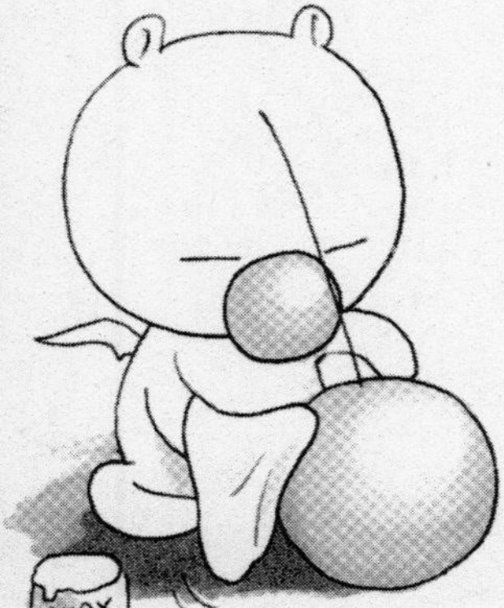
WAX

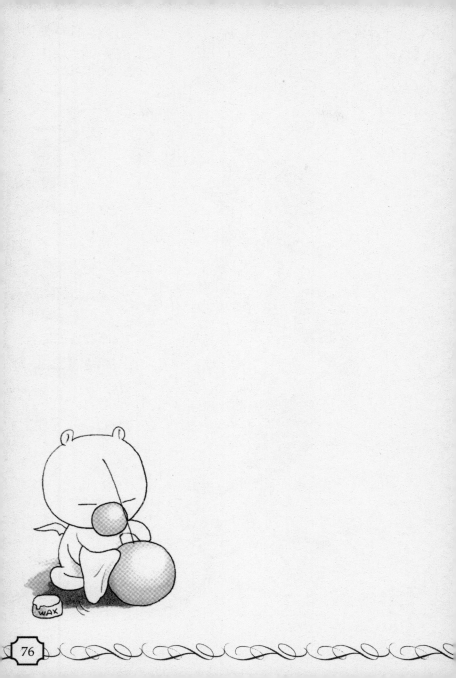

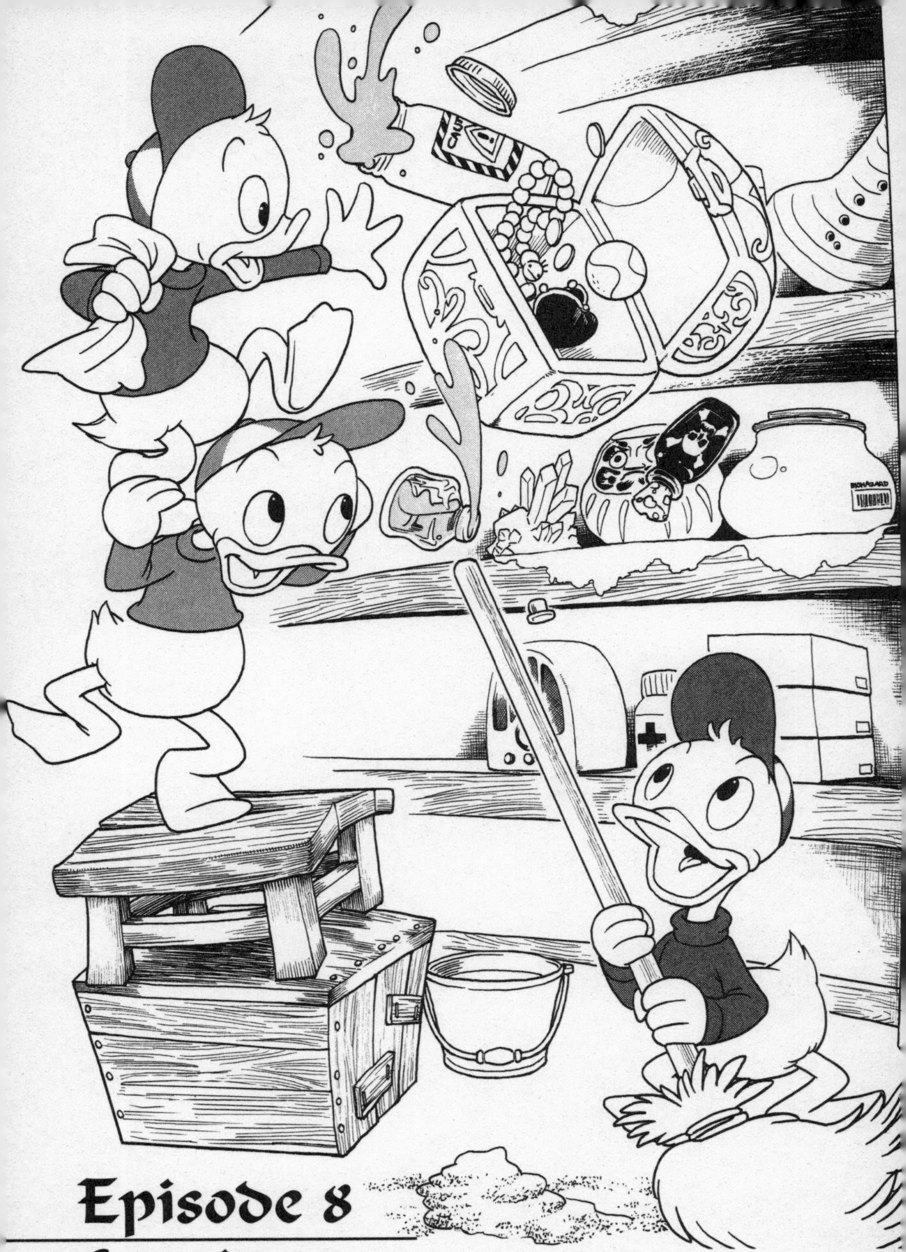

Episode 8

Conspiracy

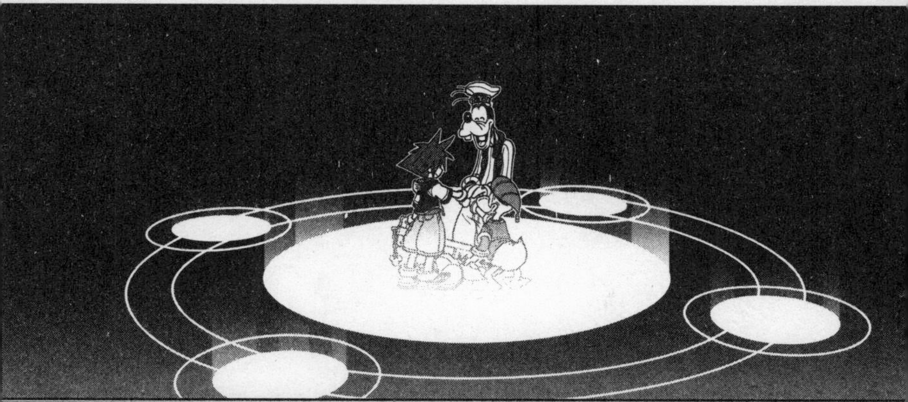

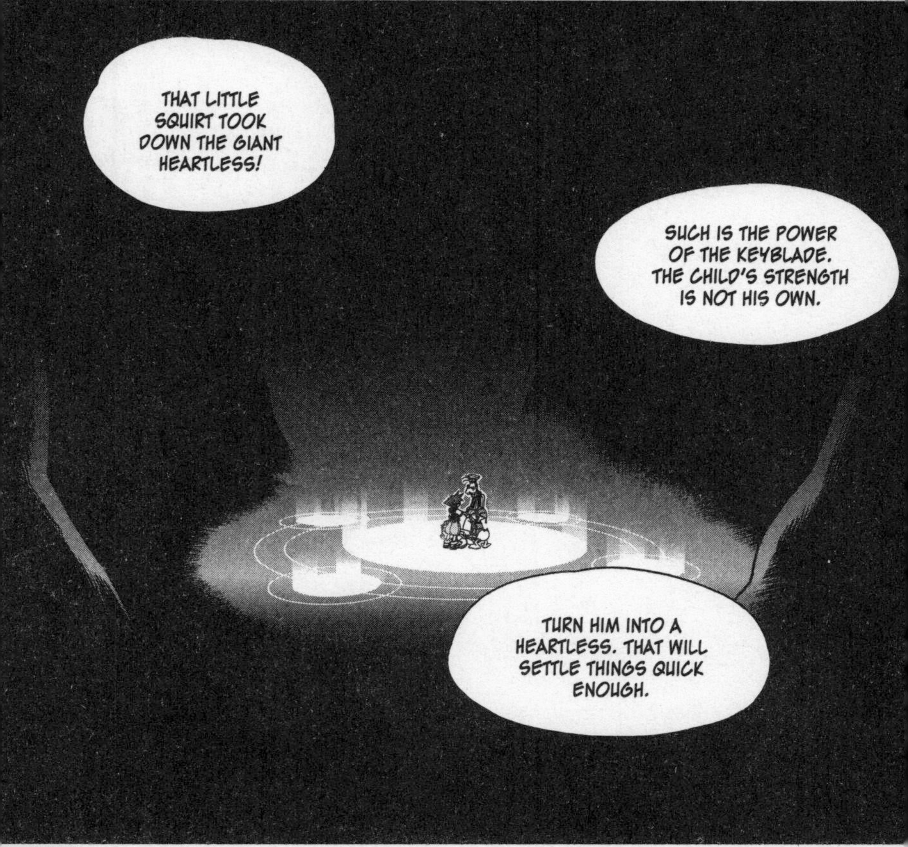
THAT LITTLE SQUIRT TOOK DOWN THE GIANT HEARTLESS!
SUCH IS THE POWER OF THE KEYBLADE. THE CHILD'S STRENGTH IS NOT HIS OWN.
TURN HIM INTO A HEARTLESS. THAT WILL SETTLE THINGS QUICK ENOUGH.

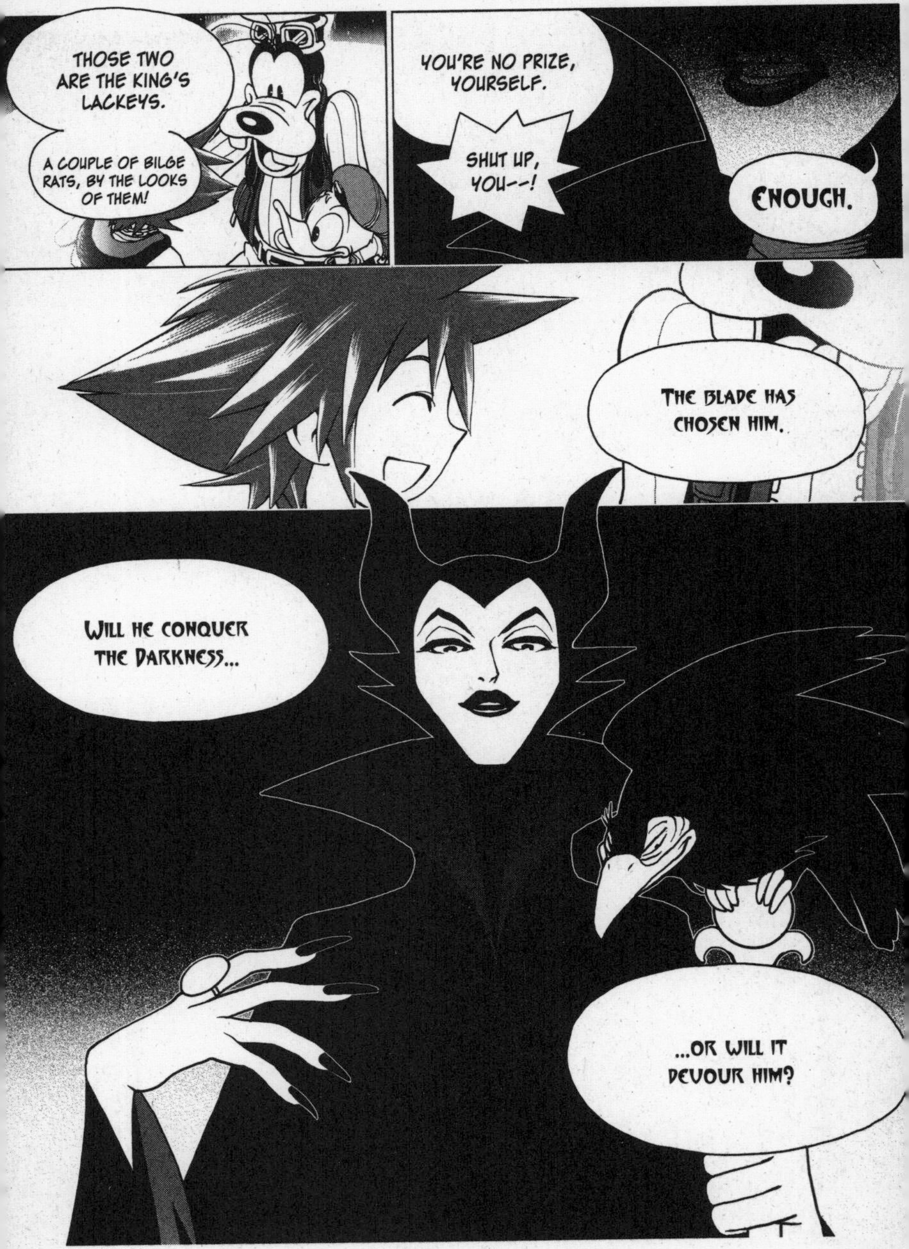
THOSE TWO ARE THE KING'S LACKEYS.
A COUPLE OF BILGE RATS, BY THE LOOKS OF THEM!
YOU'RE NO PRIZE, YOURSELF.
SHUT UP, YOU--!
ENOUGH.
THE BLADE HAS CHOSEN HIM.
WILL HE CONQUER THE DARKNESS...
...OR WILL IT DEVOUR HIM?

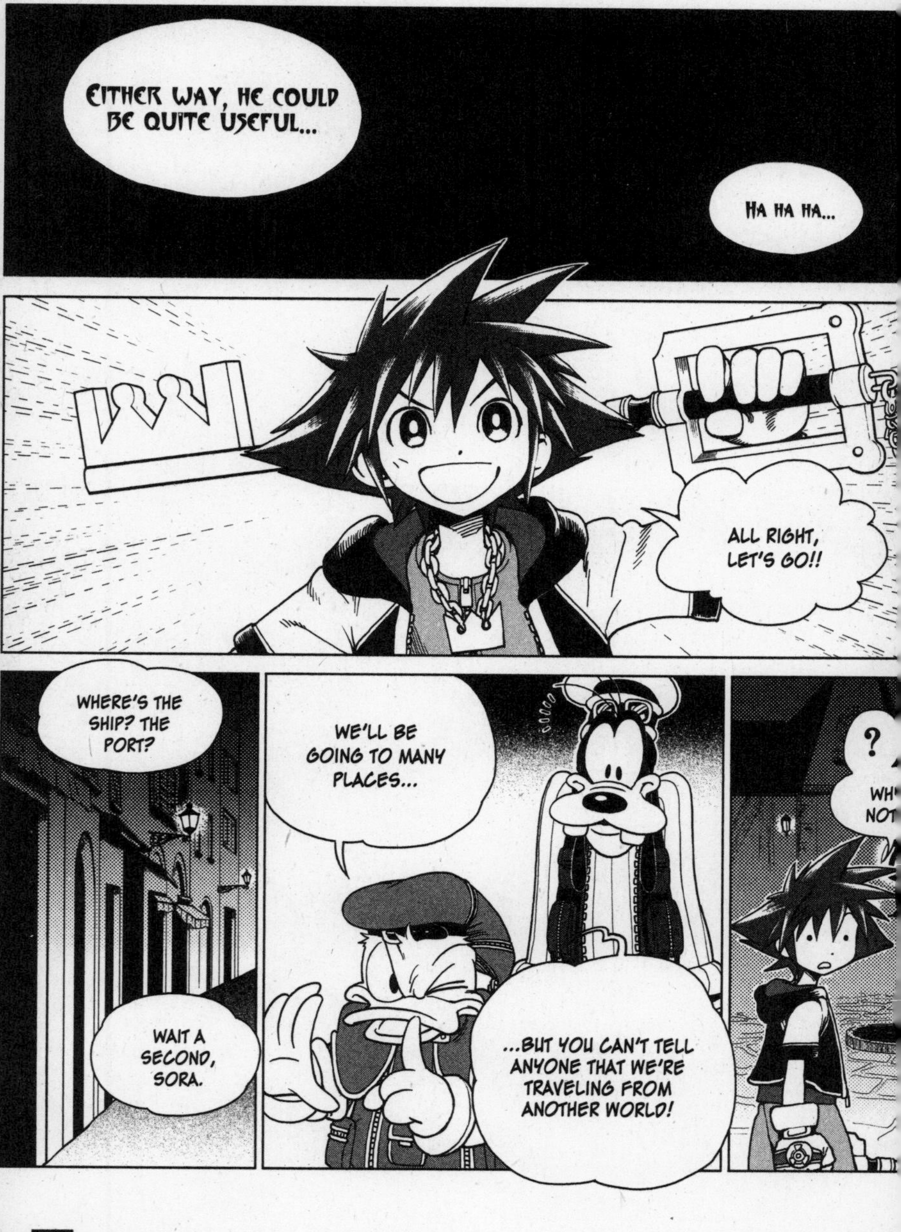
EITHER WAY, HE COULD BE QUITE USEFUL...
HA HA HA...
ALL RIGHT, LET'S GO!!
WHERE'S THE SHIP? THE PORT?
WAIT A SECOND, SORA.
WE'LL BE GOING TO MANY PLACES...
...BUT YOU CAN'T TELL ANYONE THAT WE'RE TRAVELING FROM ANOTHER WORLD!
?

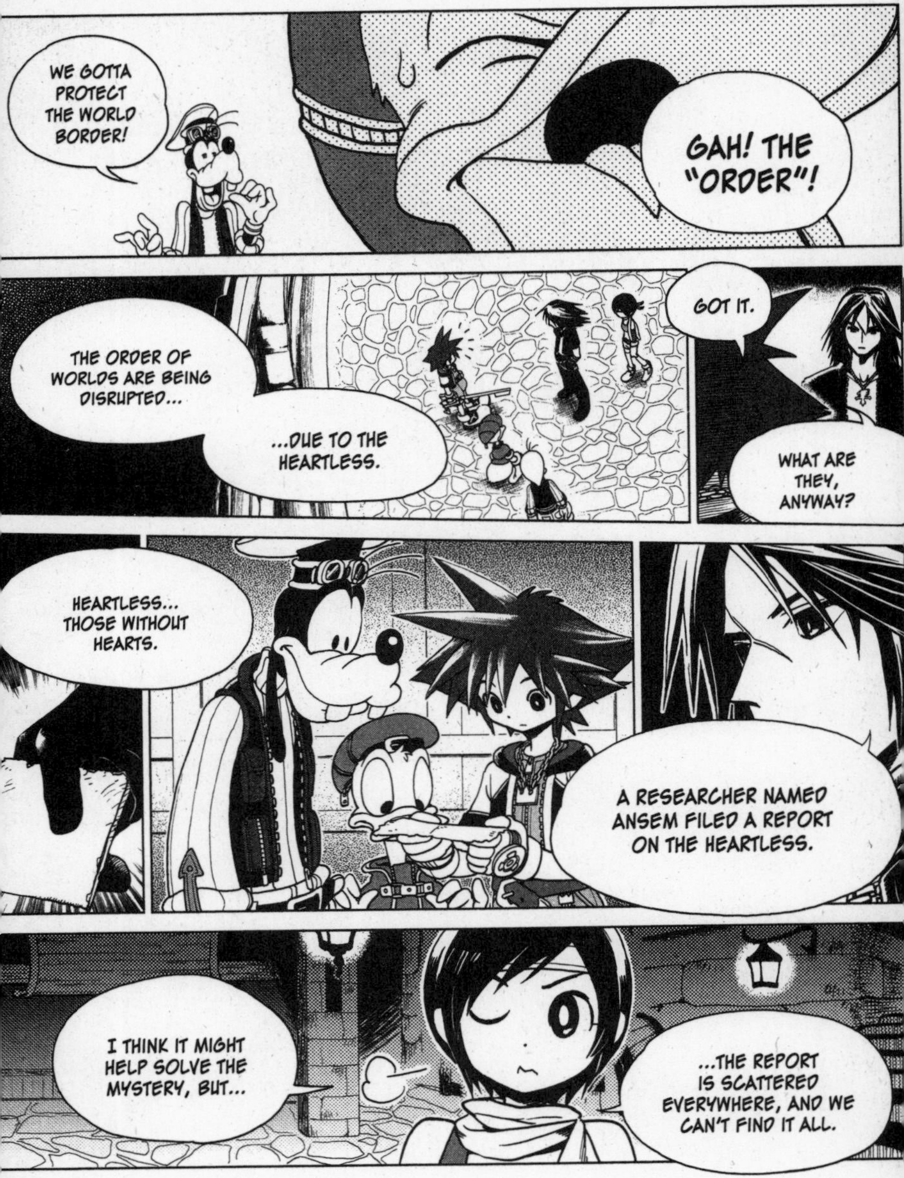
WE GOTTA PROTECT THE WORLD BORDER!
GAH! THE "ORDER"!
THE ORDER OF WORLDS ARE BEING DISRUPTED...
...DUE TO THE HEARTLESS.
GOT IT.
WHAT ARE THEY, ANYWAY?
HEARTLESS... THOSE WITHOUT HEARTS.
A RESEARCHER NAMED ANSEM FILED A REPORT ON THE HEARTLESS.
I THINK IT MIGHT HELP SOLVE THE MYSTERY, BUT...
...THE REPORT IS SCATTERED EVERYWHERE, AND WE CAN'T FIND IT ALL.

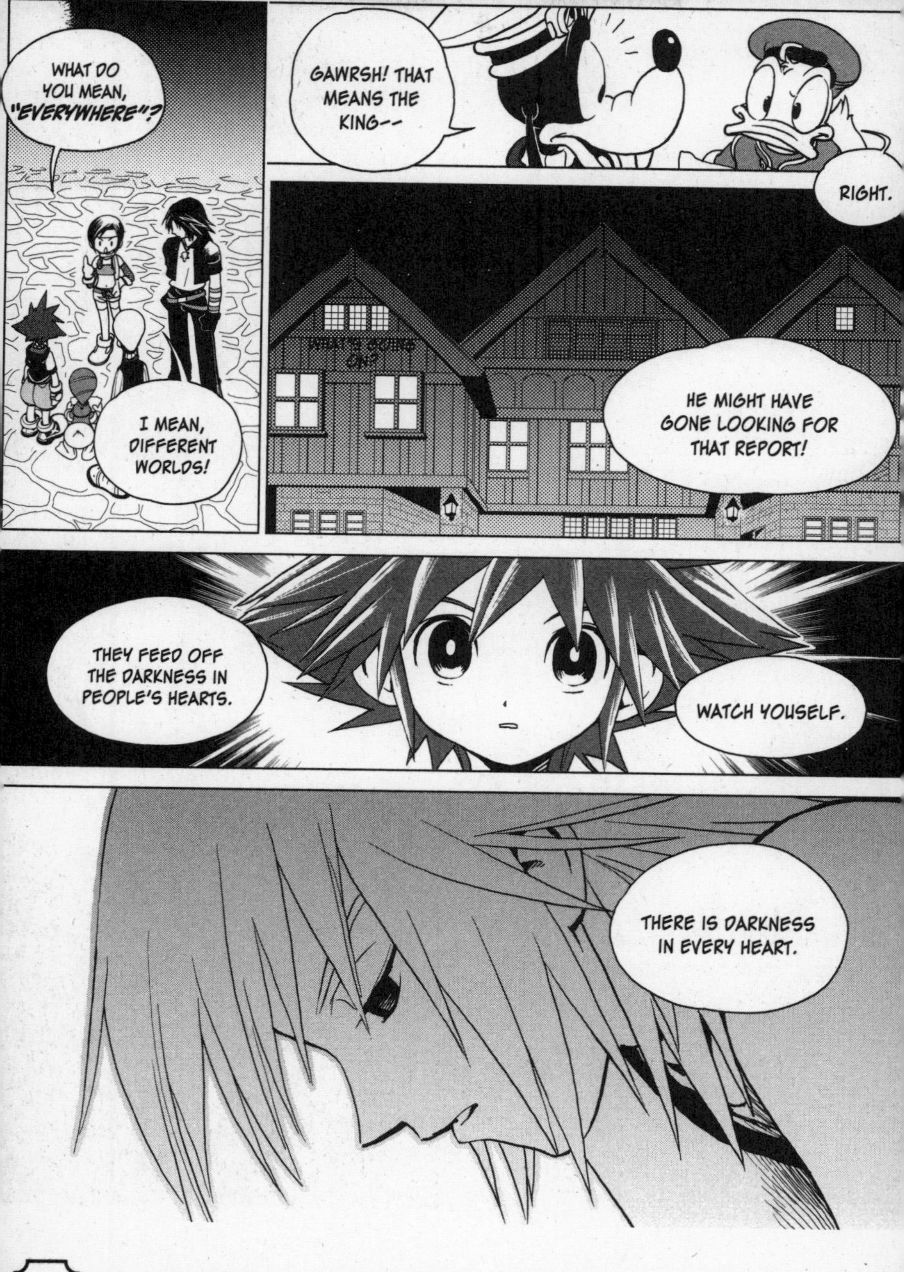
WHAT DO YOU MEAN, "EVERYWHERE"?
I MEAN, DIFFERENT WORLDS!
GAWRSH! THAT MEANS THE KING--
RIGHT.
WHAT'S GOING ON?
HE MIGHT HAVE GONE LOOKING FOR THAT REPORT!
THEY FEED OFF THE DARKNESS IN PEOPLE'S HEARTS.
WATCH YOUSELF.
THERE IS DARKNESS IN EVERY HEART.

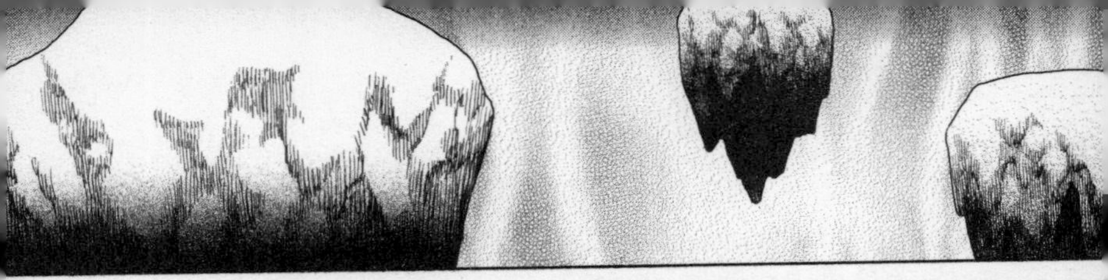

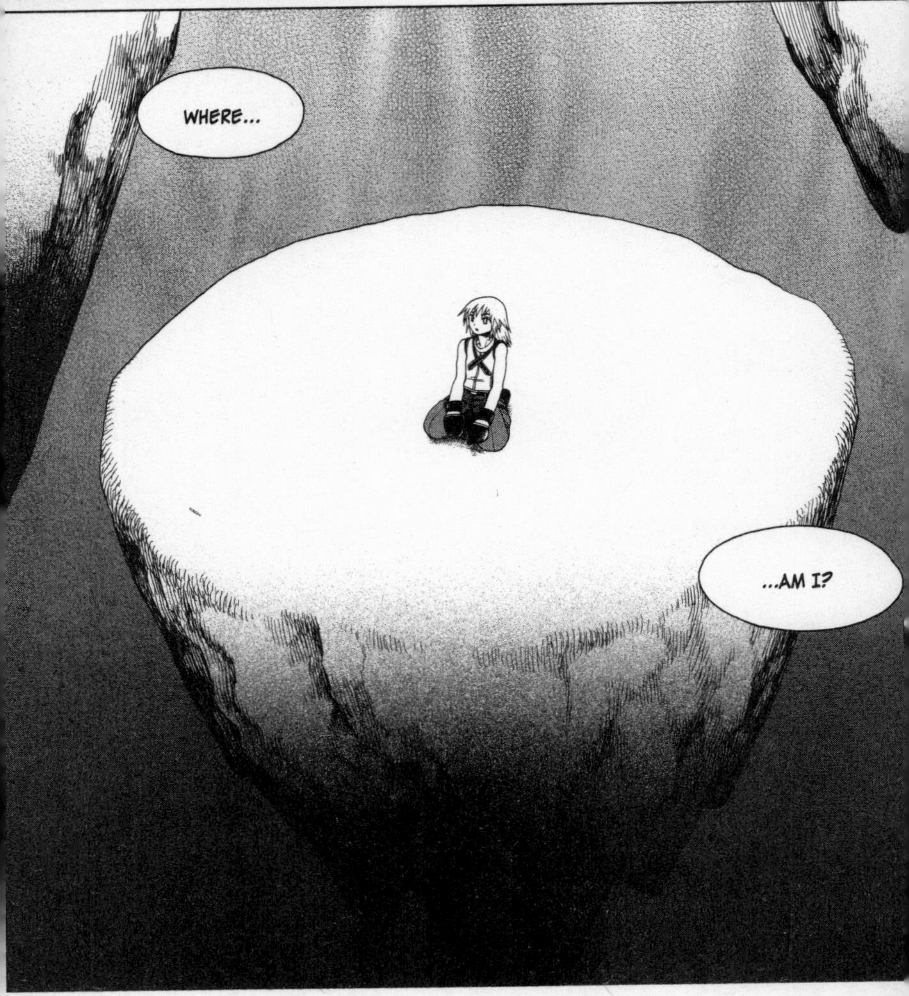
WHERE...
...AM I?

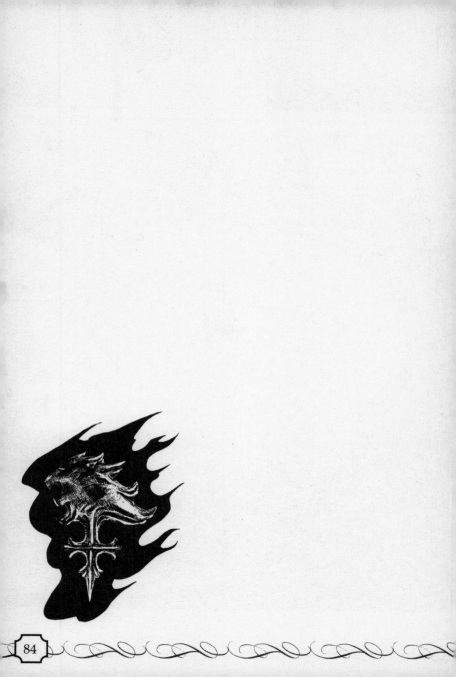

Episode 9
Departure

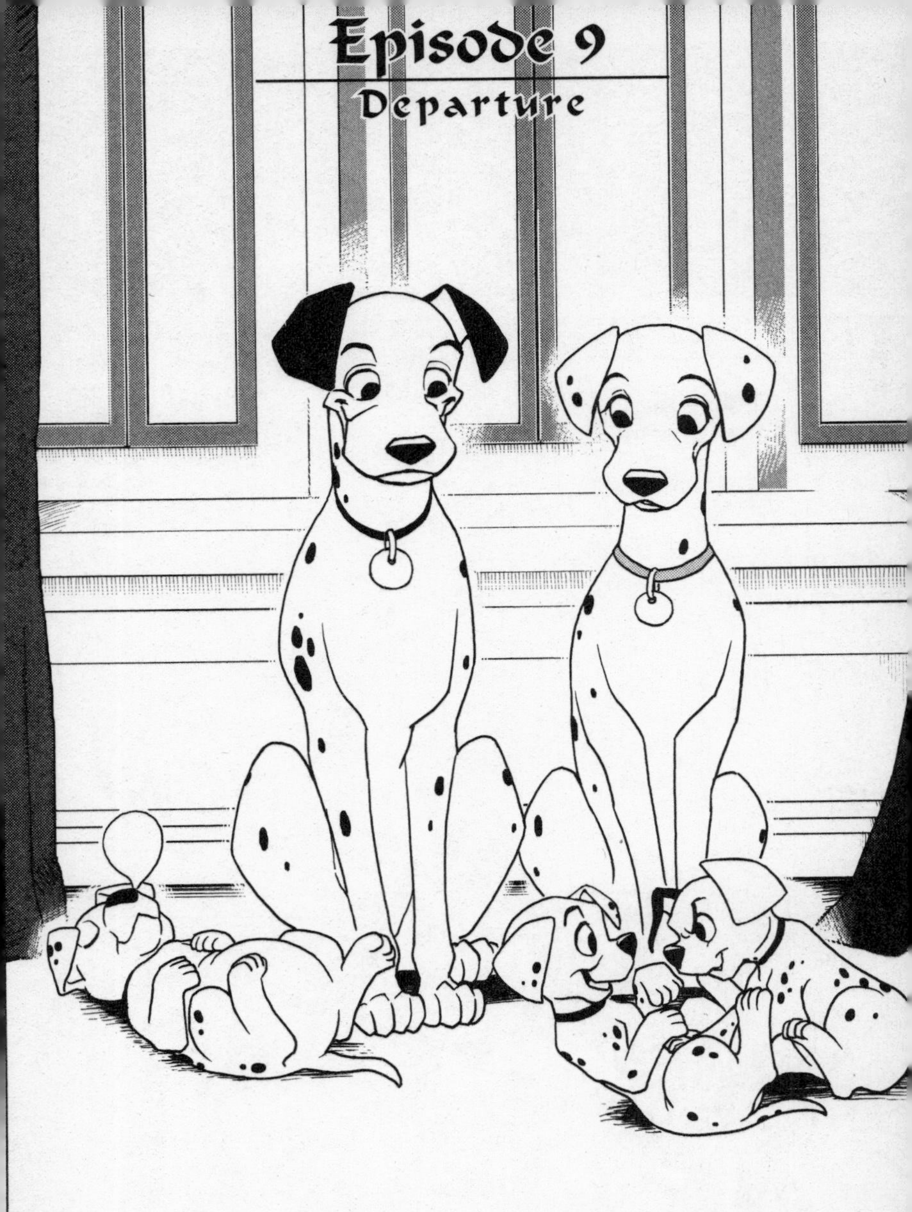

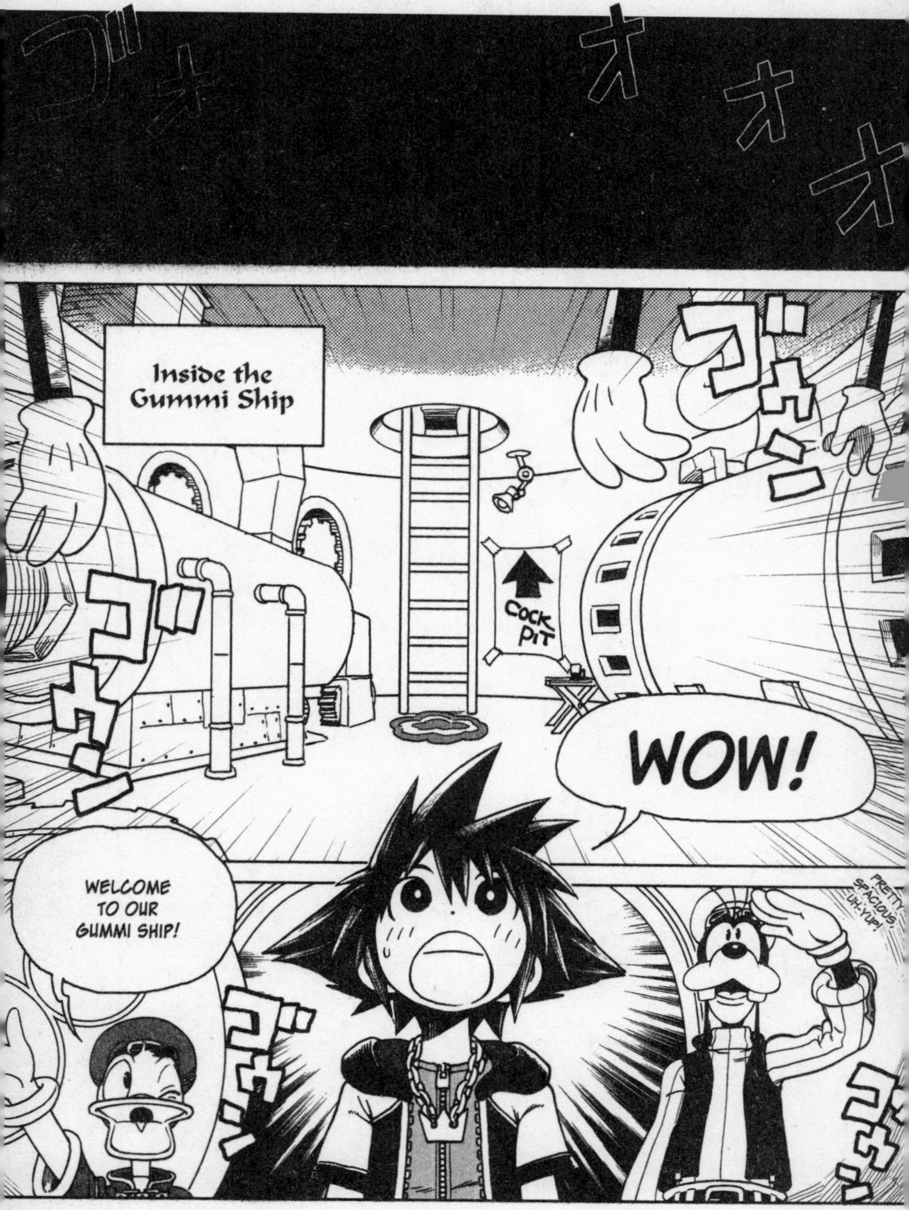
Inside the Gummi Ship
COCK PIT
WOW!
WELCOME TO OUR GUMMI SHIP!
PRETTY SPACIOUS, UH-YUP!

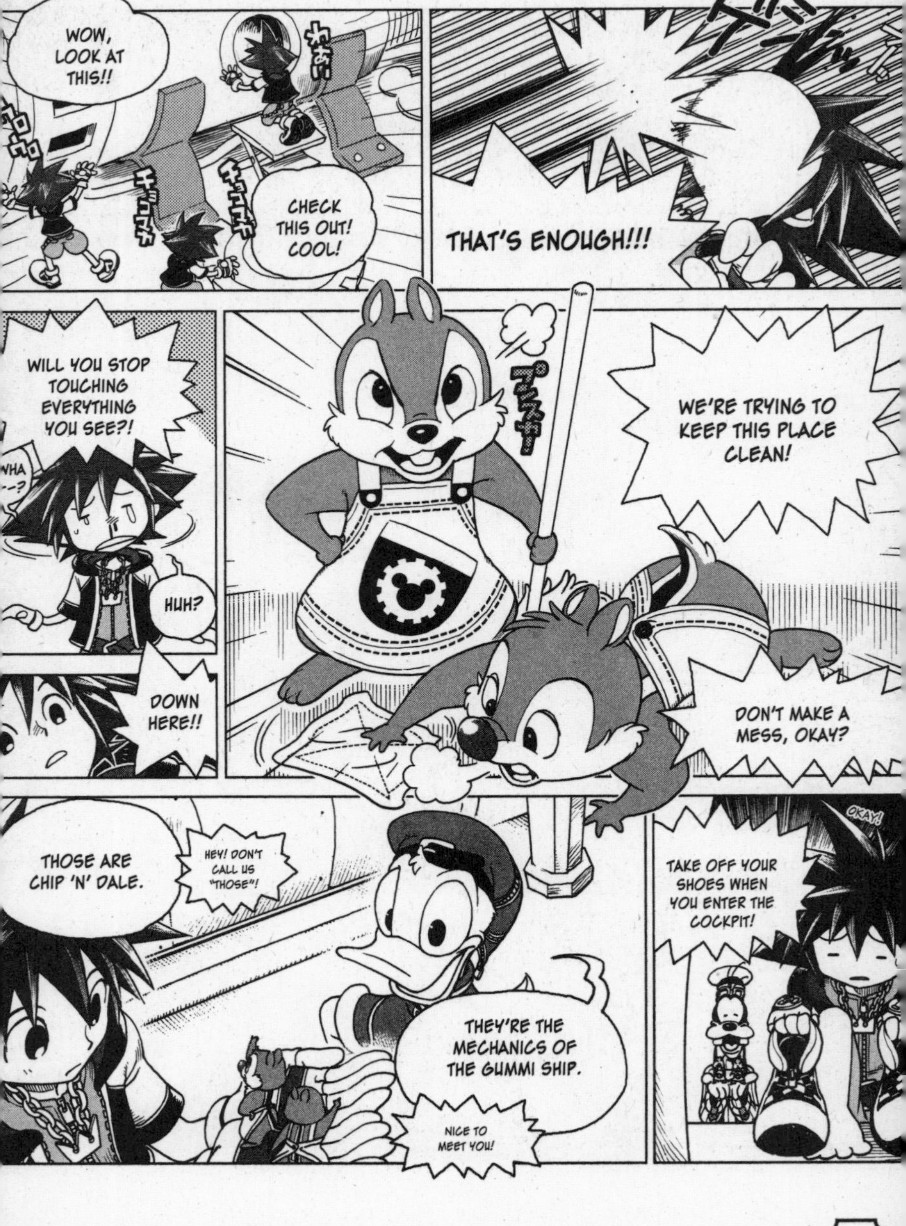
WOW, LOOK AT THIS!!
CHECK THIS OUT! COOL!
THAT'S ENOUGH!!!
WILL YOU STOP TOUCHING EVERYTHING YOU SEE?!
WHA--?
HUH?
DOWN HERE!!
WE'RE TRYING TO KEEP THIS PLACE CLEAN!
DON'T MAKE A MESS, OKAY?
THOSE ARE CHIP 'N' DALE.
HEY! DON'T CALL US "THOSE"!
THEY'RE THE MECHANICS OF THE GUMMI SHIP.
NICE TO MEET YOU!
TAKE OFF YOUR SHOES WHEN YOU ENTER THE COCKPIT!
OKAY!

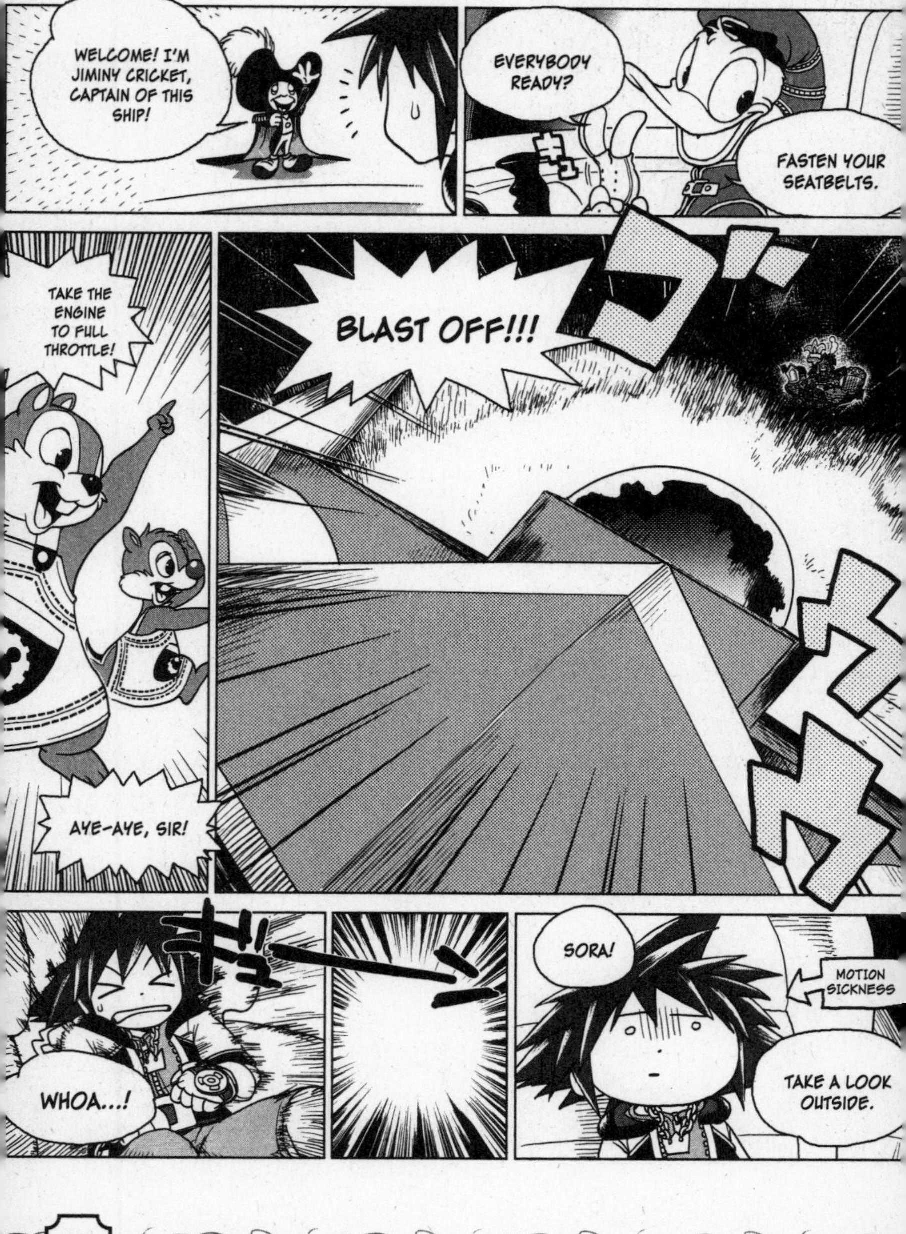
WELCOME! I'M JIMINY CRICKET, CAPTAIN OF THIS SHIP!
EVERYBODY READY?
FASTEN YOUR SEATBELTS.
TAKE THE ENGINE TO FULL THROTTLE!
AYE-AYE, SIR!
BLAST OFF!!!
WHOA...!
SORA!
MOTION SICKNESS
TAKE A LOOK OUTSIDE.

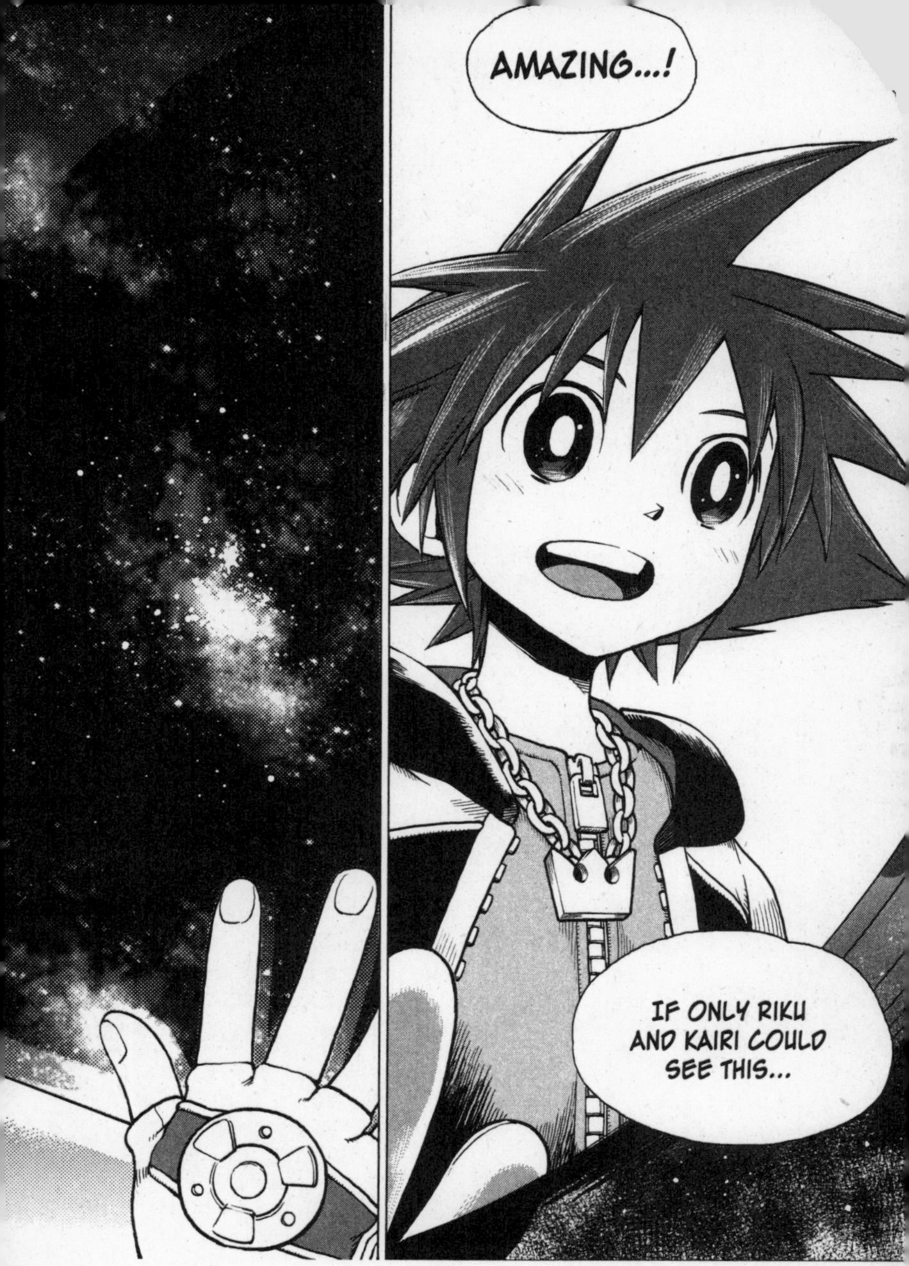
AMAZING...!
IF ONLY RIKU AND KAIRI COULD SEE THIS...

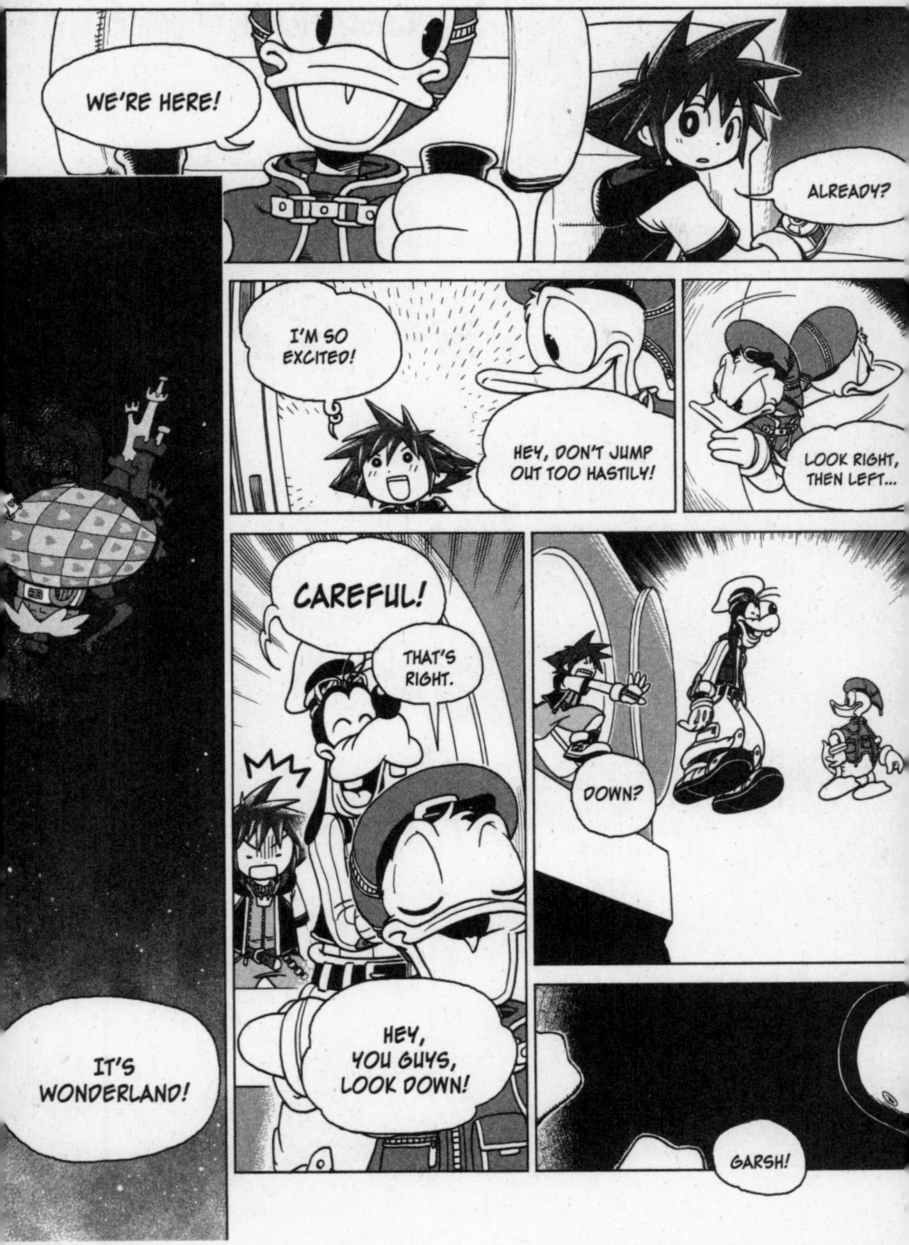
WE'RE HERE!
ALREADY?
IT'S WONDERLAND!
I'M SO EXCITED!
HEY, DON'T JUMP OUT TOO HASTILY!
LOOK RIGHT, THEN LEFT...
CAREFUL!
THAT'S RIGHT.
HEY, YOU GUYS, LOOK DOWN!
DOWN?
GARSH!

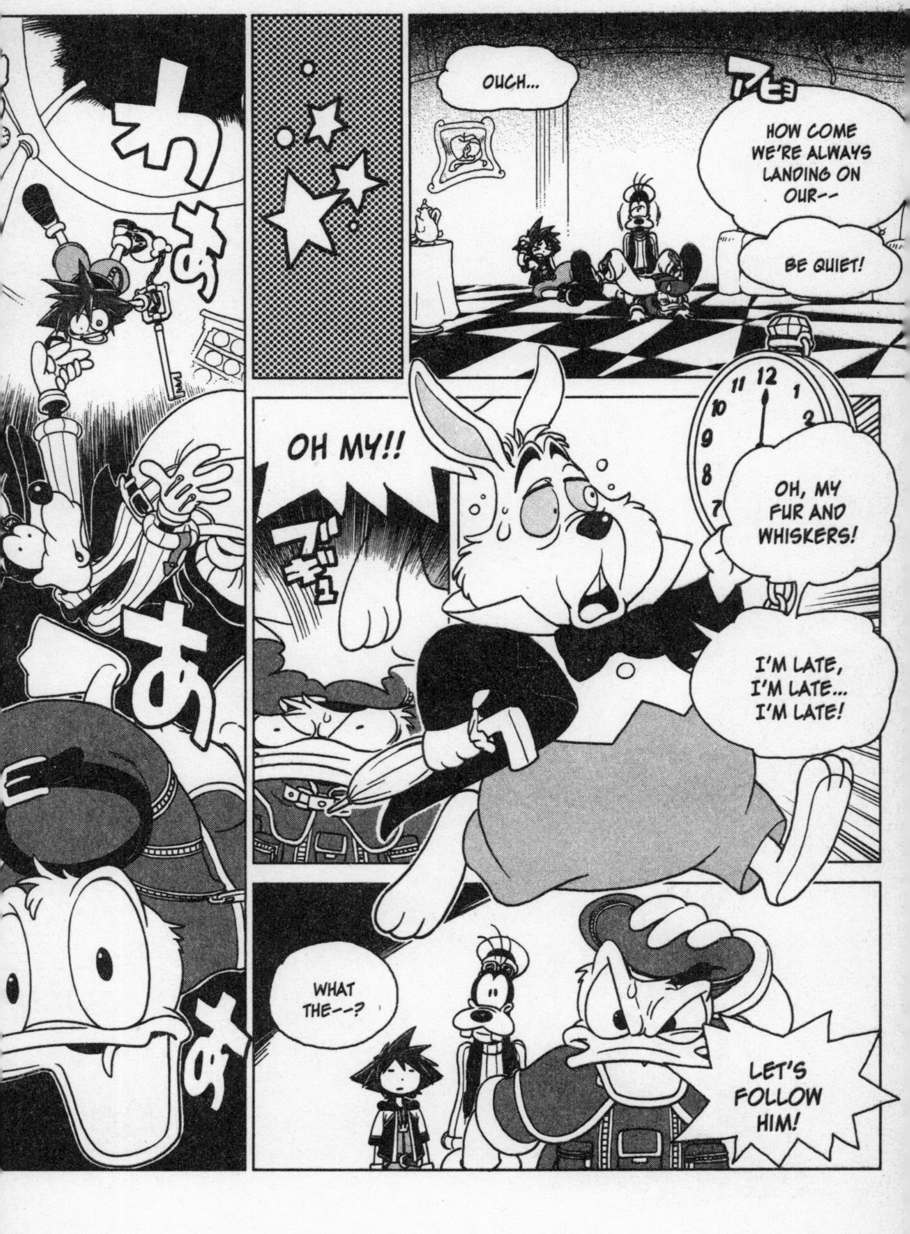

わあああ
OUCH...
アヒョ
HOW COME WE'RE ALWAYS LANDING ON OUR--
BE QUIET!
OH MY!!
ブギュ
OH, MY FUR AND WHISKERS!
I'M LATE, I'M LATE... I'M LATE!
WHAT THE--?
LET'S FOLLOW HIM!

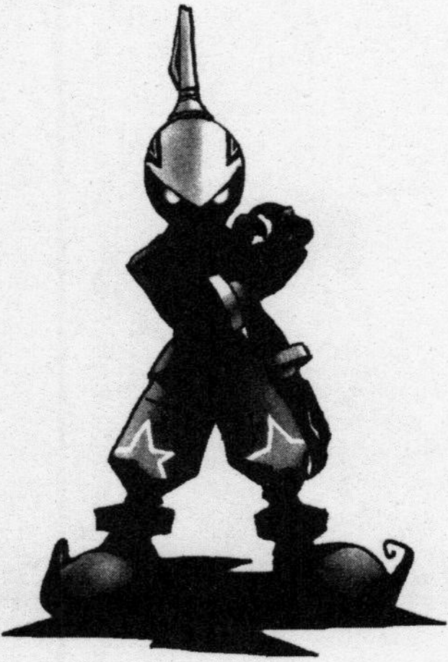

Episode 10

Kangaroo Court

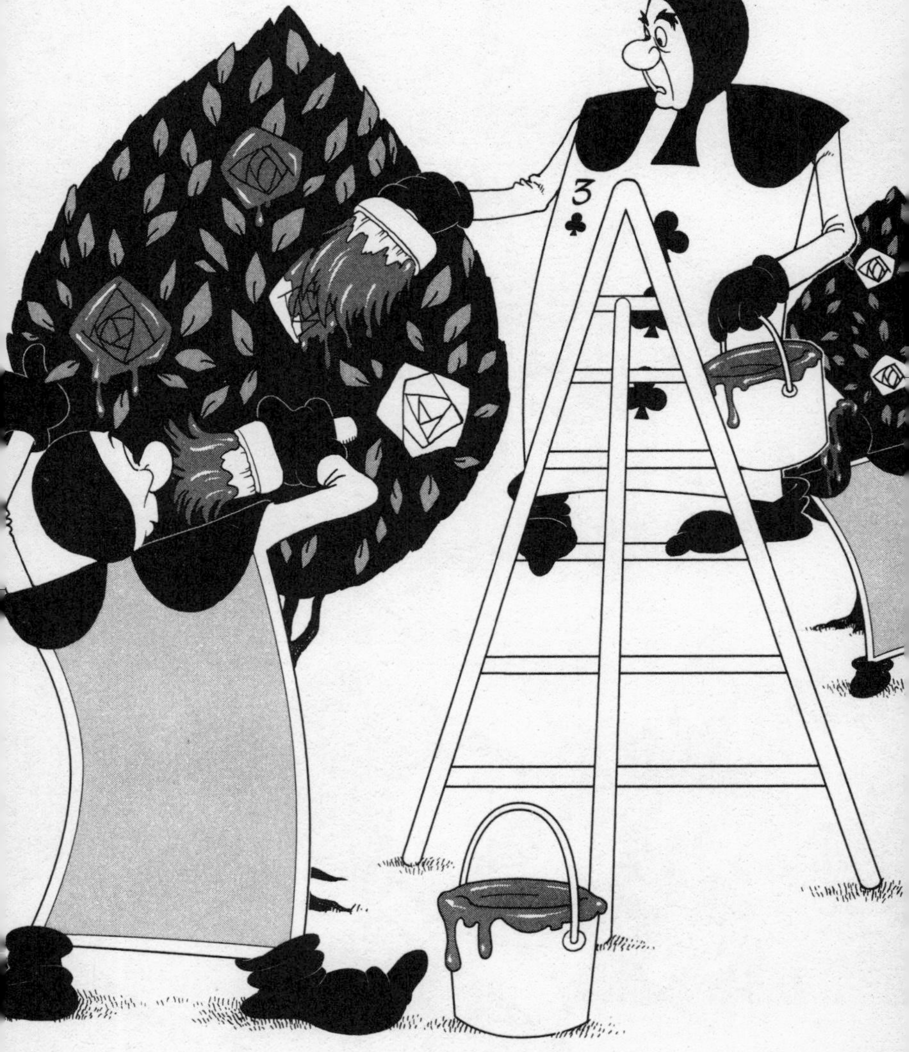
3

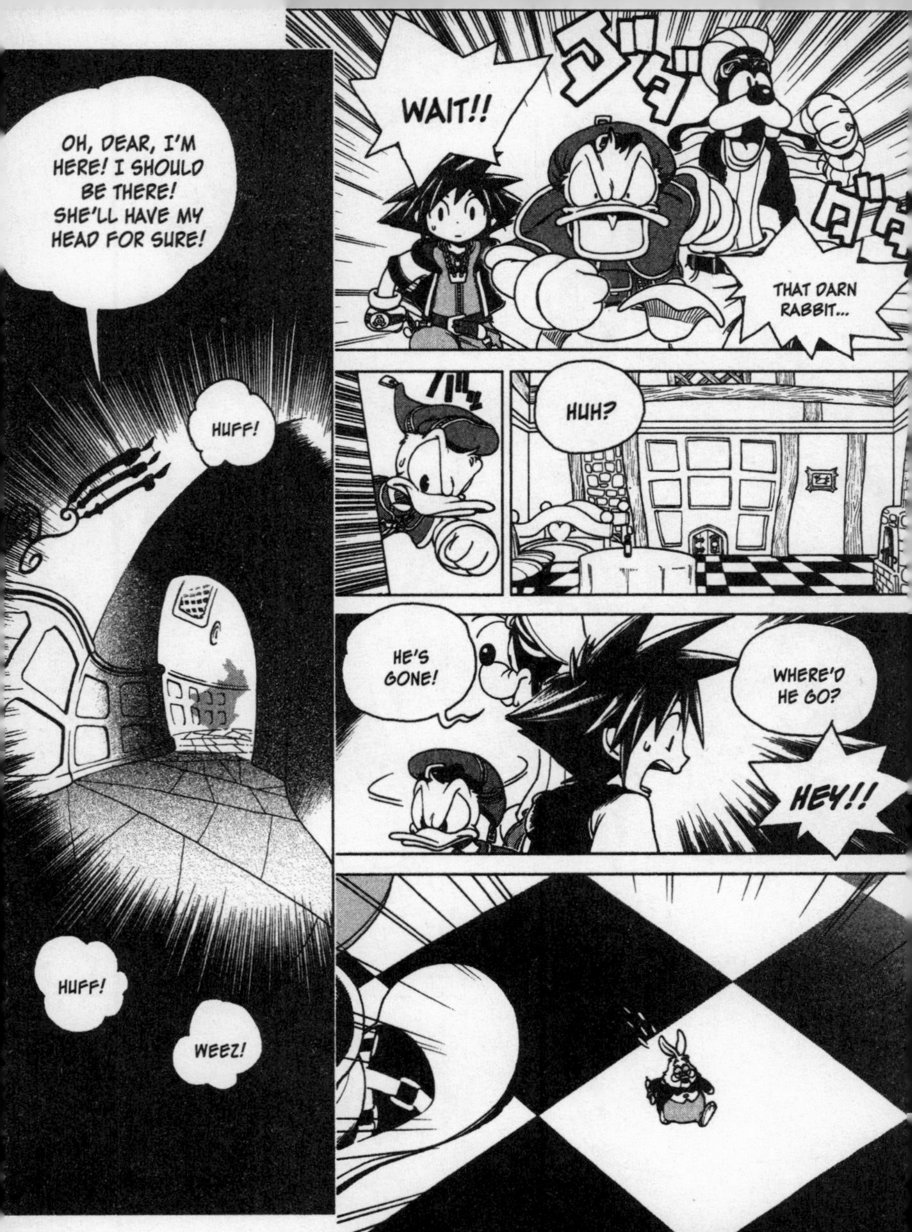
OH, DEAR, I'M HERE! I SHOULD BE THERE! SHE'LL HAVE MY HEAD FOR SURE!
HUFF!
HUFF!
WEEZ!
WAIT!!
THAT DARN RABBIT...
HUH?
HE'S GONE!
WHERE'D HE GO?
HEY!!

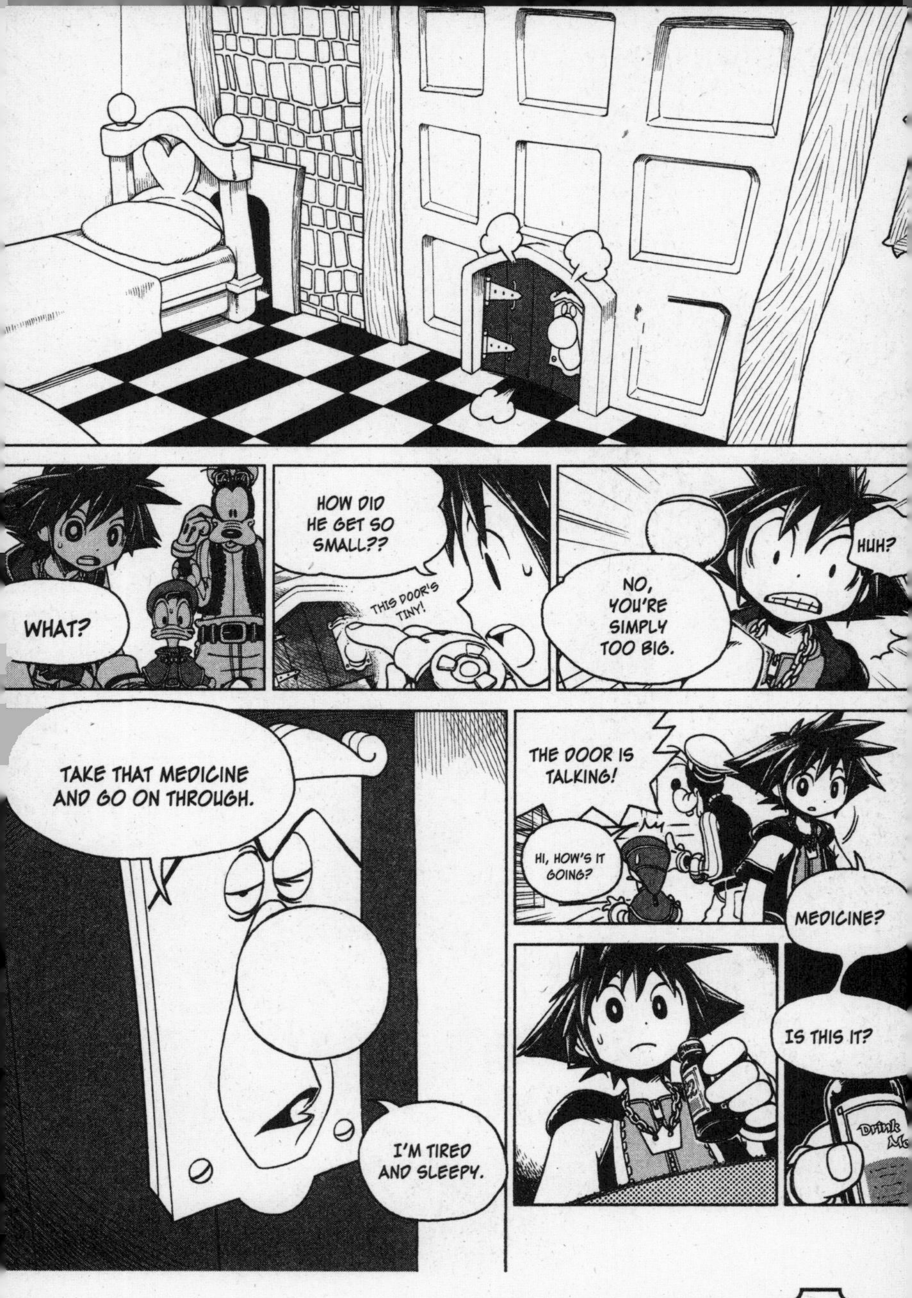
WHAT?
HOW DID HE GET SO SMALL??
THIS DOOR'S TINY!
NO, YOU'RE SIMPLY TOO BIG.
HUH?
TAKE THAT MEDICINE AND GO ON THROUGH.
I'M TIRED AND SLEEPY.
THE DOOR IS TALKING!
HI, HOW'S IT GOING?
MEDICINE?
IS THIS IT?

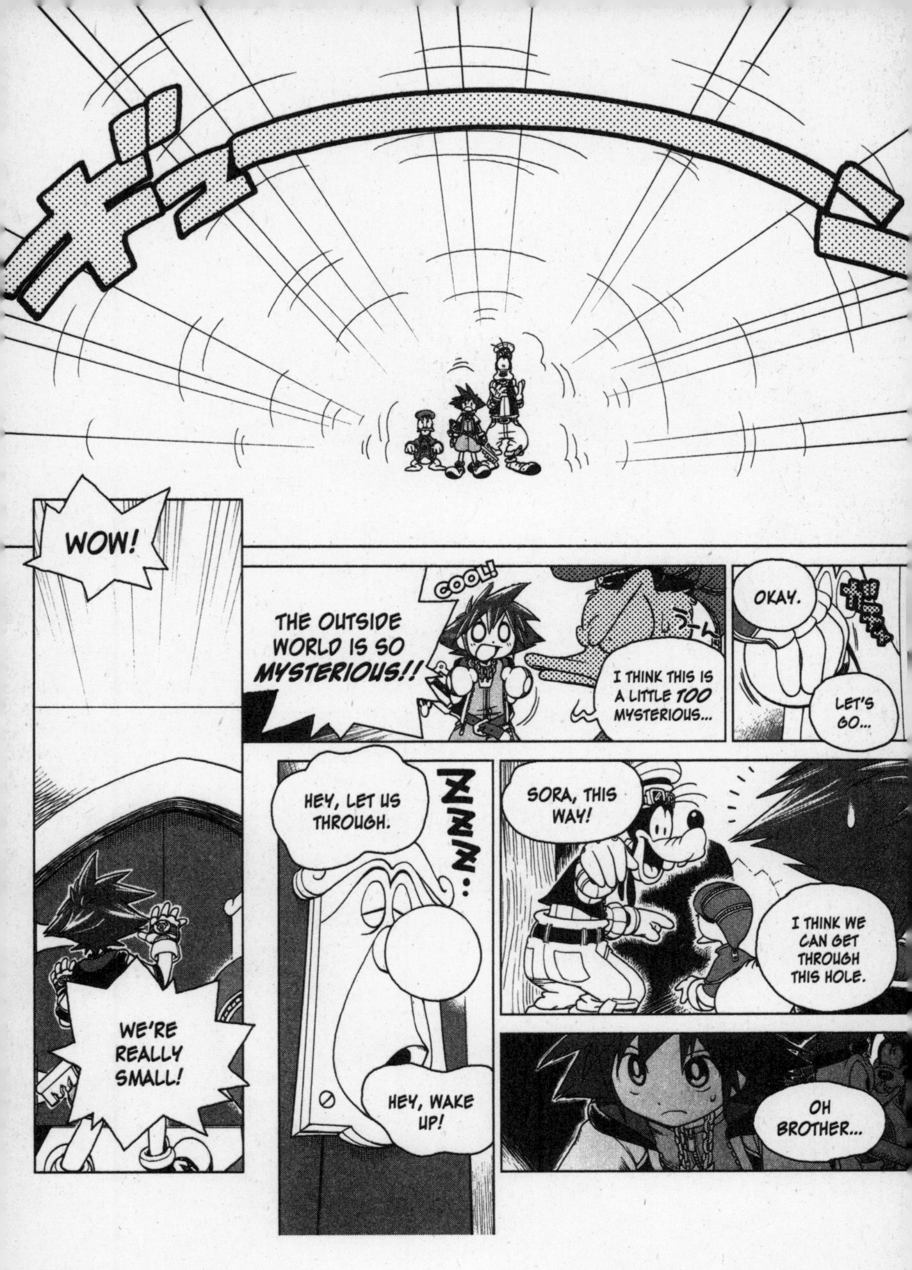
WOW!
THE OUTSIDE WORLD IS SO MYSTERIOUS!!
COOL!
I THINK THIS IS A LITTLE TOO MYSTERIOUS...
OKAY.
LET'S GO...
WE'RE REALLY SMALL!
HEY, LET US THROUGH.
ZZZ..
HEY, WAKE UP!
SORA, THIS WAY!
I THINK WE CAN GET THROUGH THIS HOLE.
OH BROTHER...

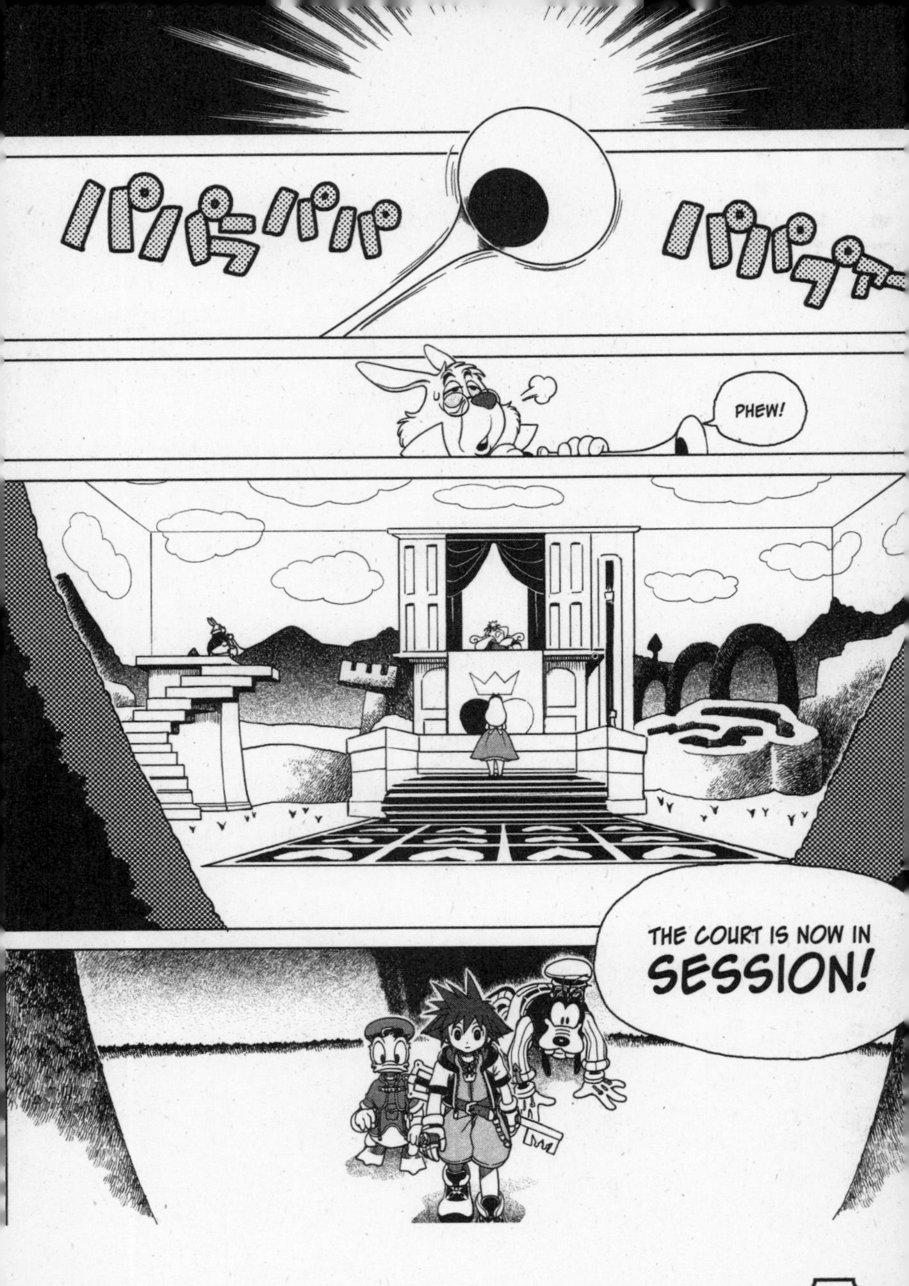
パパパパパ
パパプー
PHEW!
THE COURT IS NOW IN SESSION!

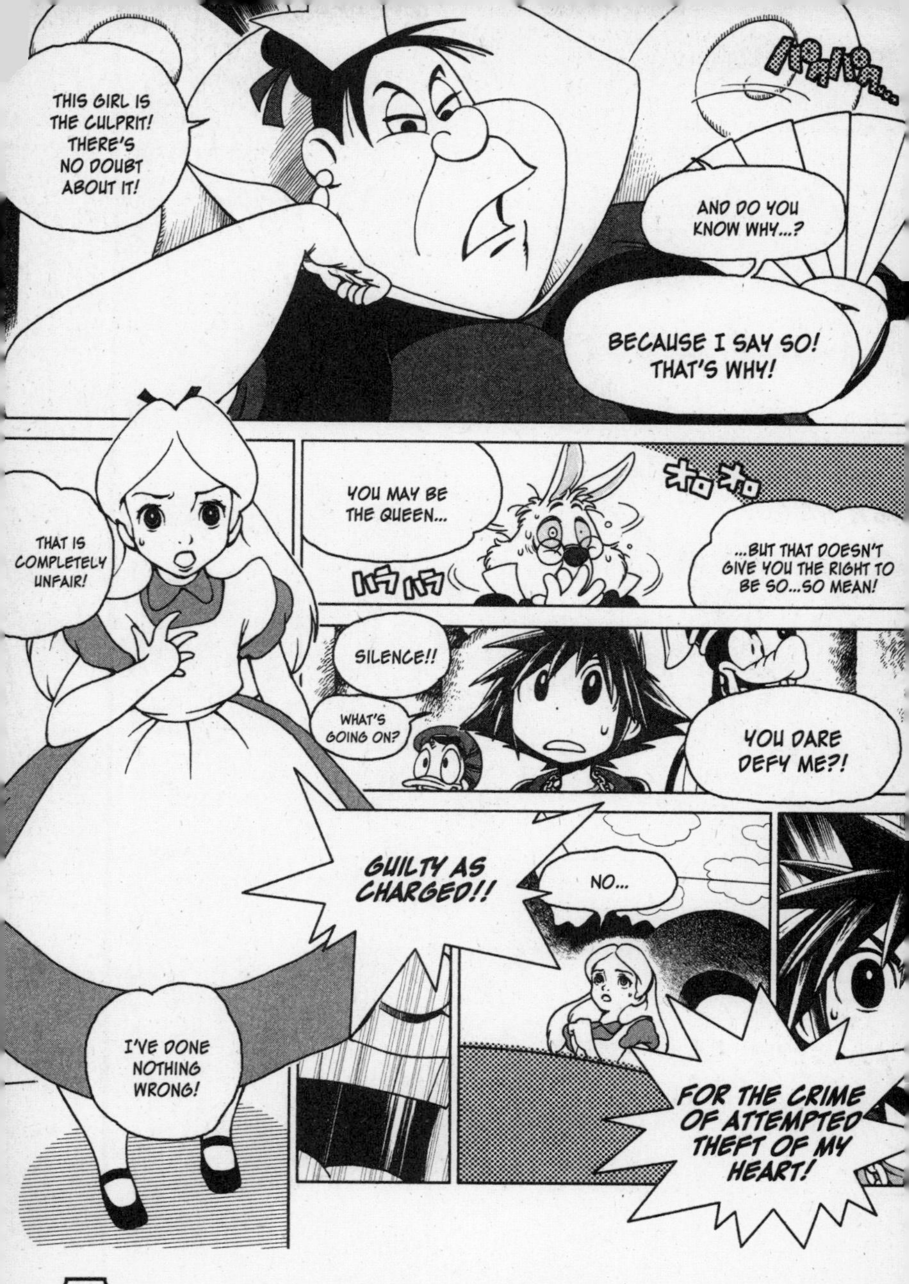
THIS GIRL IS THE CULPRIT! THERE'S NO DOUBT ABOUT IT!
パタパタ…
AND DO YOU KNOW WHY...?
BECAUSE I SAY SO! THAT'S WHY!
THAT IS COMPLETELY UNFAIR!
I'VE DONE NOTHING WRONG!
YOU MAY BE THE QUEEN...
オロオロ
ハラハラ
...BUT THAT DOESN'T GIVE YOU THE RIGHT TO BE SO...SO MEAN!
SILENCE!!
WHAT'S GOING ON?
YOU DARE DEFY ME?!
GUILTY AS CHARGED!!
NO...
FOR THE CRIME OF ATTEMPTED THEFT OF MY HEART!

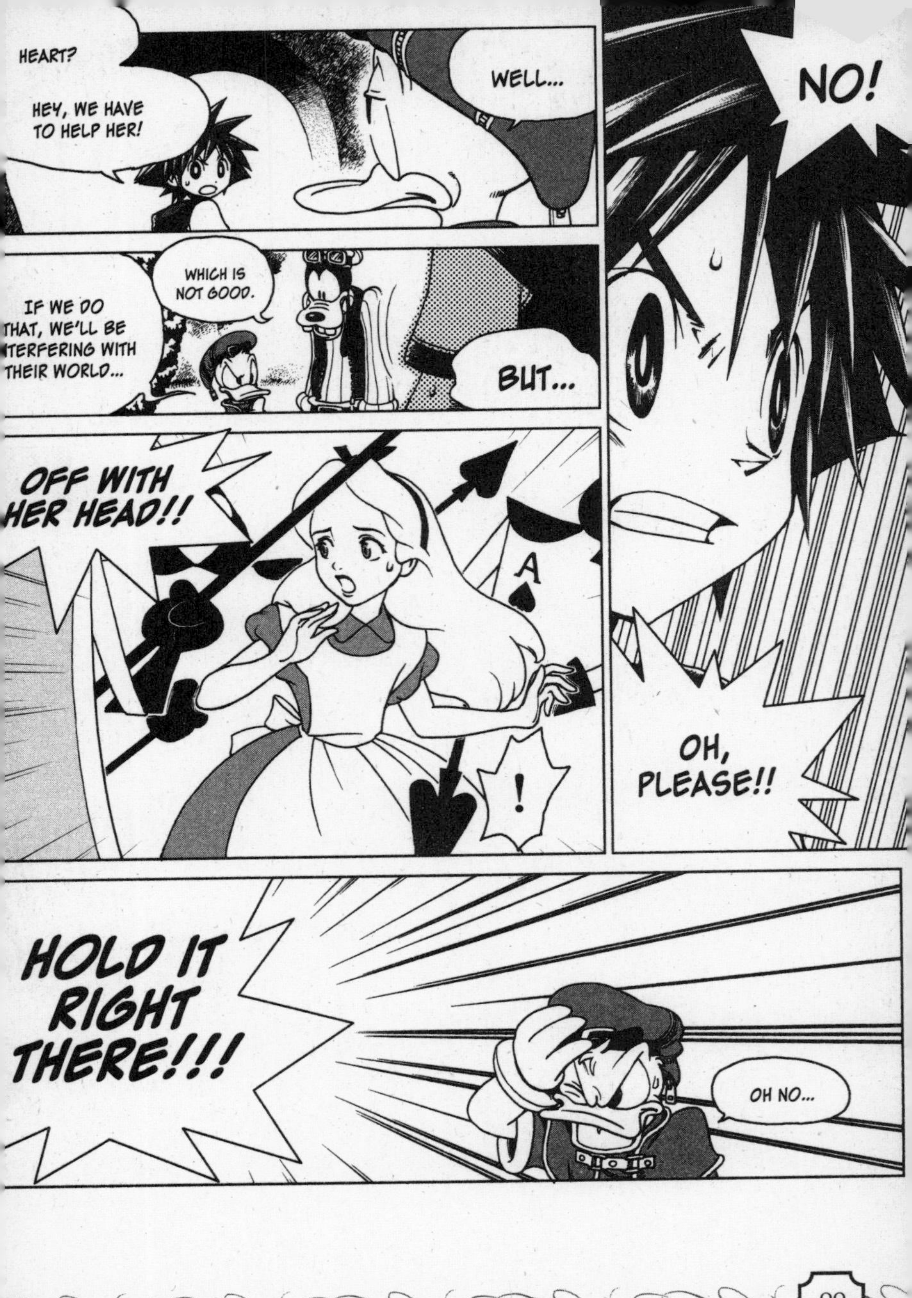
HEART?
HEY, WE HAVE TO HELP HER!
WELL...
IF WE DO THAT, WE'LL BE TERFERING WITH THEIR WORLD...
WHICH IS NOT GOOD.
BUT...
OFF WITH HER HEAD!!
A
!
NO!
OH, PLEASE!!
HOLD IT RIGHT THERE!!!
OH NO...

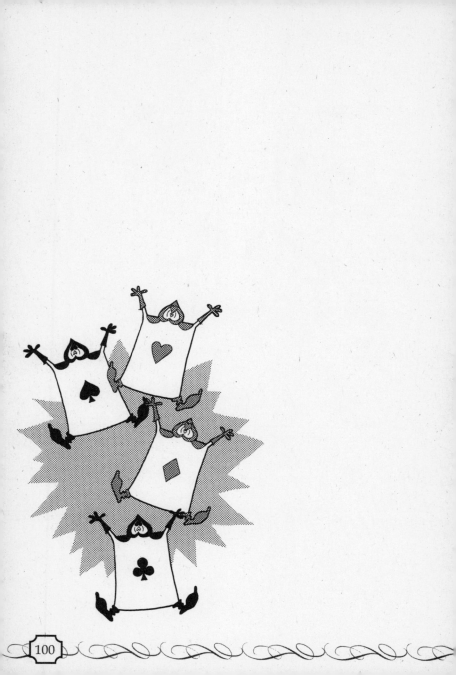

Episode 11

Find the Evidence!

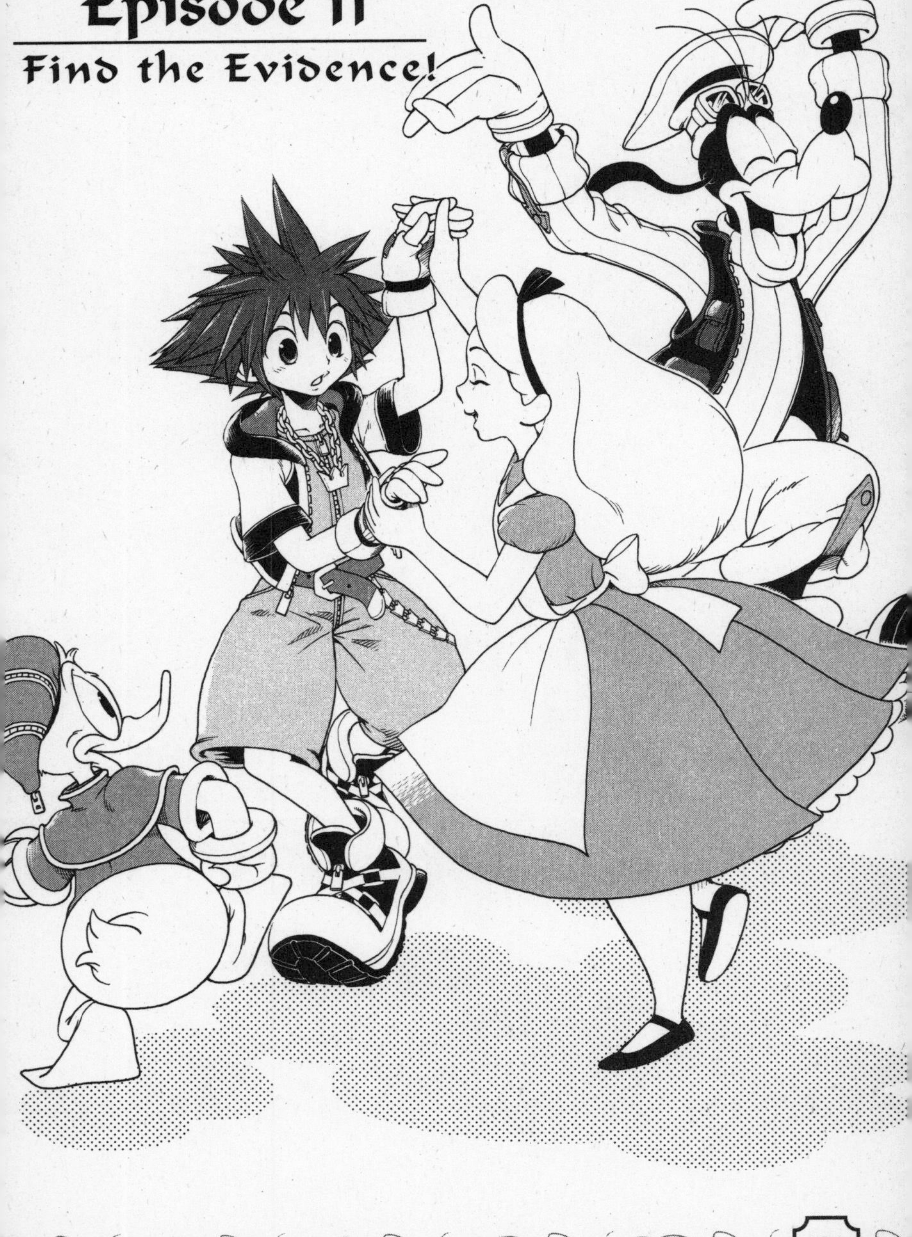

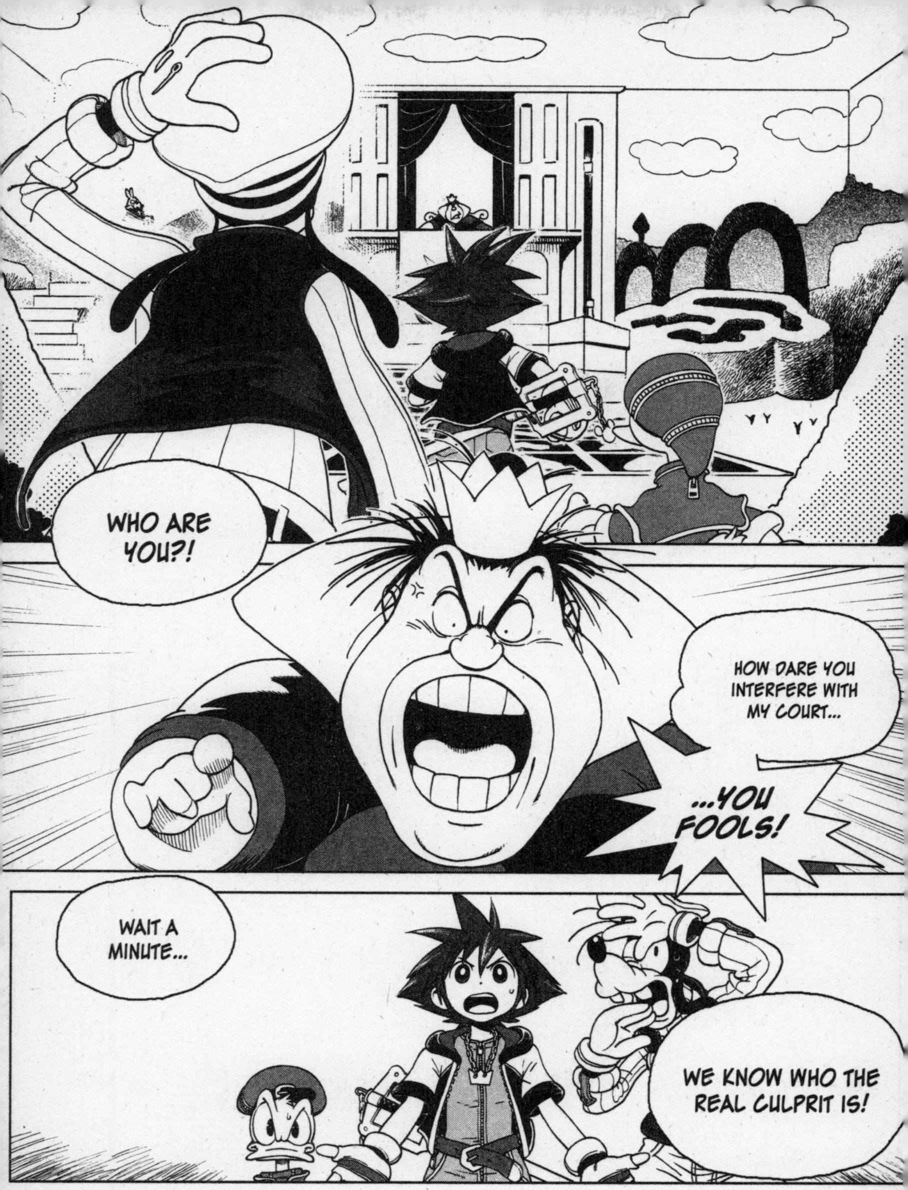
WHO ARE YOU?!
HOW DARE YOU INTERFERE WITH MY COURT...
...YOU FOOLS!
WAIT A MINUTE...
WE KNOW WHO THE REAL CULPRIT IS!

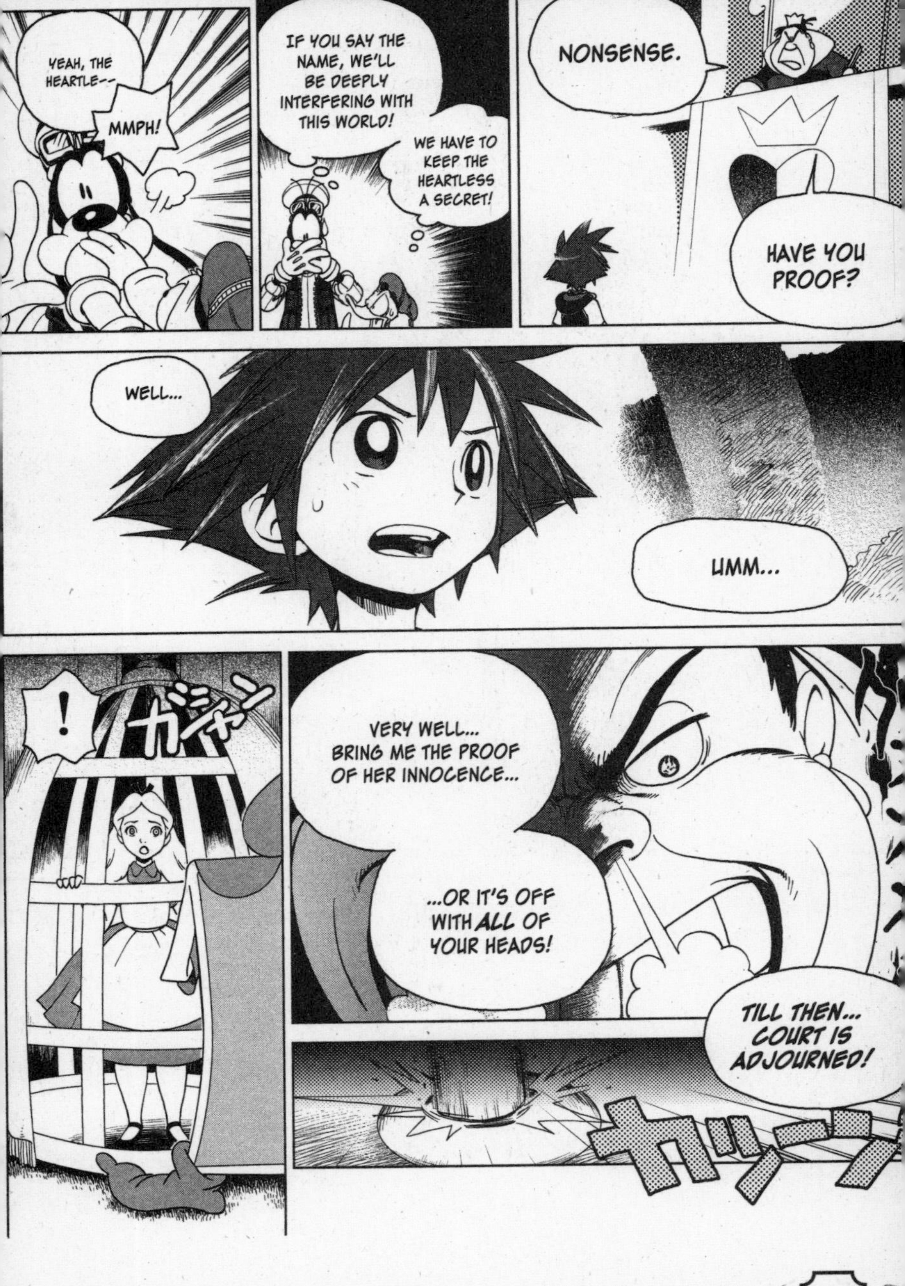
YEAH, THE HEARTLE--
MMPH!
IF YOU SAY THE NAME, WE'LL BE DEEPLY INTERFERING WITH THIS WORLD!
WE HAVE TO KEEP THE HEARTLESS A SECRET!
NONSENSE.
HAVE YOU PROOF?
WELL...
UMM...
!
ガシャン
VERY WELL... BRING ME THE PROOF OF HER INNOCENCE...
...OR IT'S OFF WITH ALL OF YOUR HEADS!
TILL THEN... COURT IS ADJOURNED!
カツーン

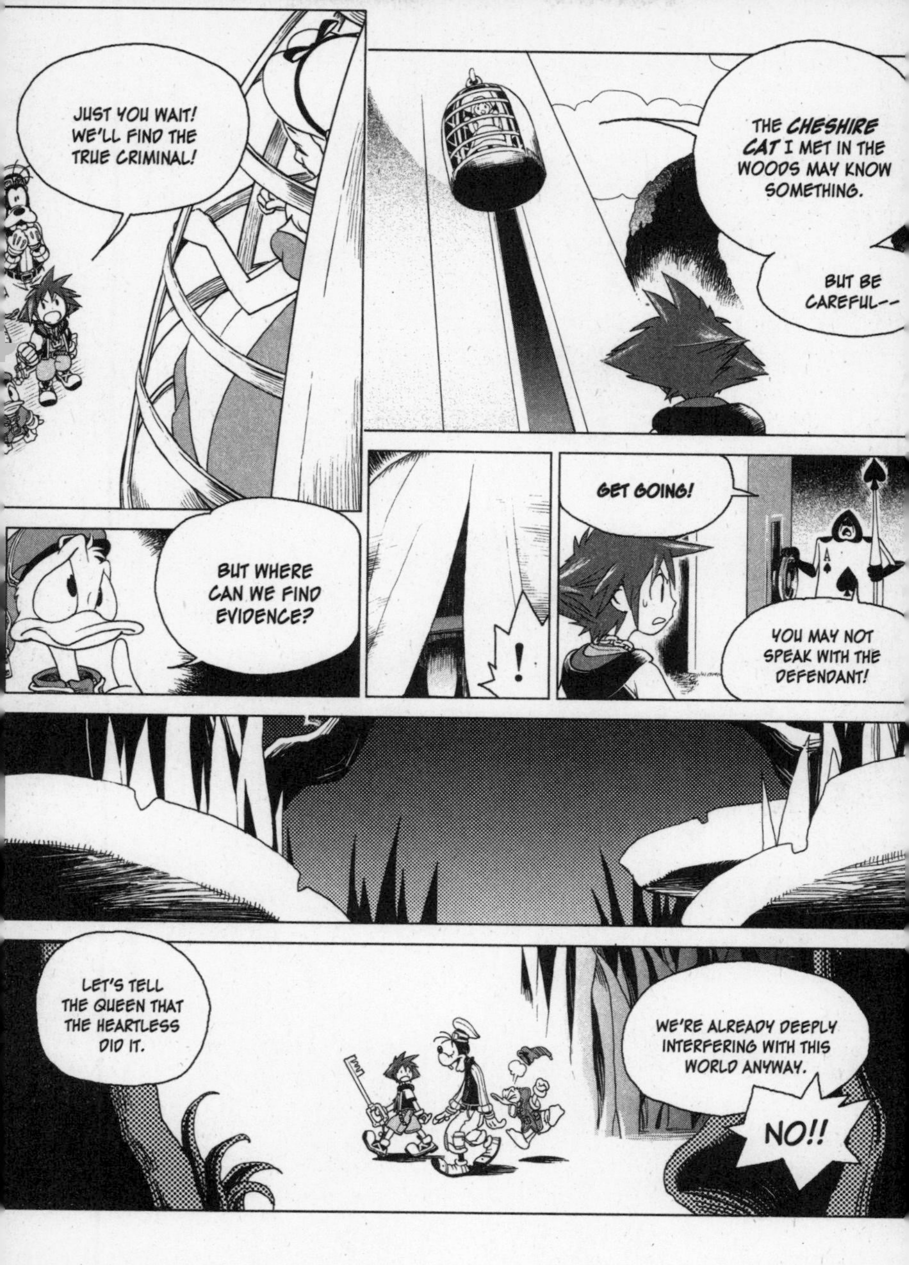
JUST YOU WAIT! WE'LL FIND THE TRUE CRIMINAL!
THE CHESHIRE CAT I MET IN THE WOODS MAY KNOW SOMETHING.
BUT BE CAREFUL--
BUT WHERE CAN WE FIND EVIDENCE?
!
GET GOING!
YOU MAY NOT SPEAK WITH THE DEFENDANT!
LET'S TELL THE QUEEN THAT THE HEARTLESS DID IT.
WE'RE ALREADY DEEPLY INTERFERING WITH THIS WORLD ANYWAY.
NO!!

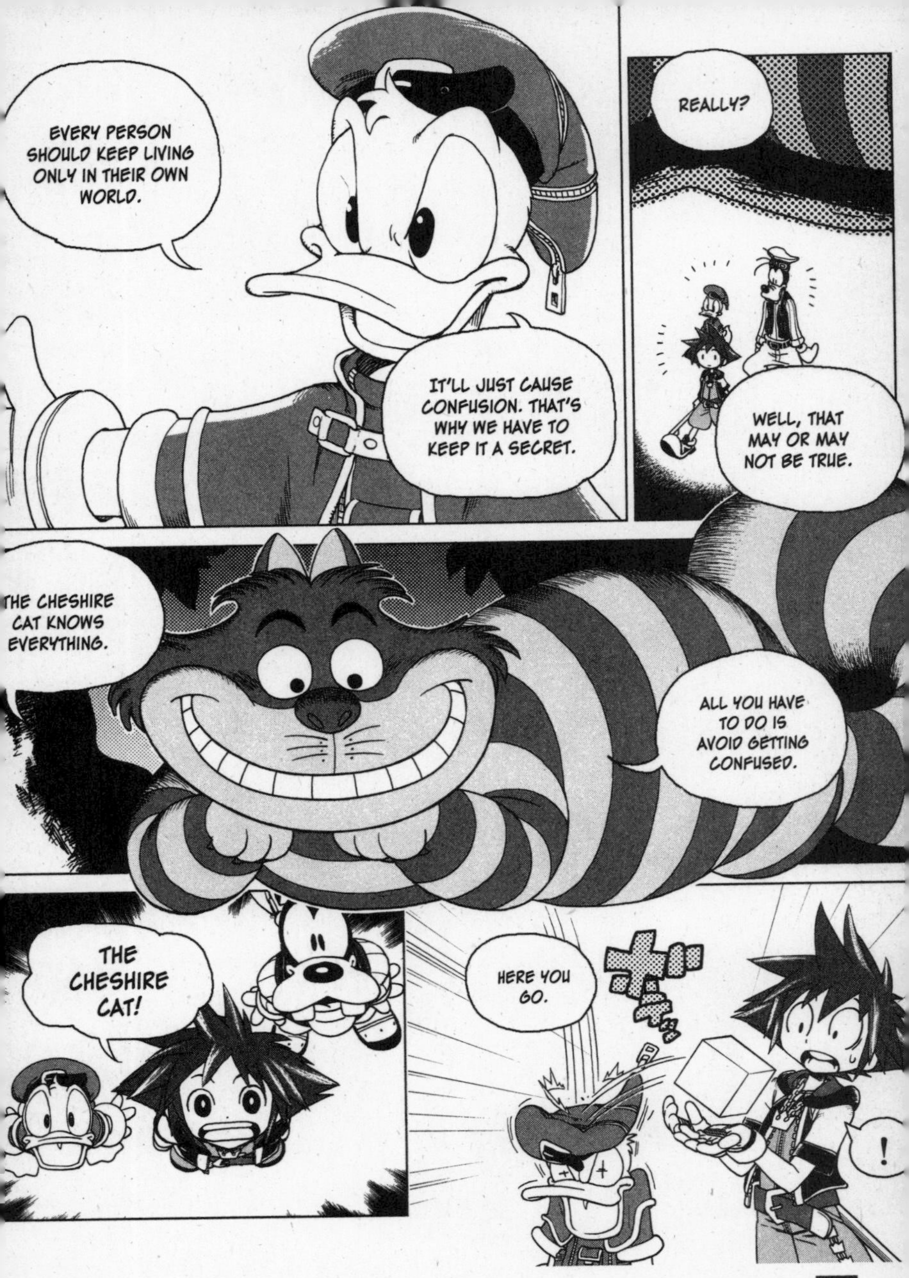
EVERY PERSON SHOULD KEEP LIVING ONLY IN THEIR OWN WORLD.
IT'LL JUST CAUSE CONFUSION. THAT'S WHY WE HAVE TO KEEP IT A SECRET.
REALLY?
WELL, THAT MAY OR MAY NOT BE TRUE.
THE CHESHIRE CAT KNOWS EVERYTHING.
ALL YOU HAVE TO DO IS AVOID GETTING CONFUSED.
THE CHESHIRE CAT!
HERE YOU GO.
!

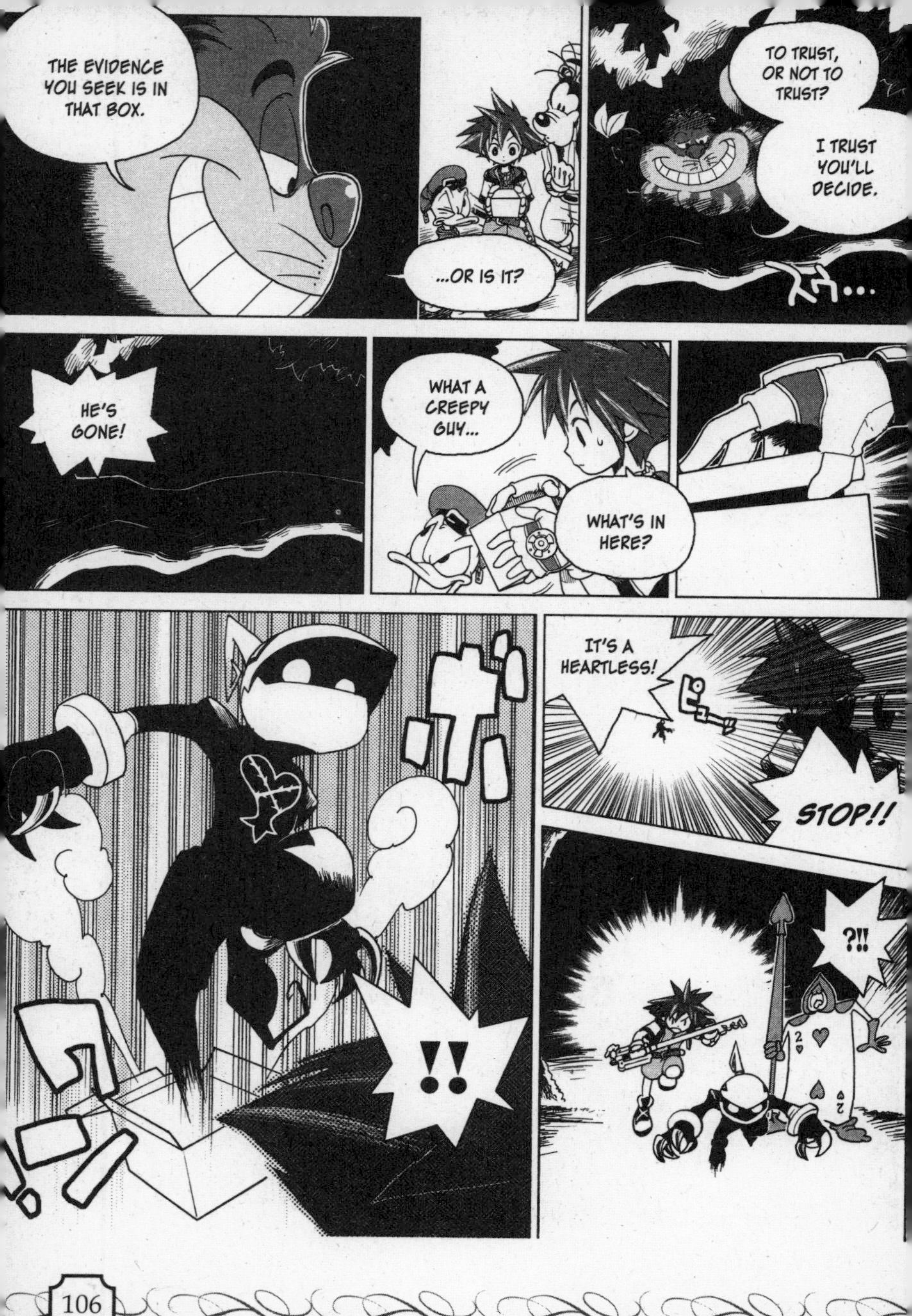
THE EVIDENCE YOU SEEK IS IN THAT BOX.
...OR IS IT?
TO TRUST, OR NOT TO TRUST?
I TRUST YOU'LL DECIDE.
HE'S GONE!
WHAT A CREEPY GUY...
WHAT'S IN HERE?
!!
IT'S A HEARTLESS!
STOP!!
?!!

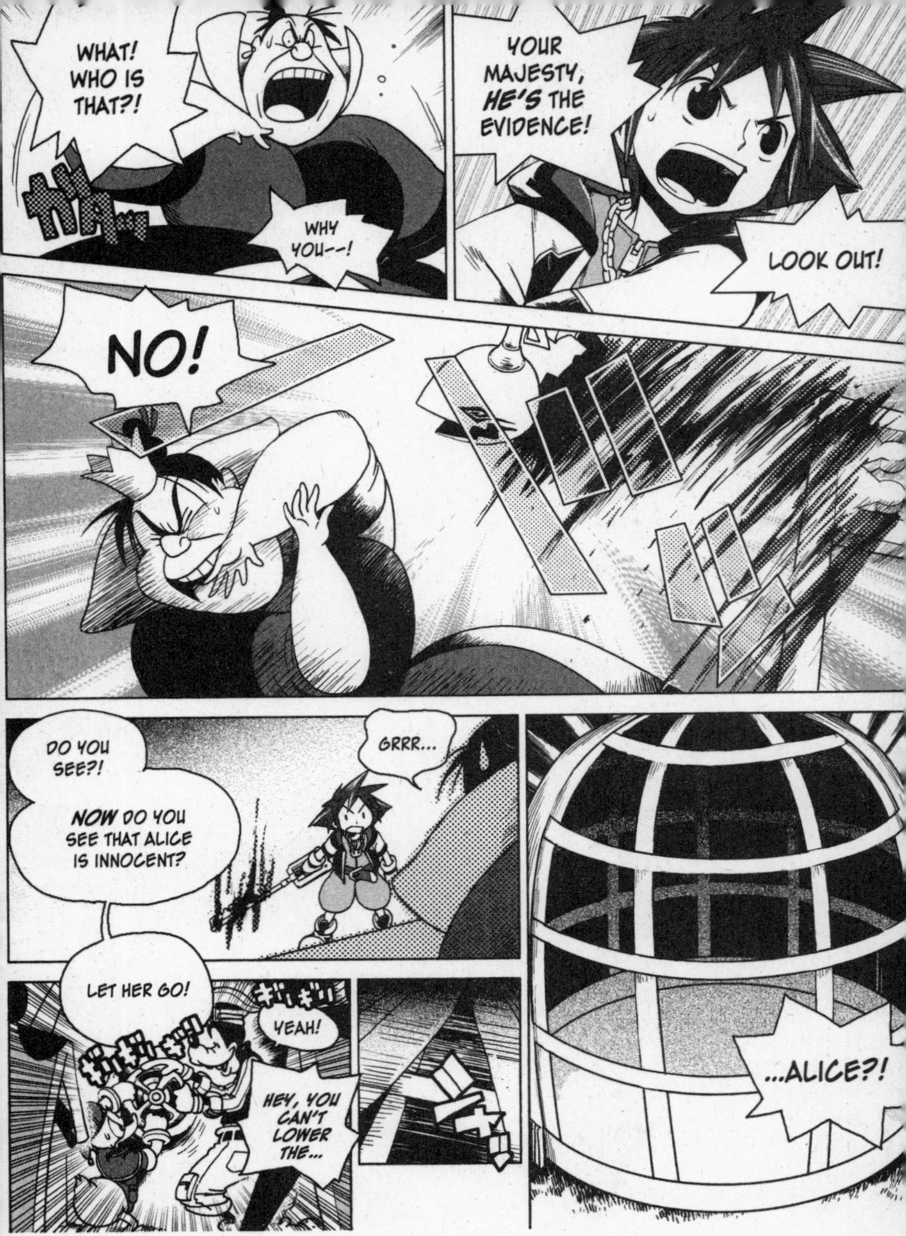
WHAT! WHO IS THAT?!
WHY YOU--!
YOUR MAJESTY, HE'S THE EVIDENCE!
LOOK OUT!
NO!
DO YOU SEE?!
NOW DO YOU SEE THAT ALICE IS INNOCENT?
GRRR...
LET HER GO!
YEAH!
HEY, YOU CAN'T LOWER THE...
...ALICE?!

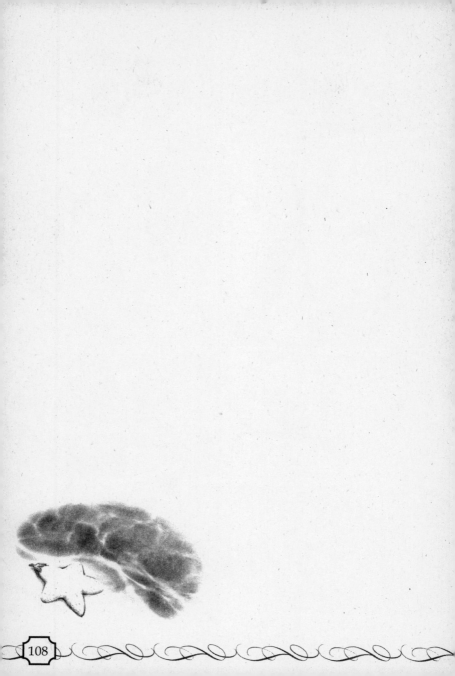

Episode 12
Helping Hand

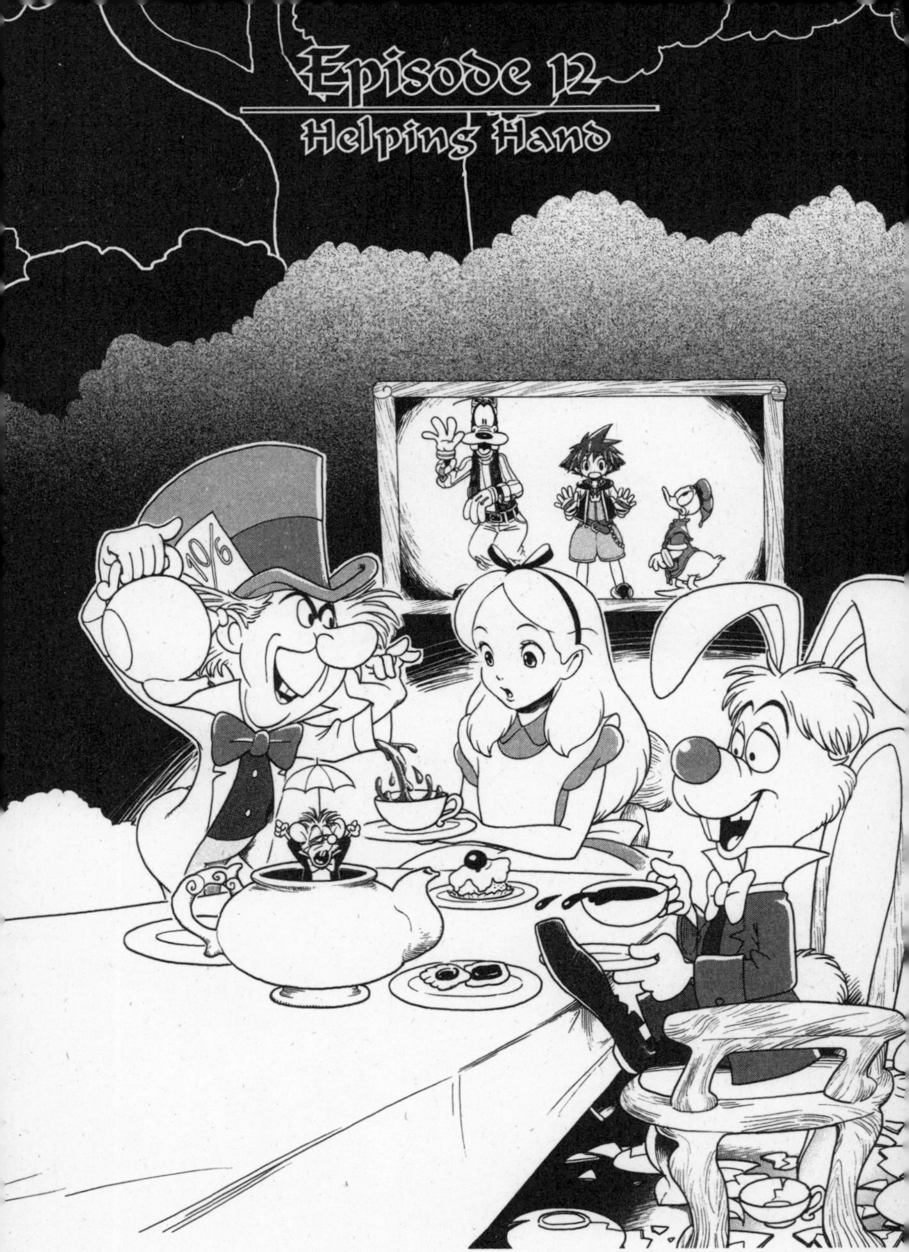

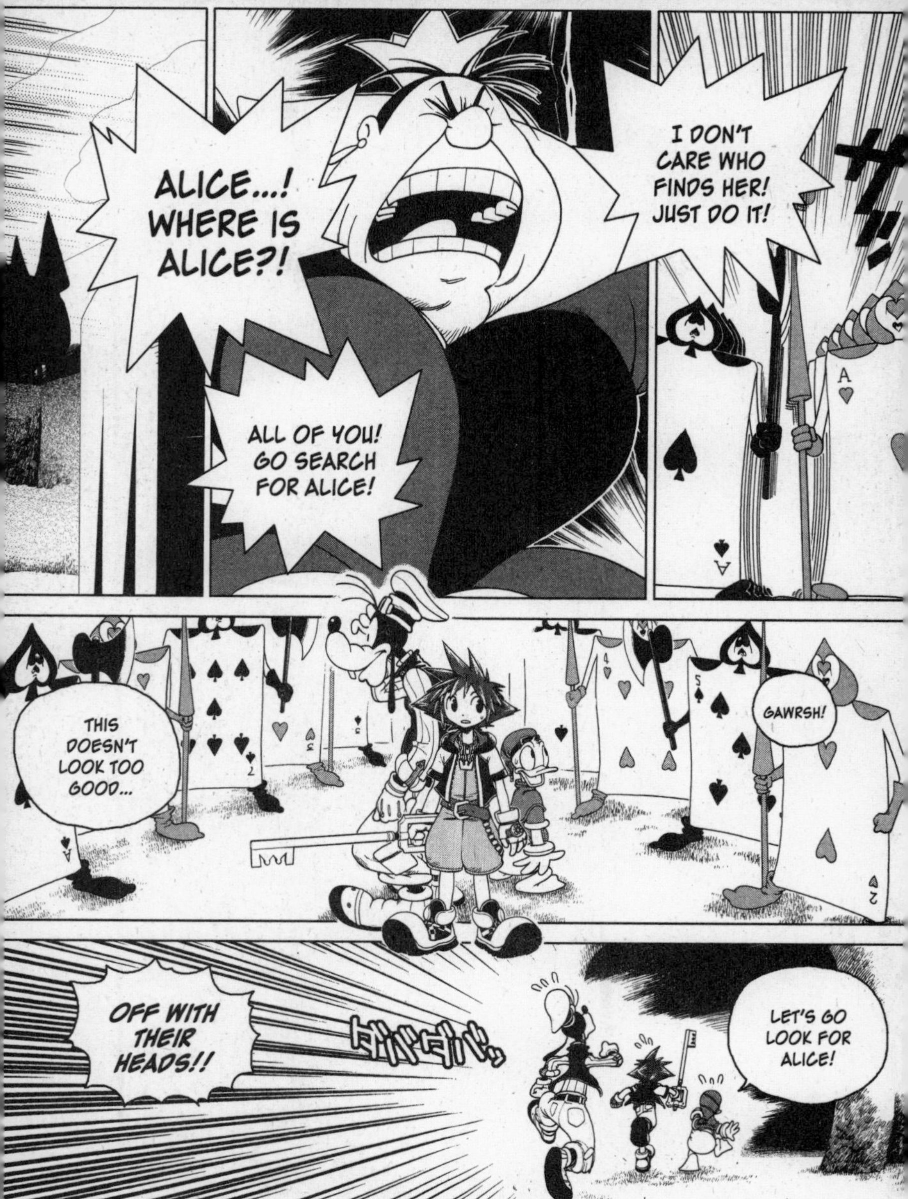
ALICE...! WHERE IS ALICE?!
ALL OF YOU! GO SEARCH FOR ALICE!
I DON'T CARE WHO FINDS HER! JUST DO IT!
THIS DOESN'T LOOK TOO GOOD...
GAWRSH!
OFF WITH THEIR HEADS!!
LET'S GO LOOK FOR ALICE!

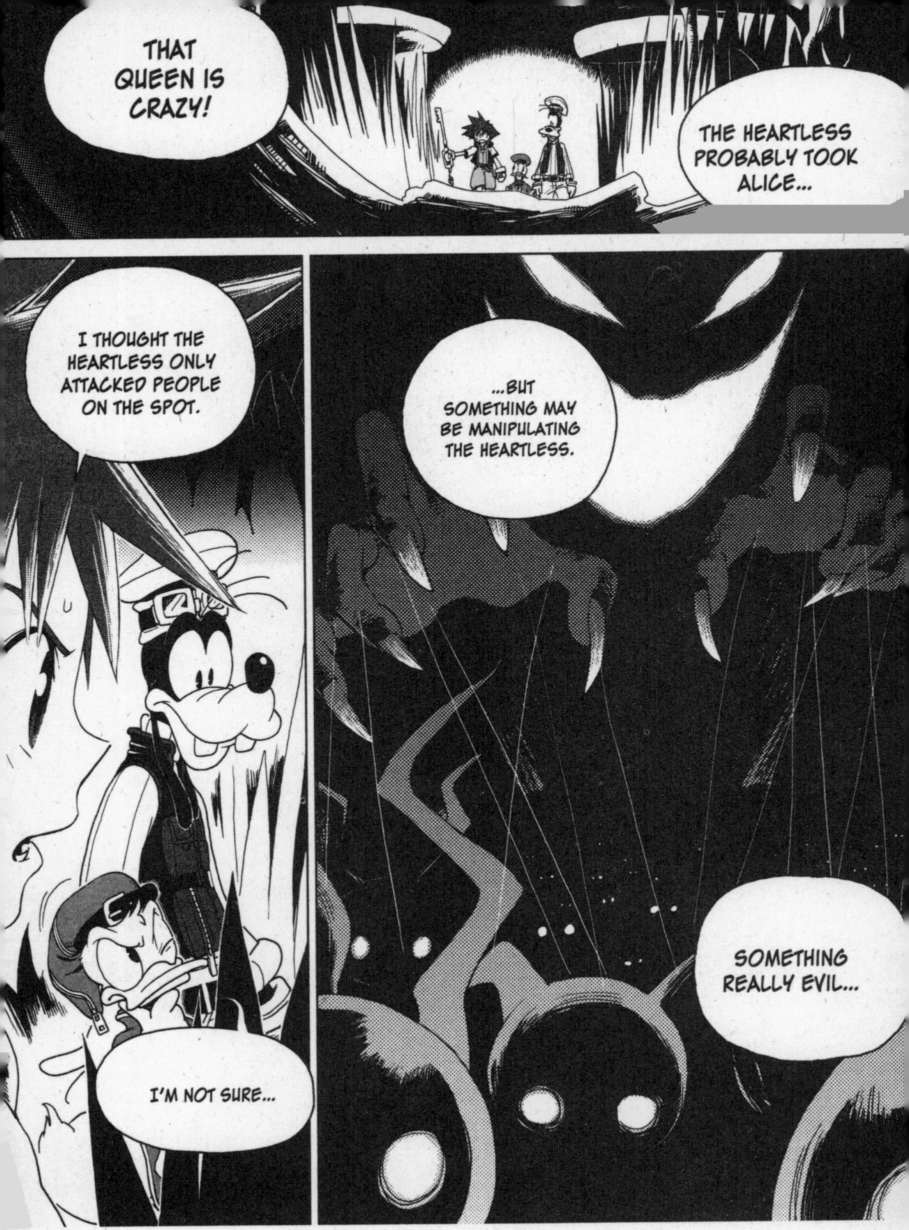
THAT QUEEN IS CRAZY!
THE HEARTLESS PROBABLY TOOK ALICE...
I THOUGHT THE HEARTLESS ONLY ATTACKED PEOPLE ON THE SPOT.
I'M NOT SURE...
...BUT SOMETHING MAY BE MANIPULATING THE HEARTLESS.
SOMETHING REALLY EVIL...

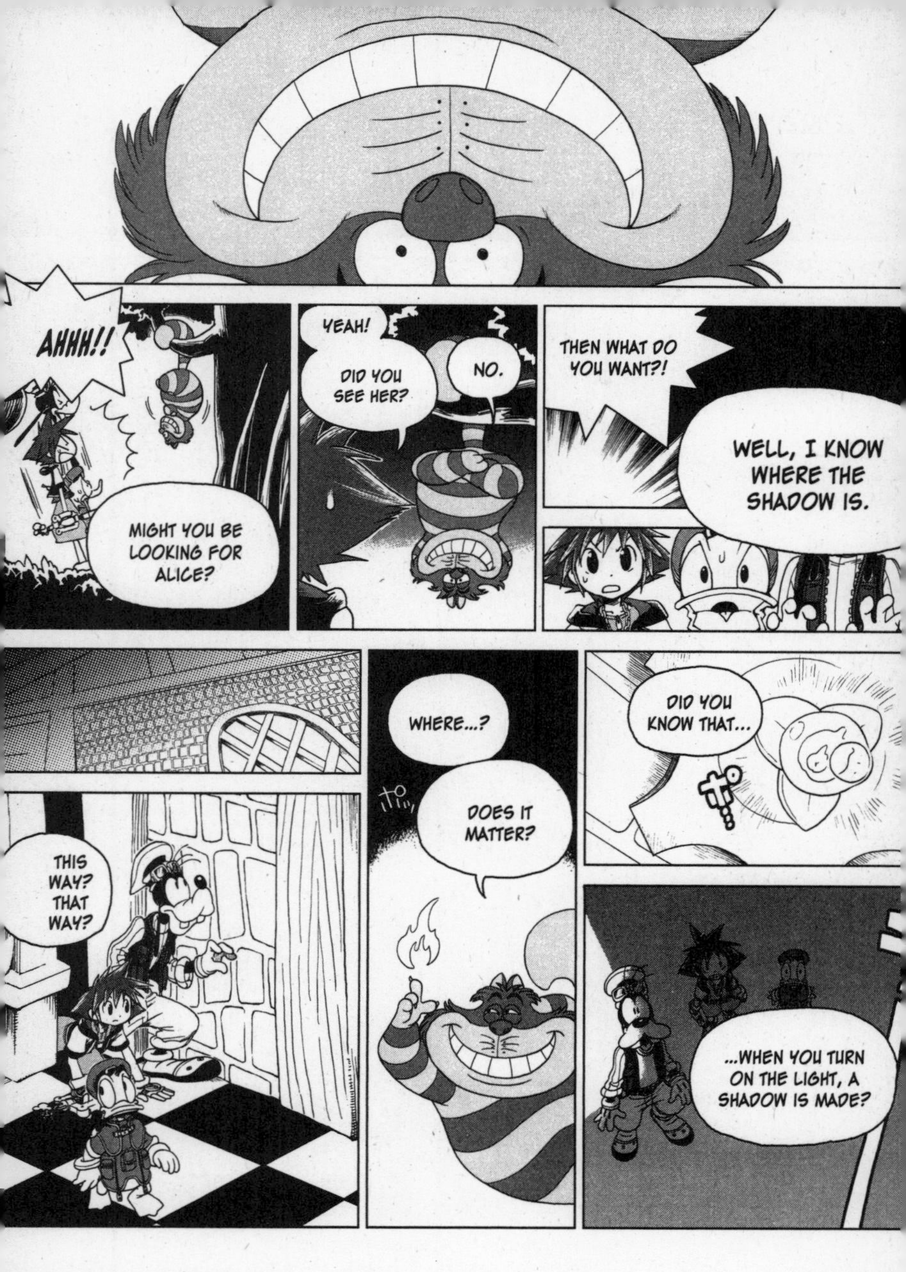
AHHH!!
MIGHT YOU BE LOOKING FOR ALICE?
YEAH!
DID YOU SEE HER?
NO.
THEN WHAT DO YOU WANT?!
WELL, I KNOW WHERE THE SHADOW IS.
THIS WAY? THAT WAY?
WHERE...?
DOES IT MATTER?
DID YOU KNOW THAT...
...WHEN YOU TURN ON THE LIGHT, A SHADOW IS MADE?

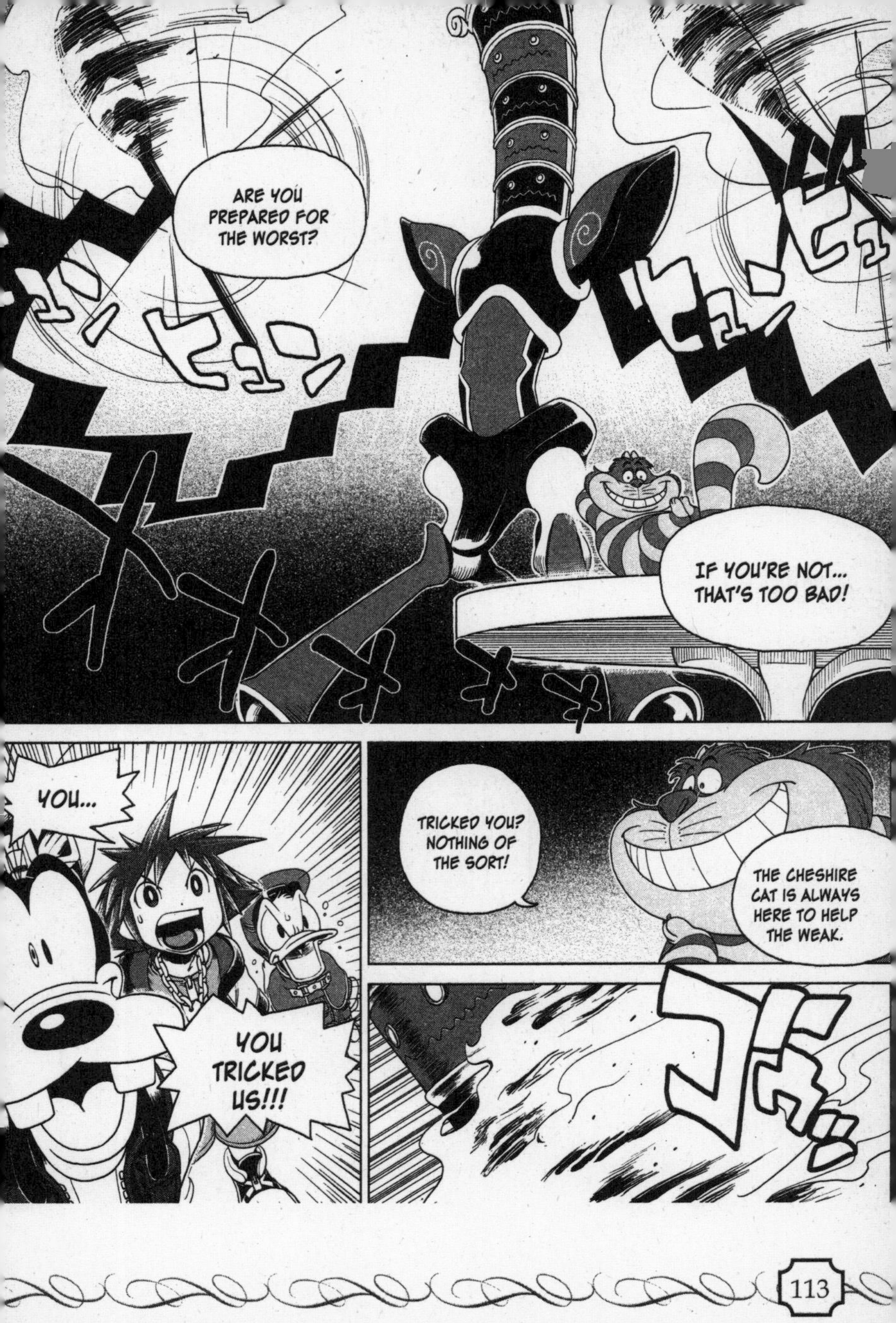
ARE YOU PREPARED FOR THE WORST?
IF YOU'RE NOT... THAT'S TOO BAD!
YOU...
YOU TRICKED US!!!
TRICKED YOU? NOTHING OF THE SORT!
THE CHESHIRE CAT IS ALWAYS HERE TO HELP THE WEAK.

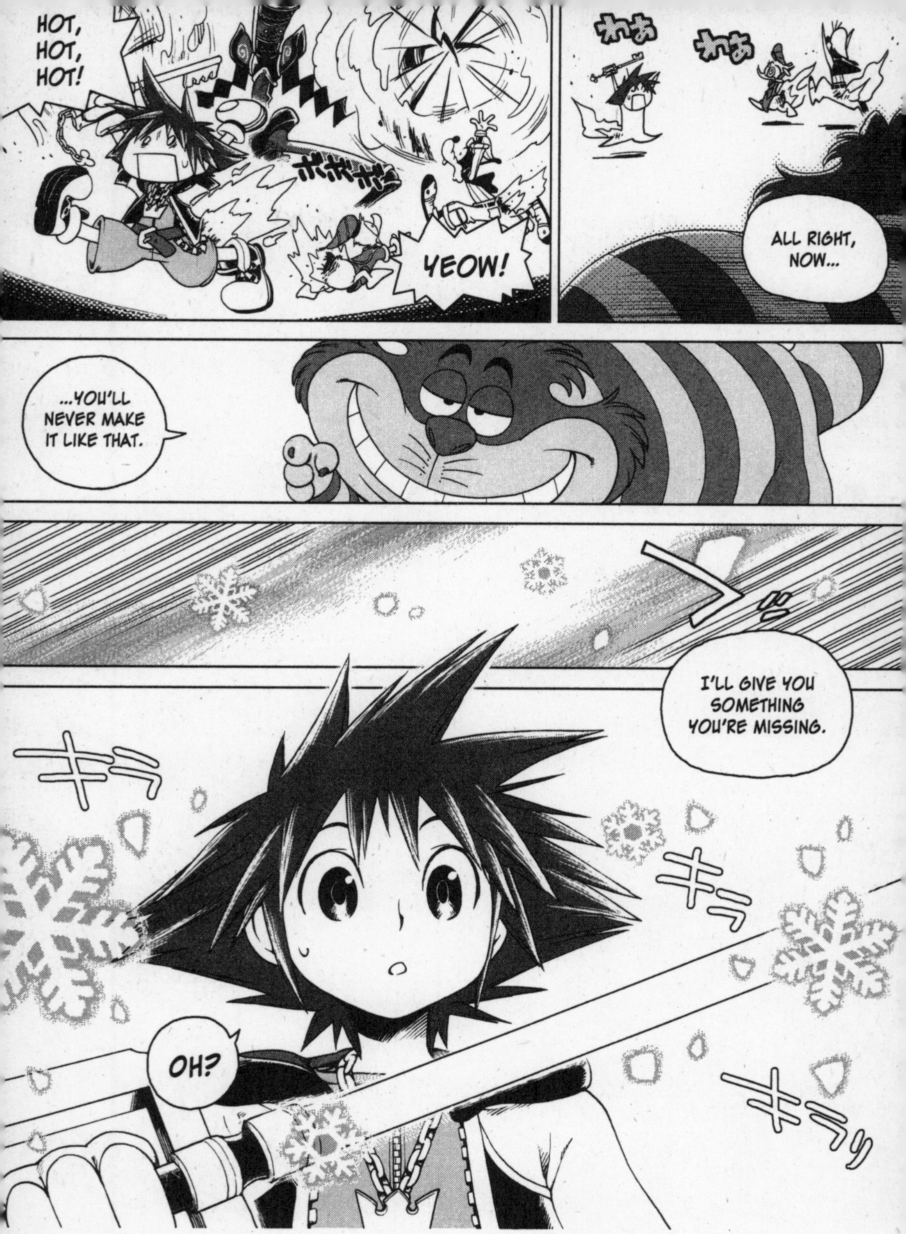
HOT, HOT, HOT!
ボボボ
YEOW!
わあ
わあ
ALL RIGHT, NOW...
...YOU'LL NEVER MAKE IT LIKE THAT.
キラ
I'LL GIVE YOU SOMETHING YOU'RE MISSING.
キラ
OH?
キラリ

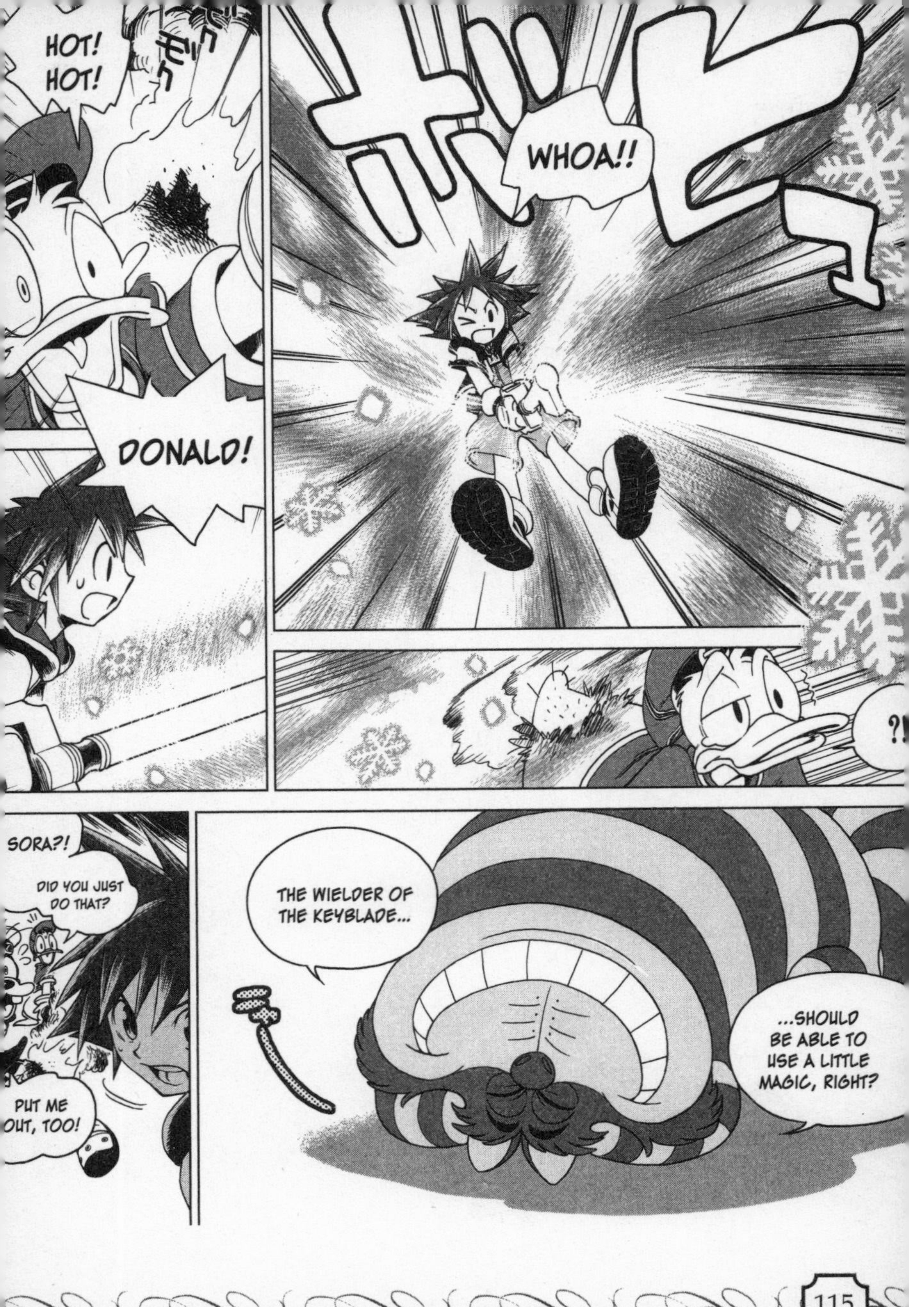

HOT! HOT!
DONALD!
WHOA!!
?!
SORA?!
DID YOU JUST DO THAT?
PUT ME OUT, TOO!
THE WIELDER OF THE KEYBLADE...
...SHOULD BE ABLE TO USE A LITTLE MAGIC, RIGHT?

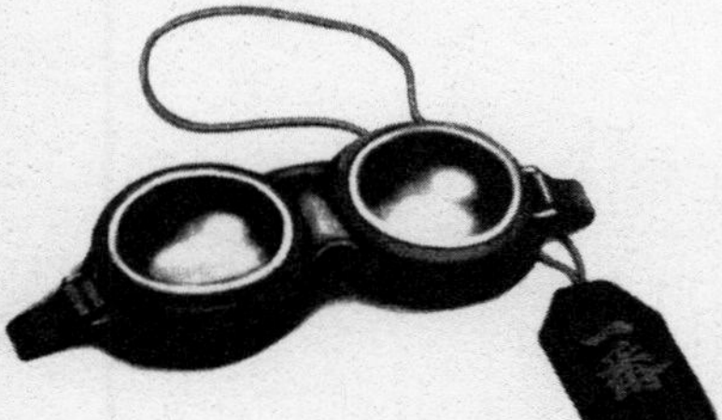

Episode 13

Keyhole

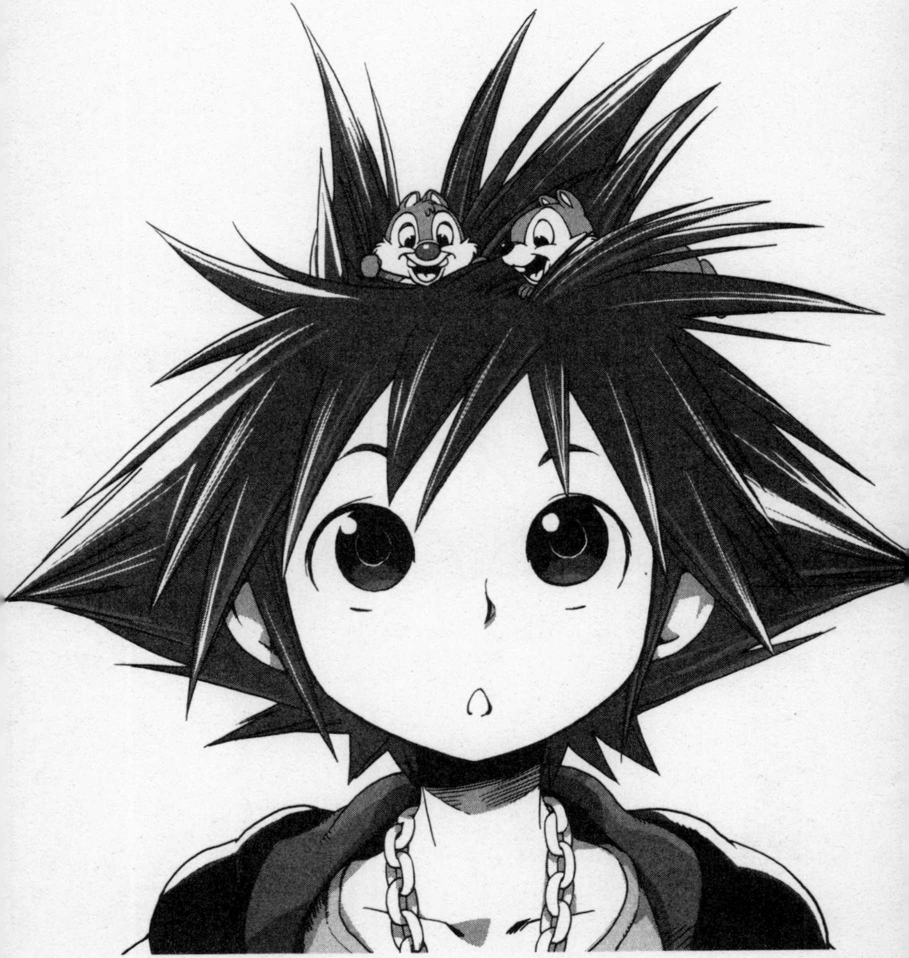

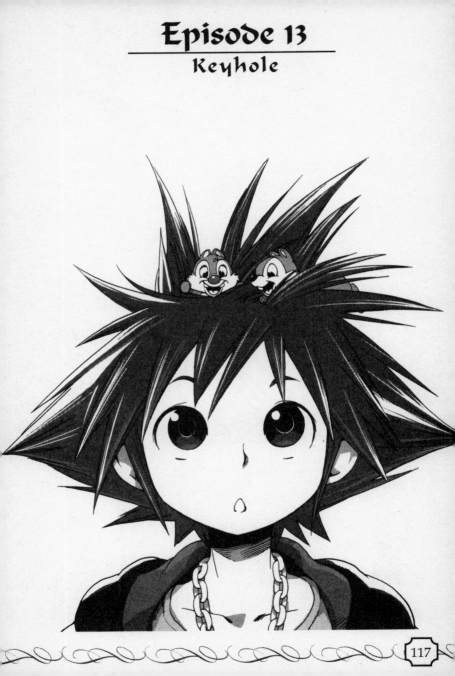

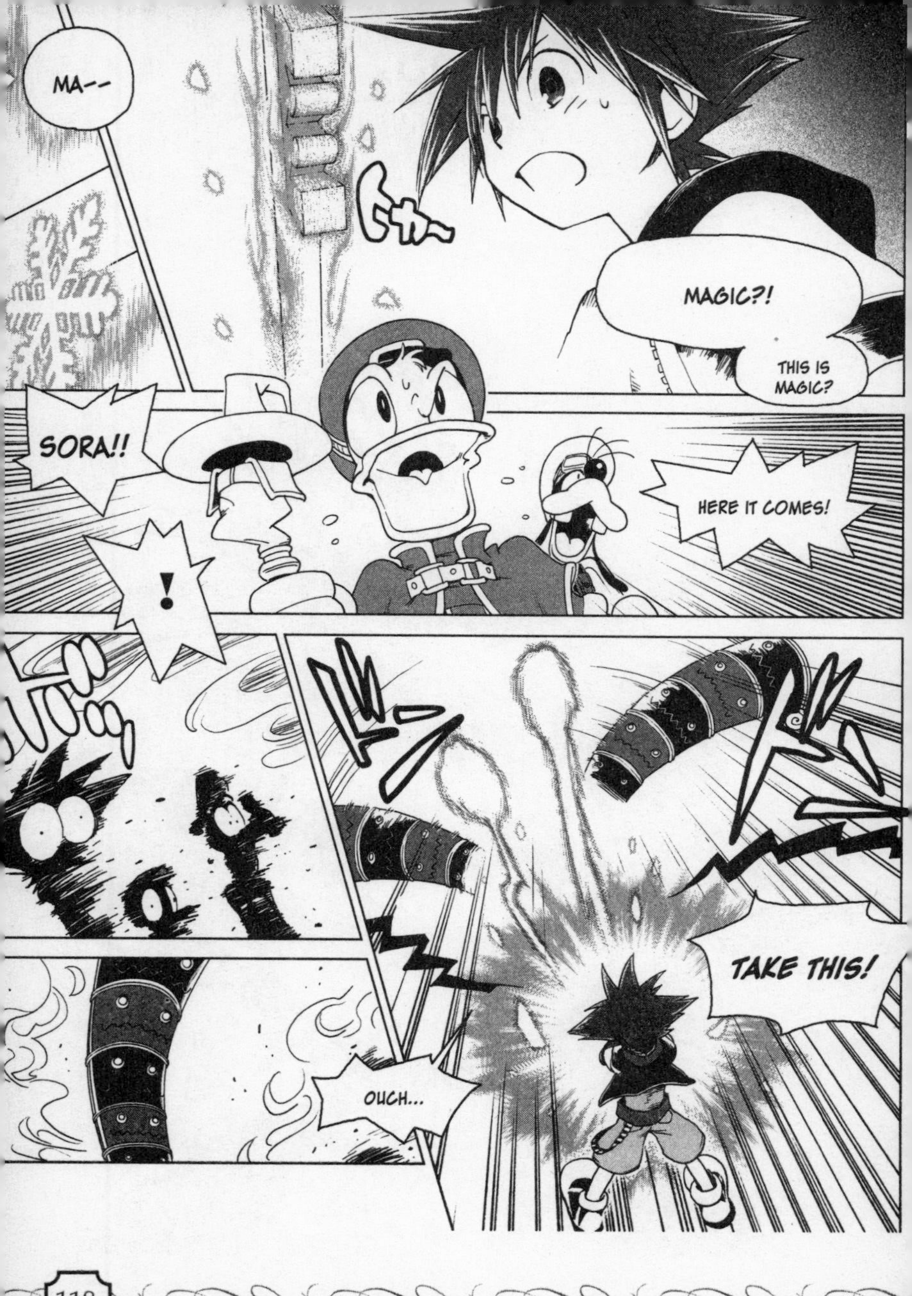
MA--
ピカー
MAGIC?!
THIS IS MAGIC?
SORA!!
HERE IT COMES!
!
OUCH...
TAKE THIS!

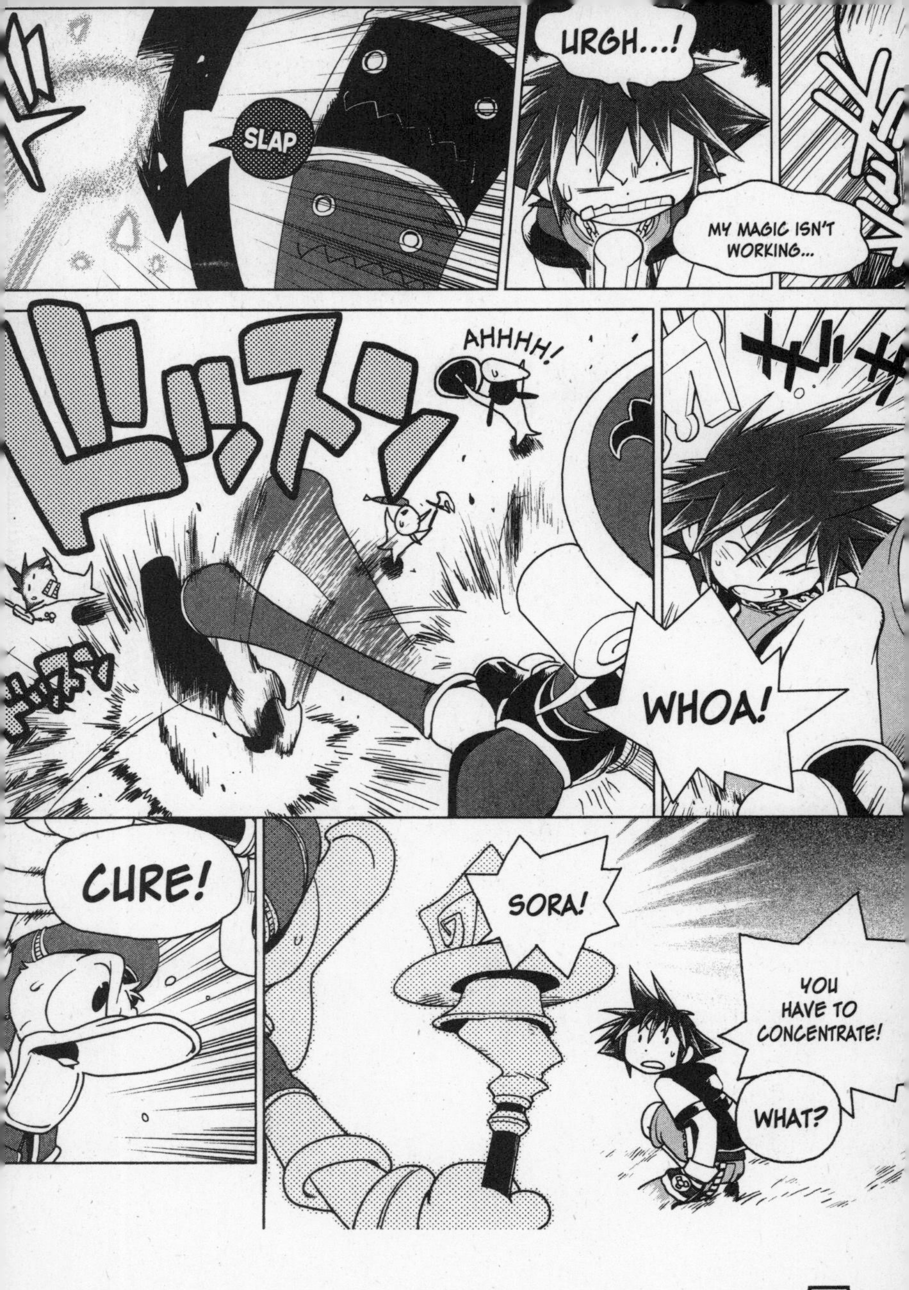
SLAP
URGH...!
MY MAGIC ISN'T WORKING...
ドッスン
AHHHH!
WHOA!
CURE!
SORA!
YOU HAVE TO CONCENTRATE!
WHAT?

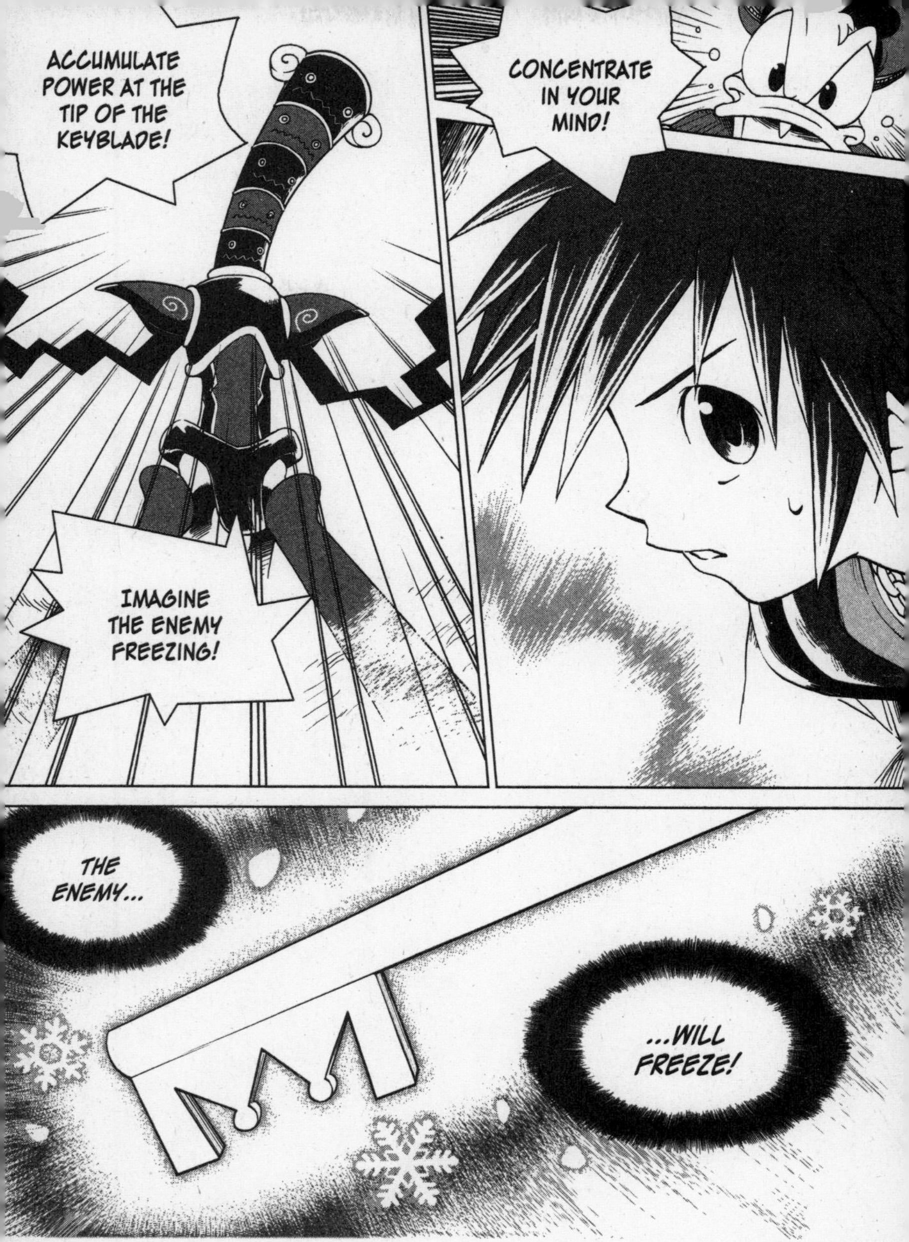
ACCUMULATE POWER AT THE TIP OF THE KEYBLADE!
IMAGINE THE ENEMY FREEZING!
CONCENTRATE IN YOUR MIND!
THE ENEMY...
...WILL FREEZE!

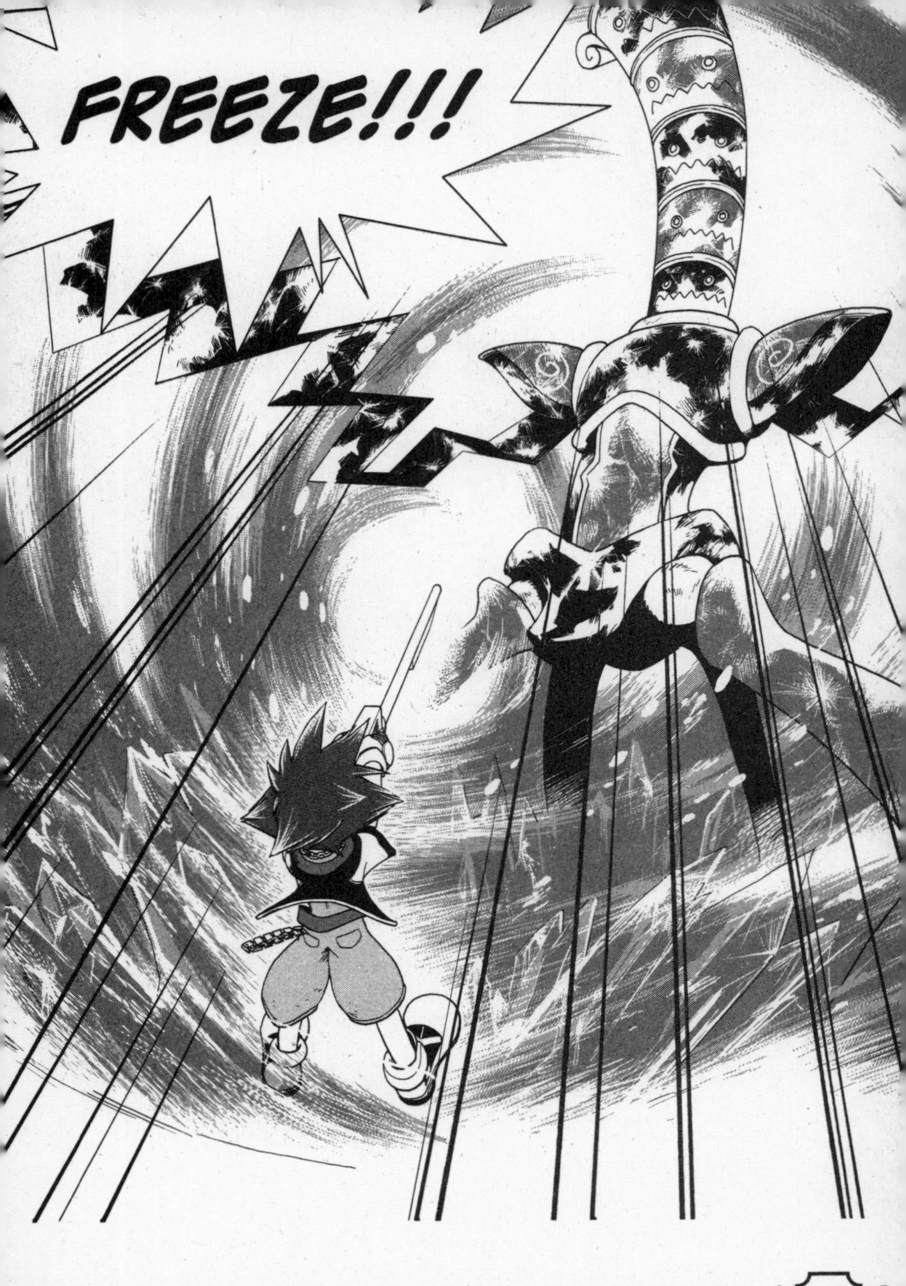
FREEZE!!!

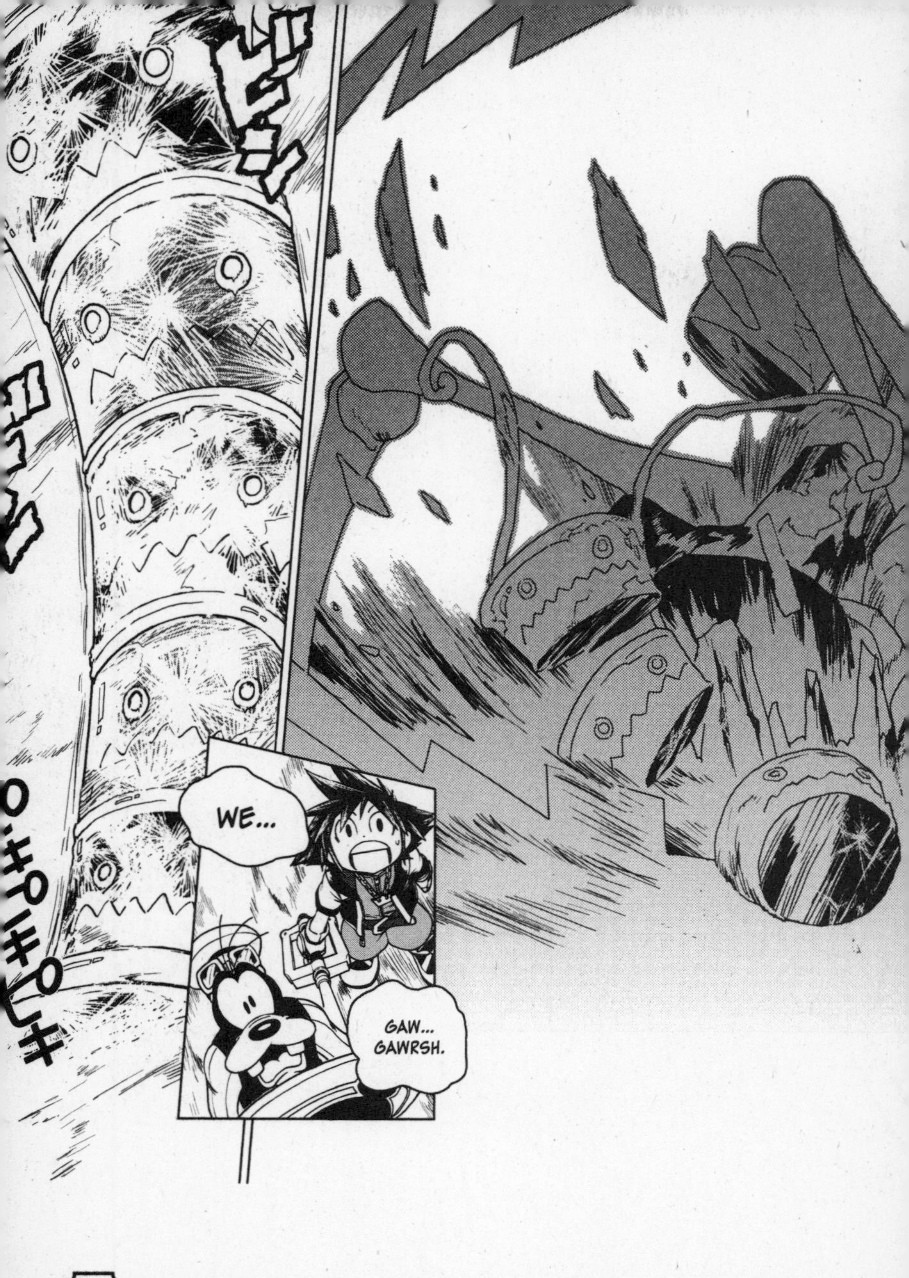
WE...
GAW... GAWRSH.

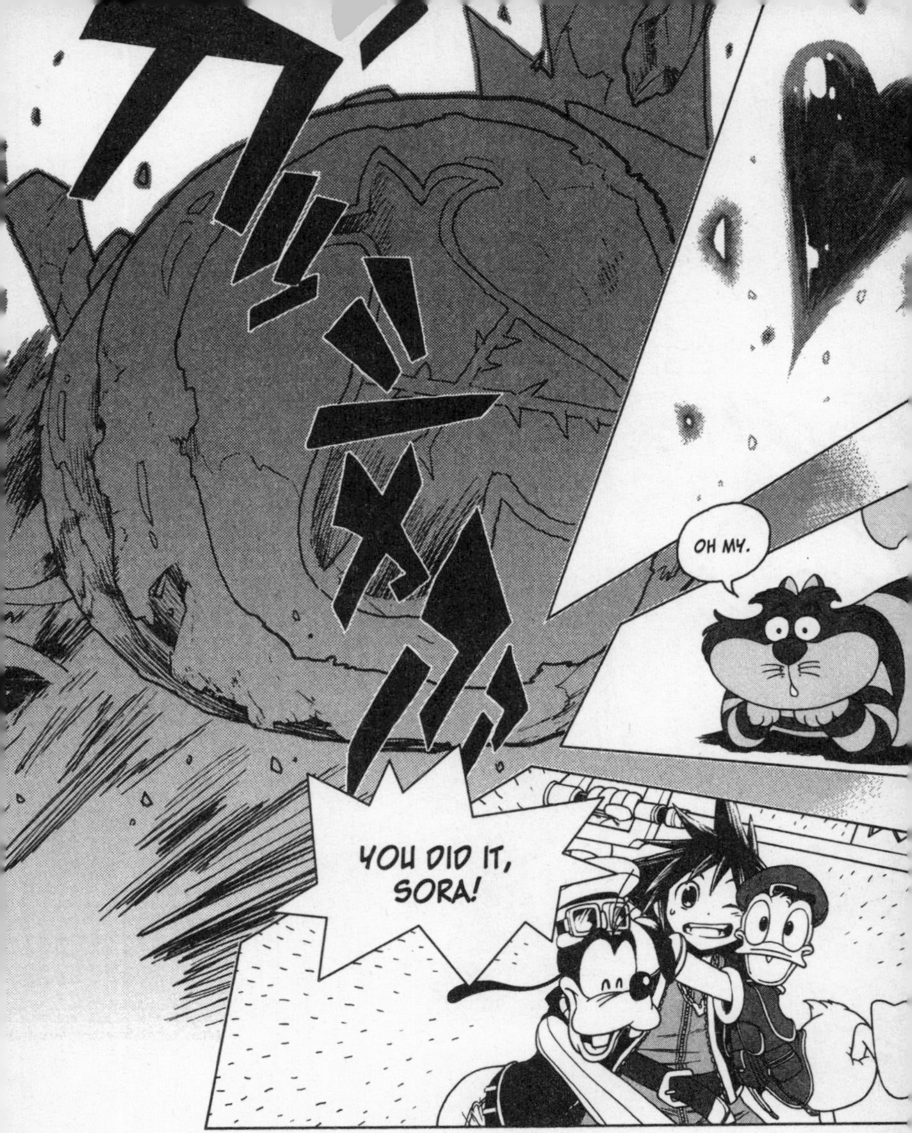
OH MY.
YOU DID IT, SORA!

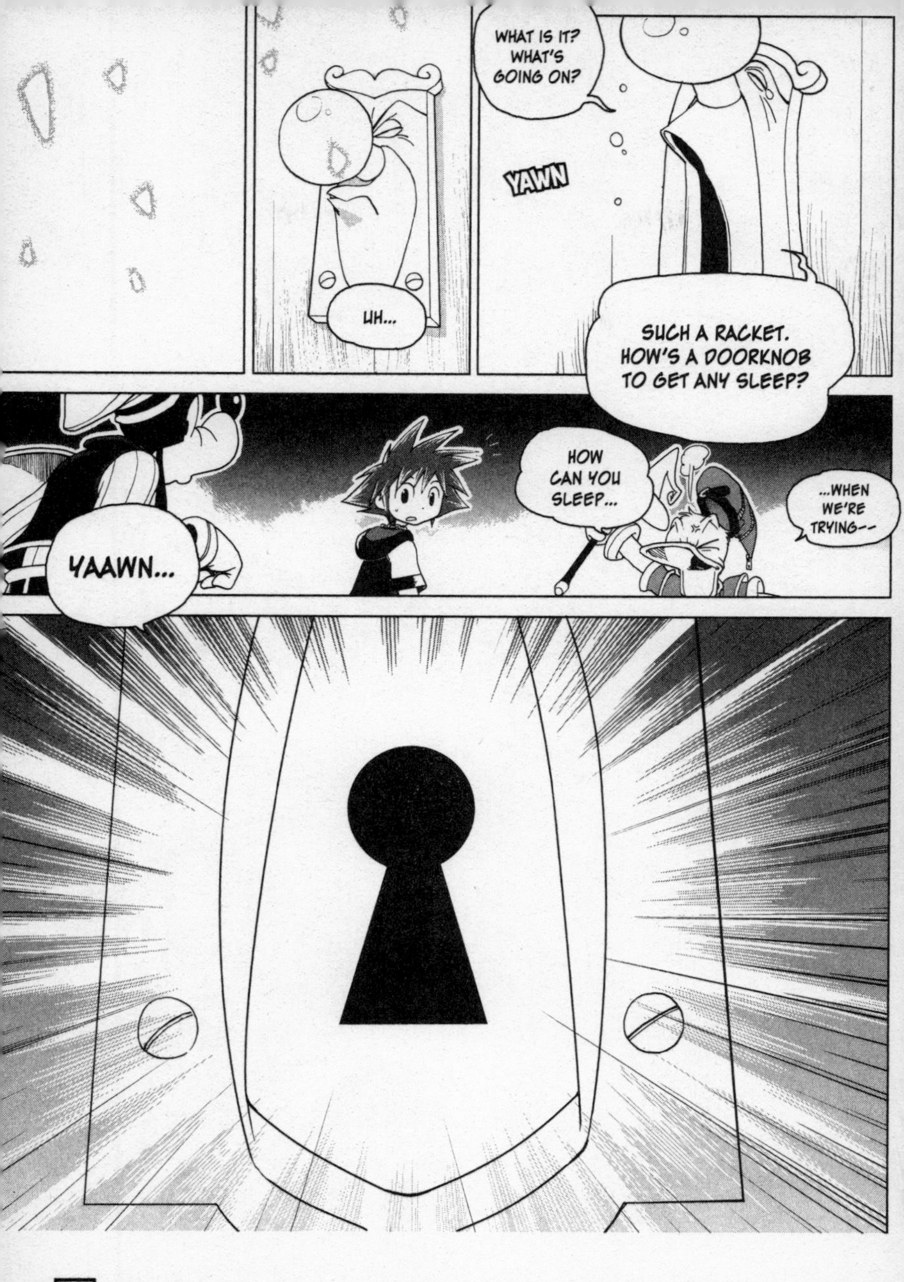
UH...
WHAT IS IT? WHAT'S GOING ON?
YAWN
SUCH A RACKET. HOW'S A DOORKNOB TO GET ANY SLEEP?
YAAWN...
HOW CAN YOU SLEEP...
...WHEN WE'RE TRYING--

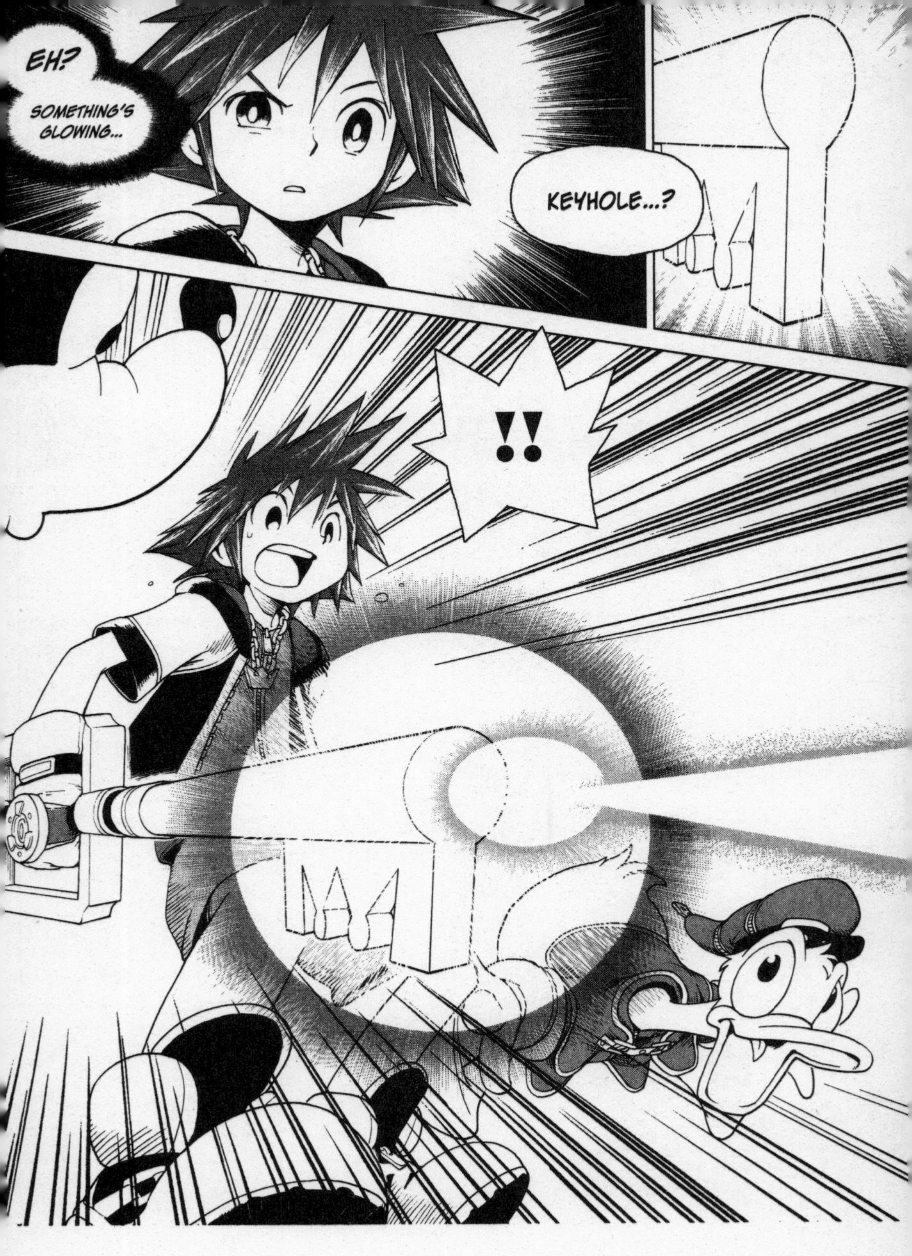

EH?
SOMETHING'S GLOWING...
KEYHOLE...?
!!

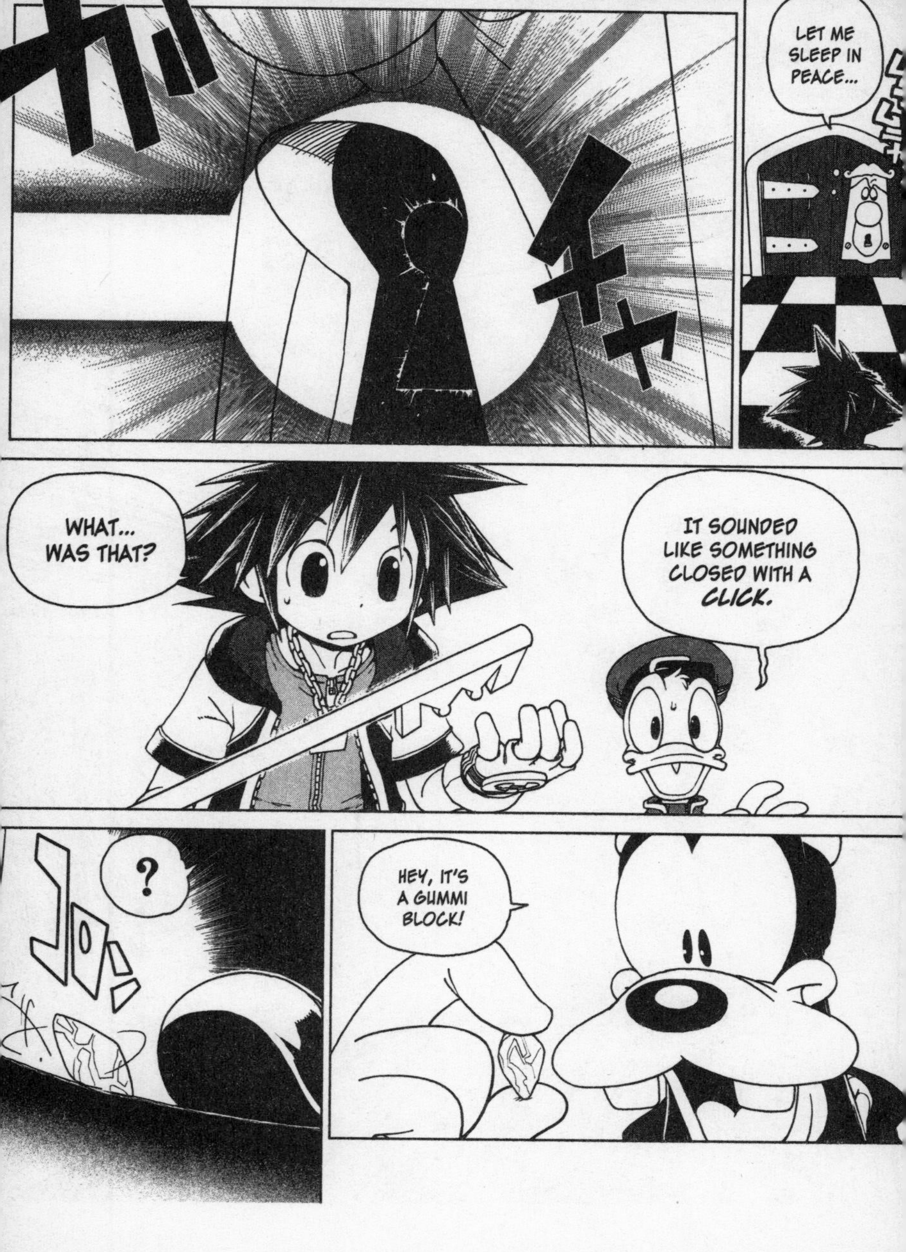
LET ME SLEEP IN PEACE...
WHAT... WAS THAT?
IT SOUNDED LIKE SOMETHING CLOSED WITH A CLICK.
?
HEY, IT'S A GUMMI BLOCK!

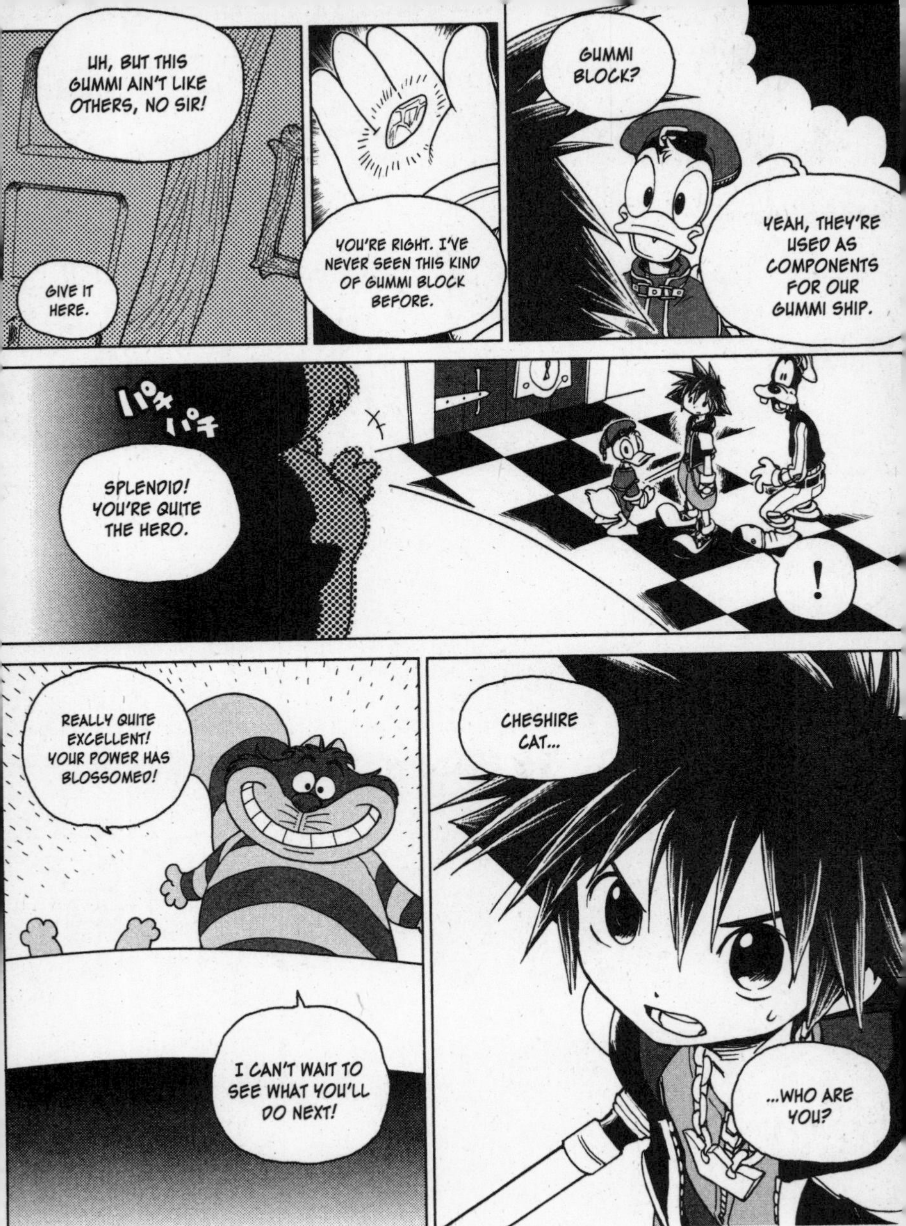
UH, BUT THIS GUMMI AIN'T LIKE OTHERS, NO SIR!
GIVE IT HERE.
YOU'RE RIGHT. I'VE NEVER SEEN THIS KIND OF GUMMI BLOCK BEFORE.
GUMMI BLOCK?
YEAH, THEY'RE USED AS COMPONENTS FOR OUR GUMMI SHIP.
パチパチ
SPLENDID! YOU'RE QUITE THE HERO.
!
REALLY QUITE EXCELLENT! YOUR POWER HAS BLOSSOMED!
I CAN'T WAIT TO SEE WHAT YOU'LL DO NEXT!
CHESHIRE CAT...
...WHO ARE YOU?

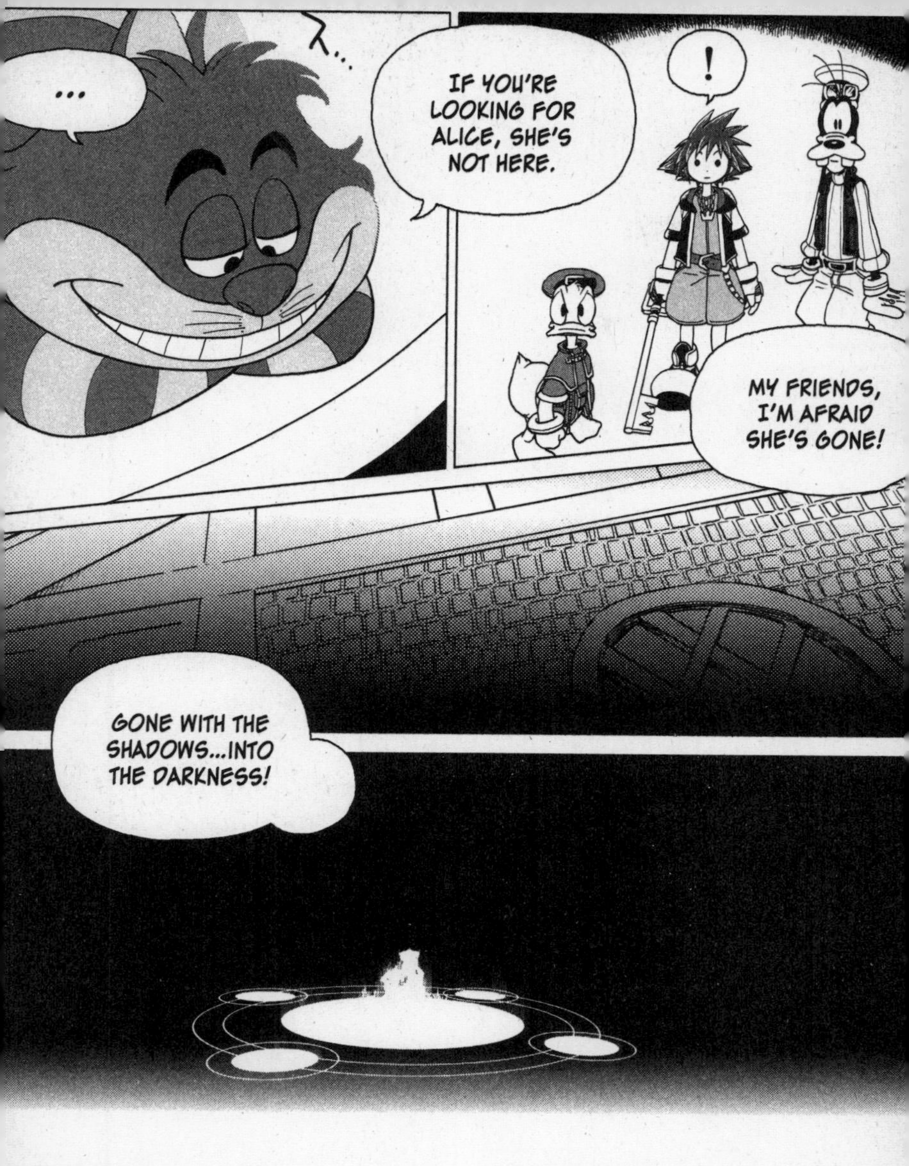
...
IF YOU'RE LOOKING FOR ALICE, SHE'S NOT HERE.
!
MY FRIENDS, I'M AFRAID SHE'S GONE!
GONE WITH THE SHADOWS...INTO THE DARKNESS!

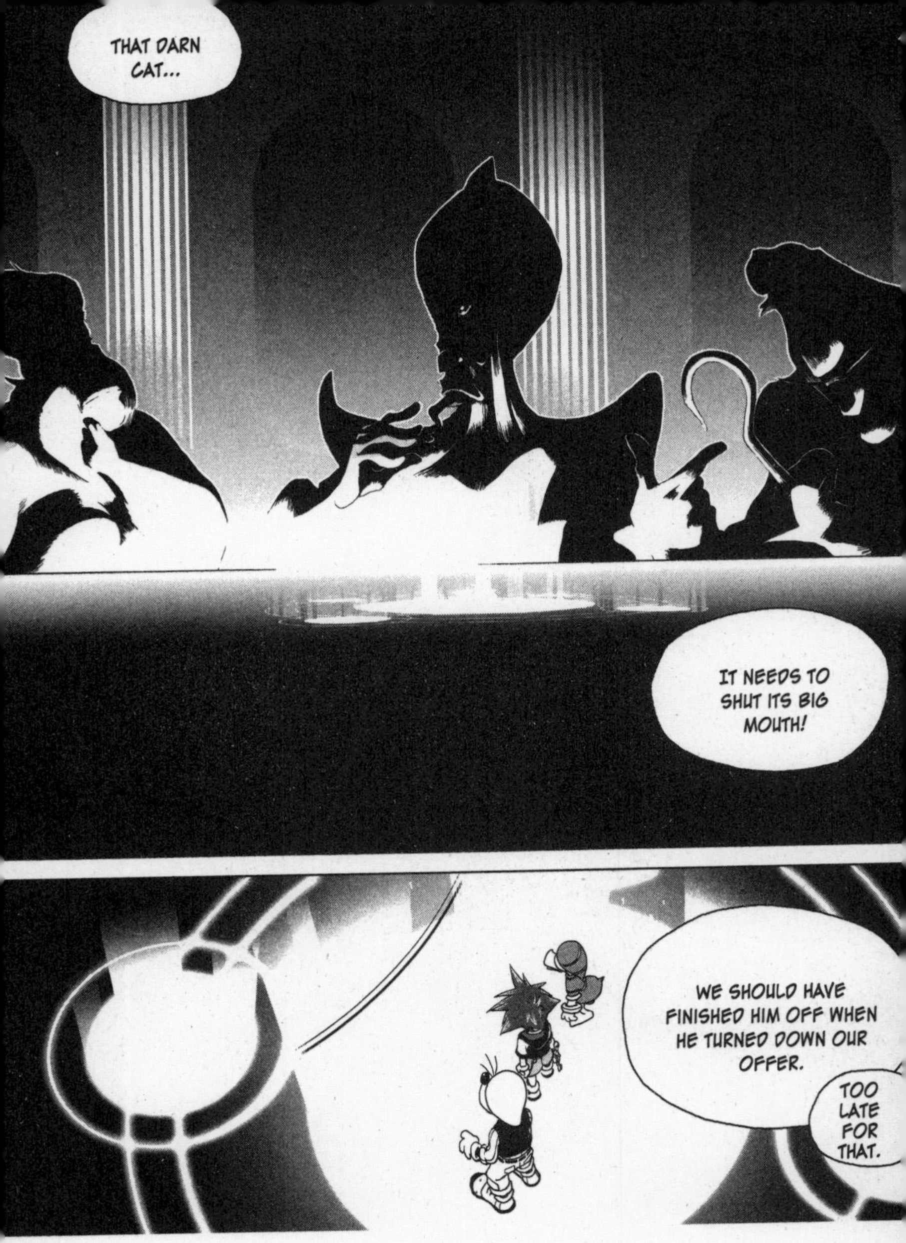
THAT DARN CAT...
IT NEEDS TO SHUT ITS BIG MOUTH!
WE SHOULD HAVE FINISHED HIM OFF WHEN HE TURNED DOWN OUR OFFER.
TOO LATE FOR THAT.

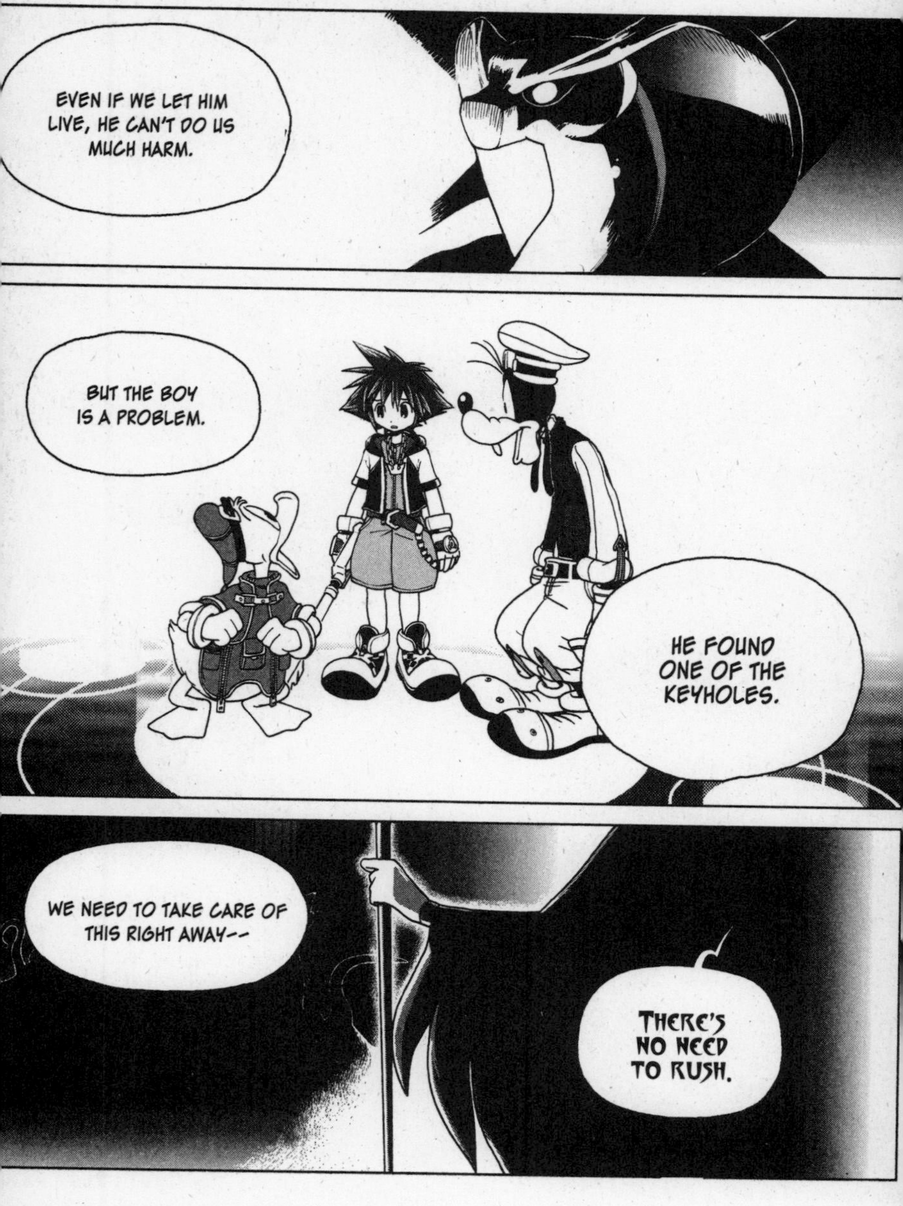
EVEN IF WE LET HIM LIVE, HE CAN'T DO US MUCH HARM.
BUT THE BOY IS A PROBLEM.
HE FOUND ONE OF THE KEYHOLES.
WE NEED TO TAKE CARE OF THIS RIGHT AWAY--
THERE'S NO NEED TO RUSH.

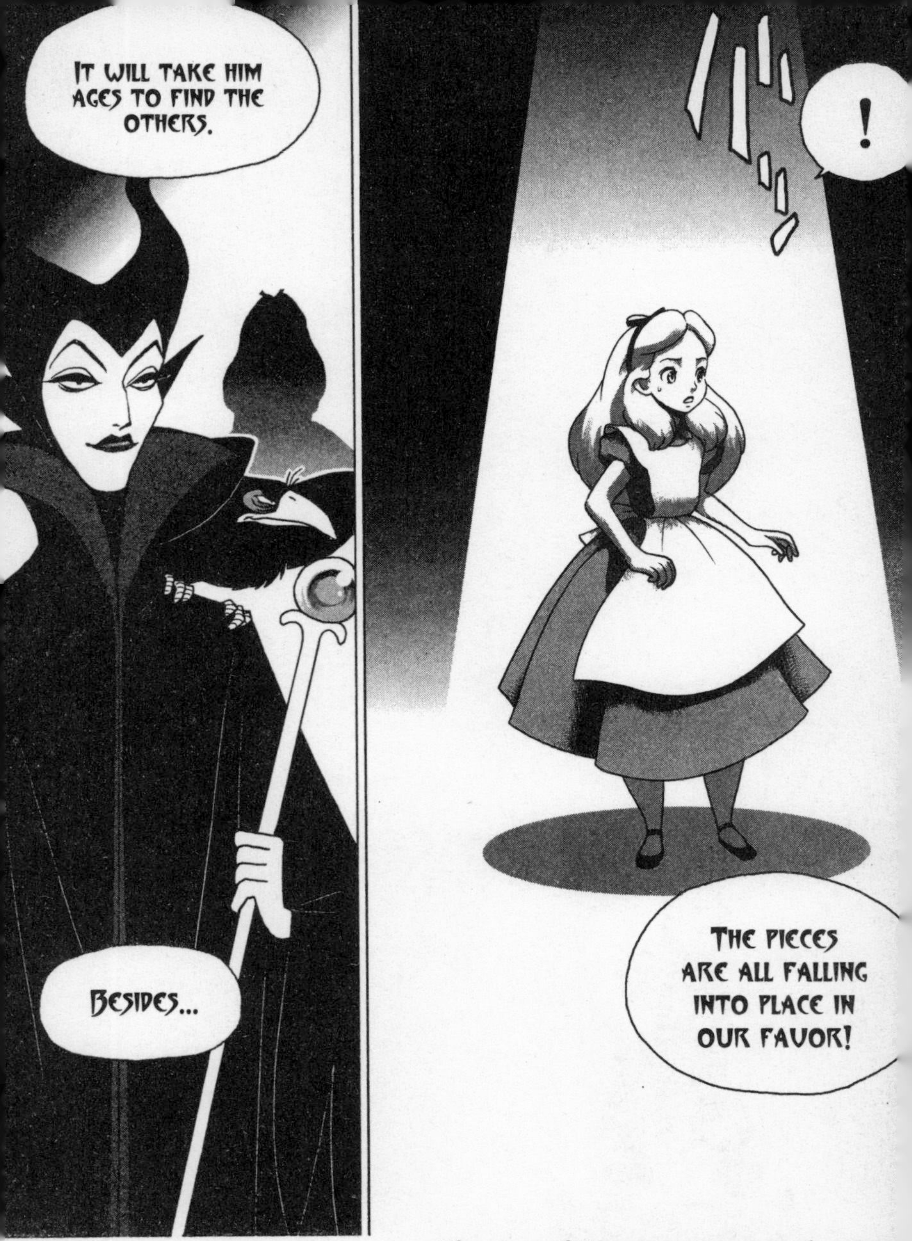
IT WILL TAKE HIM AGES TO FIND THE OTHERS.
BESIDES...
!
THE PIECES ARE ALL FALLING INTO PLACE IN OUR FAVOR!

The End of Kingdom Hearts volume 1

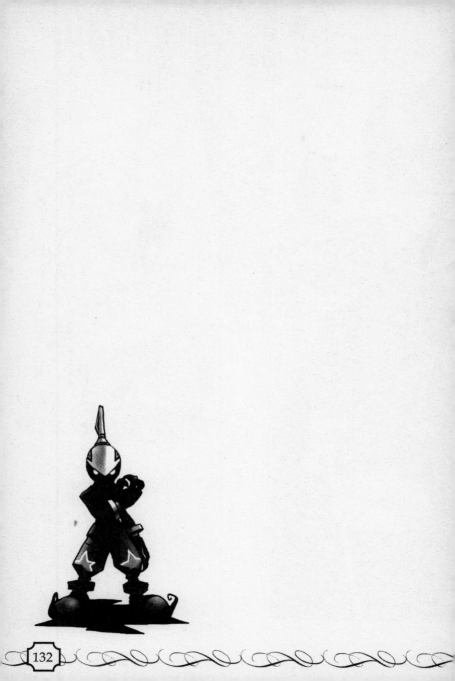

EXTRAS! SHIRO AMANO'S ROUGH CHARACTER SKETCHES!!

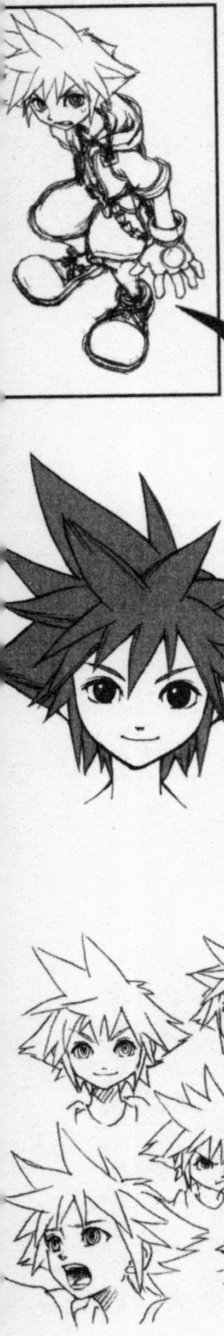

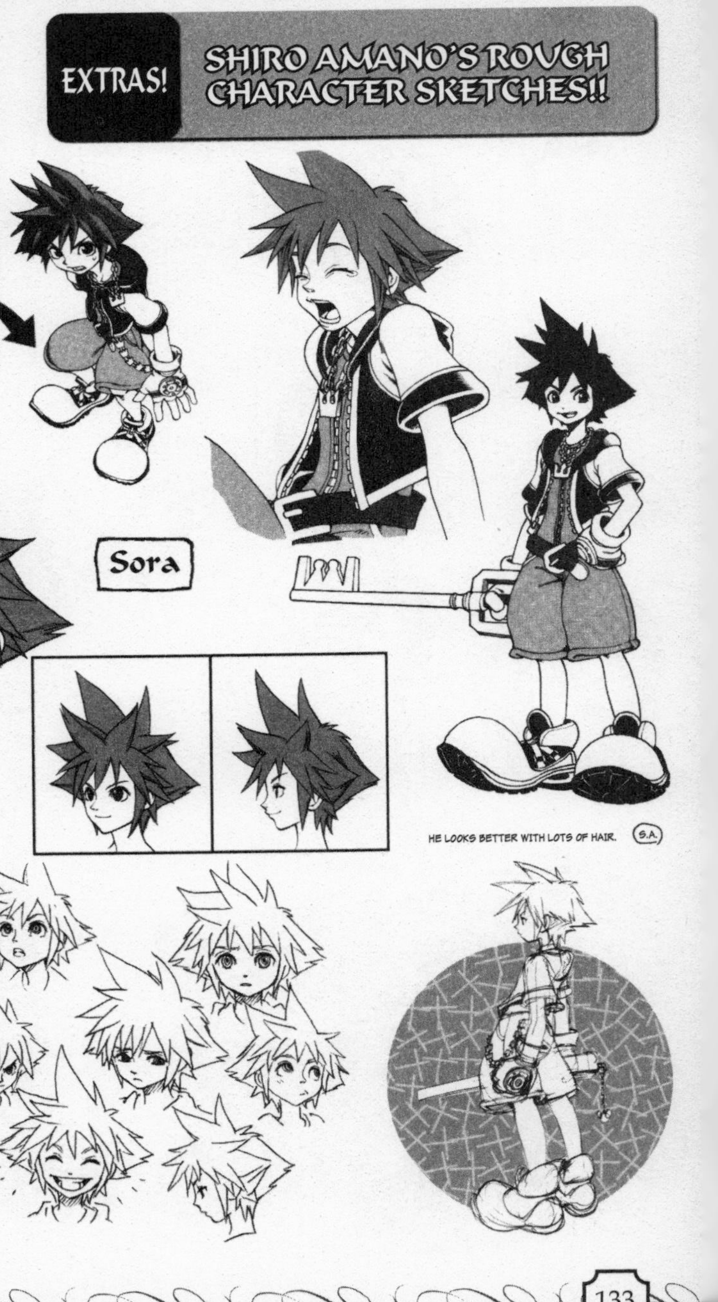
Sora

HE LOOKS BETTER WITH LOTS OF HAIR. (S.A.)

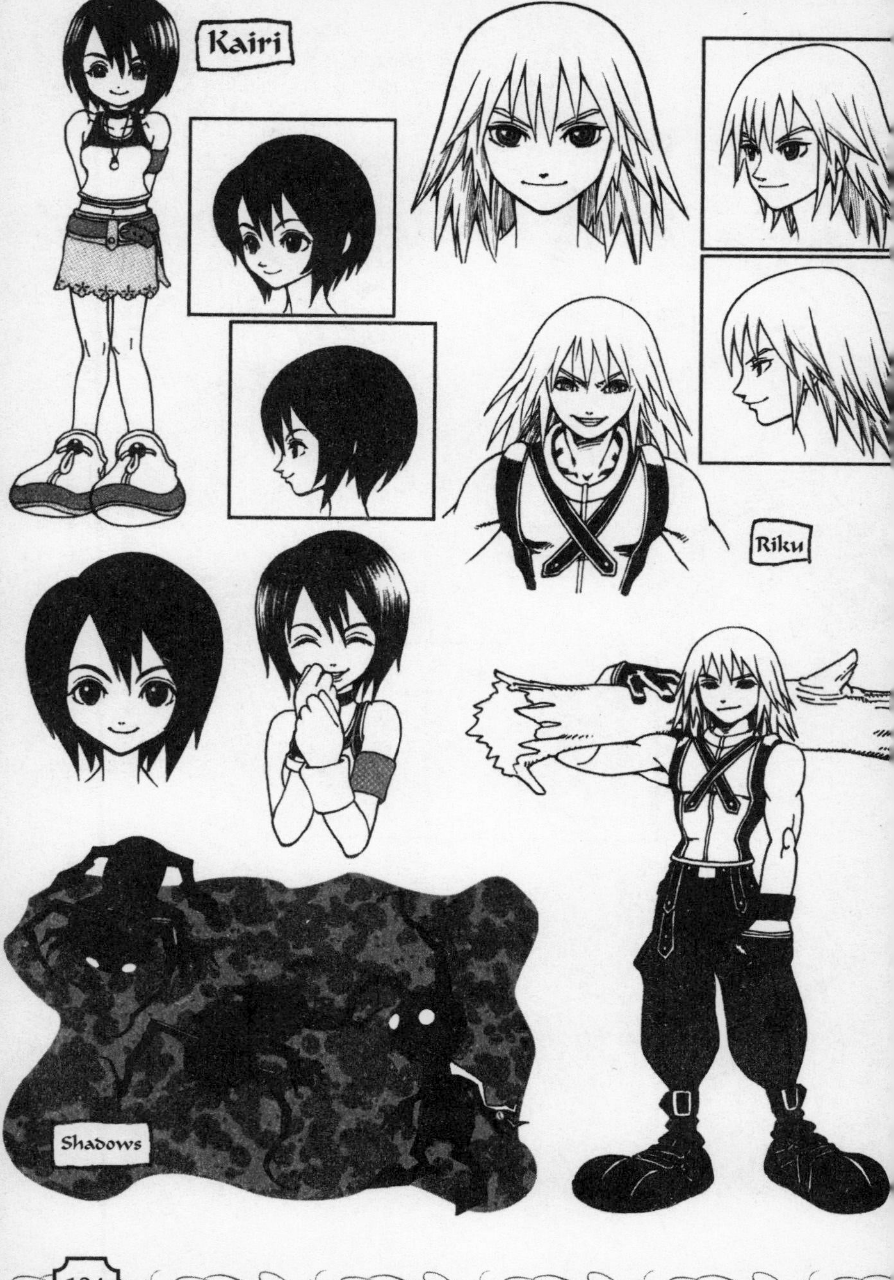
Kairi
Riku
Shadows

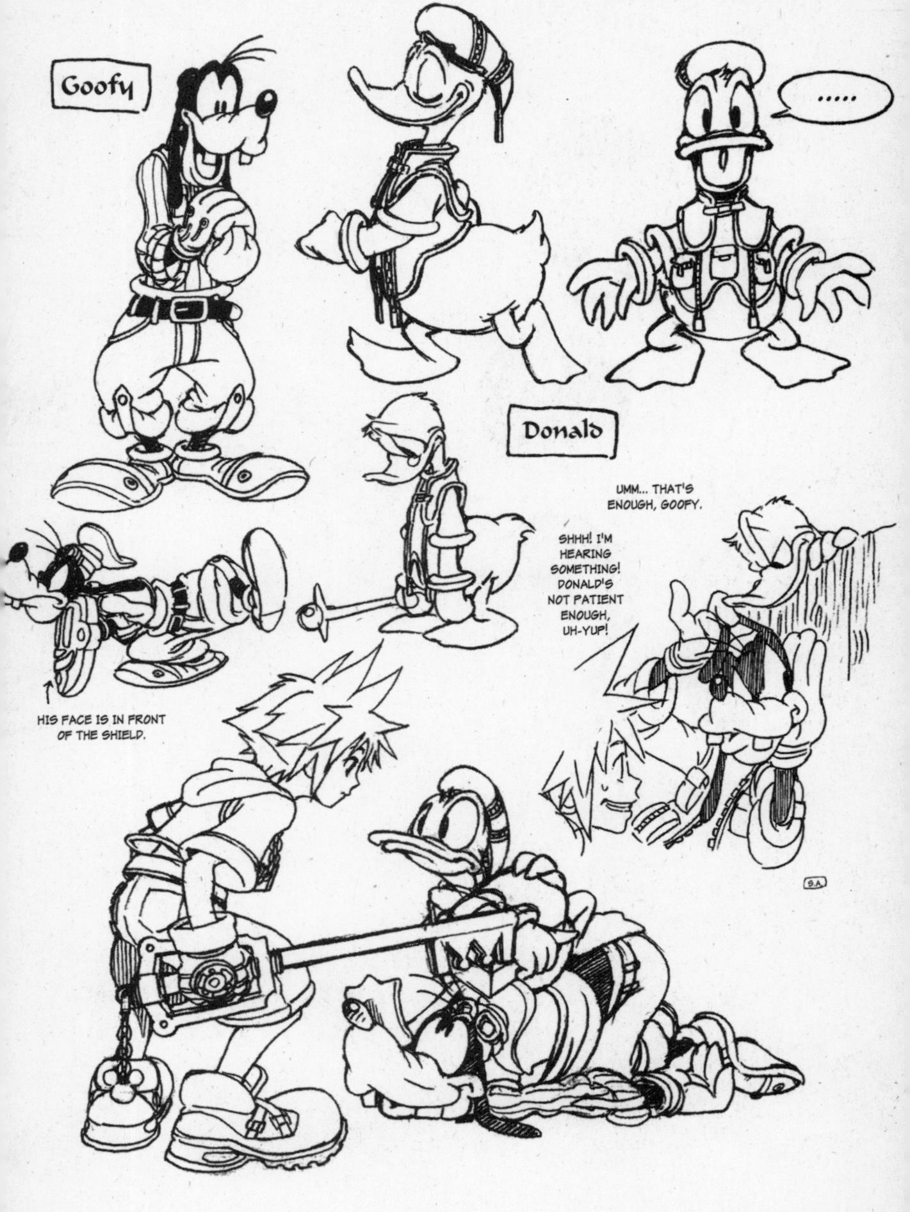
Goofy
.....
Donald
UMM... THAT'S ENOUGH, GOOFY.
SHHH! I'M HEARING SOMETHING! DONALD'S NOT PATIENT ENOUGH, UH-YUP!
HIS FACE IS IN FRONT OF THE SHIELD.
S.A.

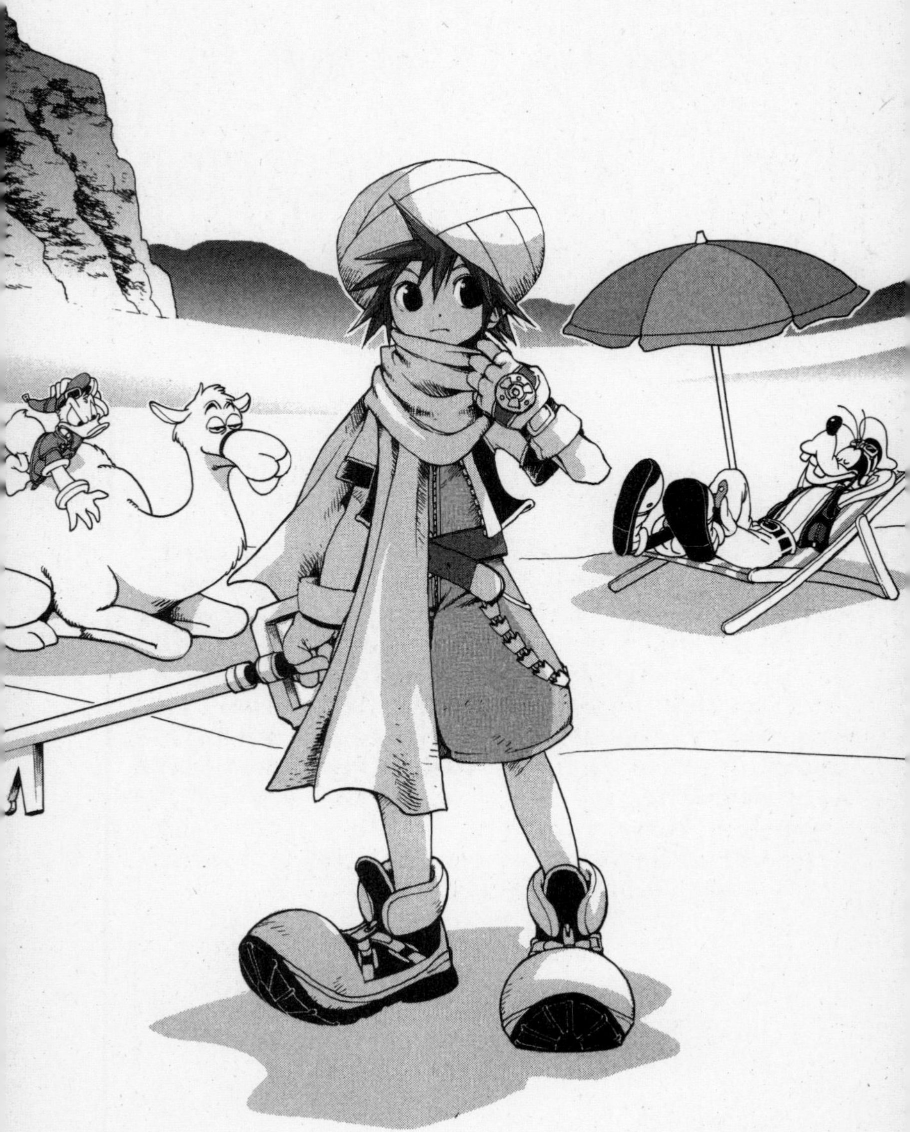

IN THE NEXT VOLUME OF

KINGDOM HEARTS

The journey continues as Sora, Goofy and Donald Duck travel through exciting and mysterious new worlds! Using the power of the Keyblade, the trio hopes to protect the denizens of these far-flung lands from Maleficent and her terrible hordes of the Heartless! Along the way they're making new friends, learning new fighting techniques and uncovering new clues about Maleficent's evil plans to rule over all the worlds. Now, everyone's safety rests in the power of Sora's Keyblade and the strength of his young heart!

ALSO AVAILABLE FROM TOKYOPOP®

MANGA

.HACK//LEGEND OF THE TWILIGHT
ALICHINO
ANGELIC LAYER
BABY BIRTH
BRAIN POWERED
BRIGADOON
B'TX
CANDIDATE FOR GODDESS, THE
CARDCAPTOR SAKURA
CARDCAPTOR SAKURA - MASTER OF THE CLOW
CHRONICLES OF THE CURSED SWORD
CLAMP SCHOOL DETECTIVES
CLOVER
COMIC PARTY
CORRECTOR YUI
COWBOY BEBOP
COWBOY BEBOP: SHOOTING STAR
CRESCENT MOON
CROSS
CULDCEPT
CYBORG 009
D•N•ANGEL
DEARS
DEMON DIARY
DEMON ORORON, THE
DIGIMON
DIGIMON TAMERS
DIGIMON ZERO TWO
DRAGON HUNTER
DRAGON KNIGHTS
DRAGON VOICE
DREAM SAGA
DUKLYON: CLAMP SCHOOL DEFENDERS
ET CETERA
ETERNITY
FAERIES' LANDING
FLCL
FLOWER OF THE DEEP SLEEP
FORBIDDEN DANCE
FRUITS BASKET
G GUNDAM
GATEKEEPERS
GIRL GOT GAME
GUNDAM SEED ASTRAY
GUNDAM SEED ASTRAY R
GUNDAM WING
GUNDAM WING: BATTLEFIELD OF PACIFISTS
GUNDAM WING: ENDLESS WALTZ
GUNDAM WING: THE LAST OUTPOST (G-UNIT)
HANDS OFF!

HARLEM BEAT
HYPER RUNE
I.N.V.U.
INITIAL D
INSTANT TEEN: JUST ADD NUTS
JING: KING OF BANDITS
JING: KING OF BANDITS - TWILIGHT TALES
JULINE
KARE KANO
KILL ME, KISS ME
KINDAICHI CASE FILES, THE
KING OF HELL
KODOCHA: SANA'S STAGE
LAGOON ENGINE
LEGEND OF CHUN HYANG, THE
LILING-PO
LOVE OR MONEY
MAGIC KNIGHT RAYEARTH I
MAGIC KNIGHT RAYEARTH II
MAN OF MANY FACES
MARMALADE BOY
MARS
MARS: HORSE WITH NO NAME
MINK
MIRACLE GIRLS
MODEL
MOURYOU KIDEN: LEGEND OF THE NYMPH
NECK AND NECK
ONE
ONE I LOVE, THE
PEACH FUZZ
PEACH GIRL
PEACH GIRL: CHANGE OF HEART
PHD: PHANTASY DEGREE
PITA-TEN
PLANET BLOOD
PLANET LADDER
PLANETES
PRESIDENT DAD
PRINCESS AI
PSYCHIC ACADEMY
QUEEN'S KNIGHT, THE
RAGNAROK
RAVE MASTER
REALITY CHECK
REBIRTH
REBOUND
RISING STARS OF MANGA™, THE
SAILOR MOON
SAINT TAIL
SAMURAI GIRL™ REAL BOUT HIGH SCHOOL

10.19.0

ALSO AVAILABLE FROM 🐾 TOKYOPOP®

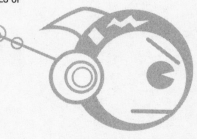

10.19.04Y

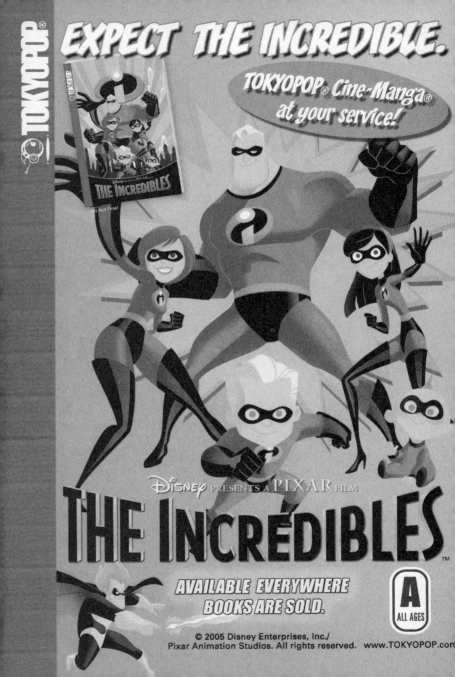

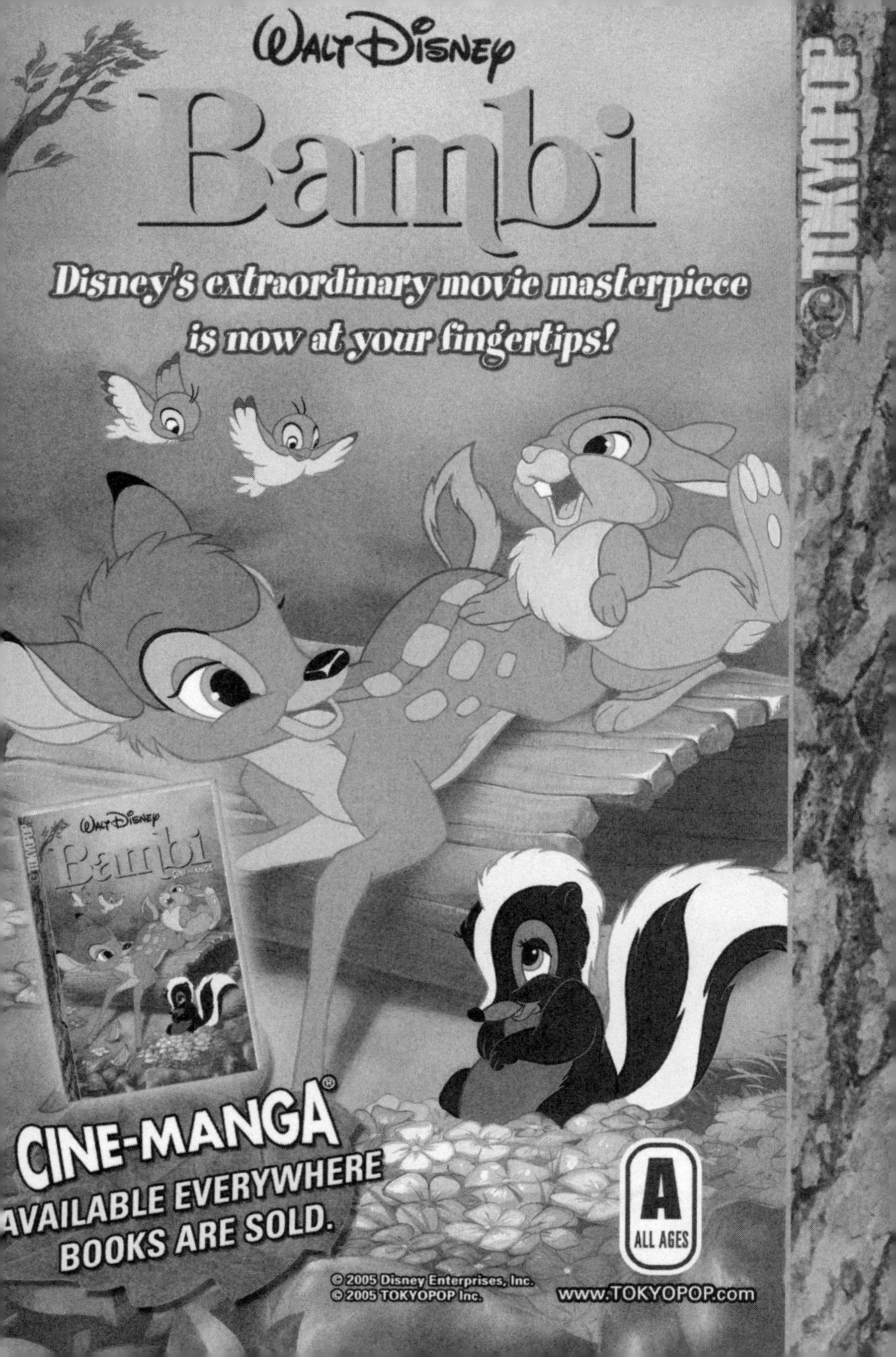

WALT DISNEY
Bambi
Disney's extraordinary movie masterpiece is now at your fingertips!
CINE-MANGA®
AVAILABLE EVERYWHERE BOOKS ARE SOLD.
A ALL AGES
© 2005 Disney Enterprises, Inc.
© 2005 TOKYOPOP Inc.
www.TOKYOPOP.com
TOKYOPOP

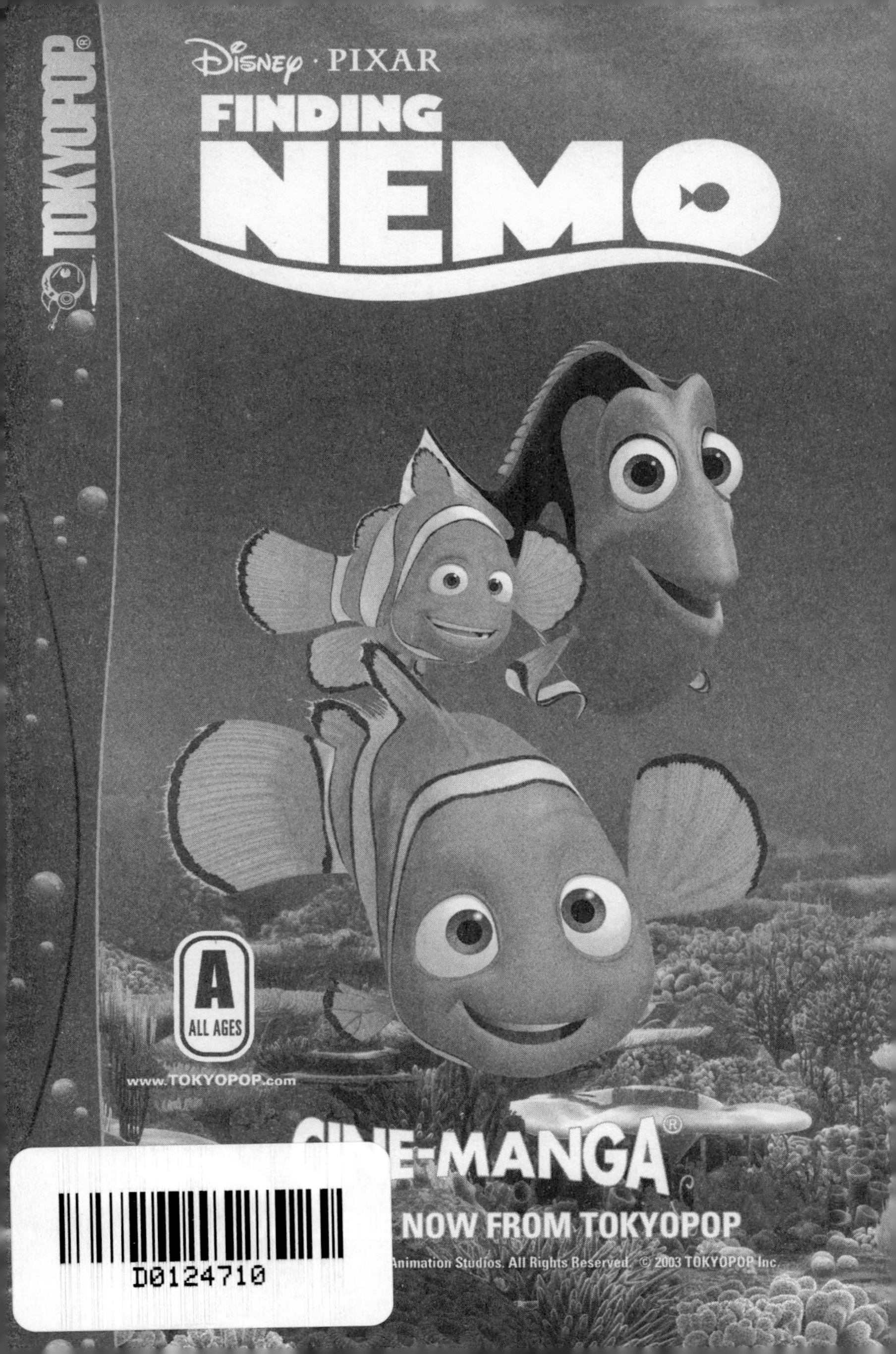
TOKYOPOP
Disney · PIXAR
FINDING
NEMO
A
ALL AGES
www.TOKYOPOP.com
CINE-MANGA®
NOW FROM TOKYOPOP
Animation Studios. All Rights Reserved. © 2003 TOKYOPOP Inc.